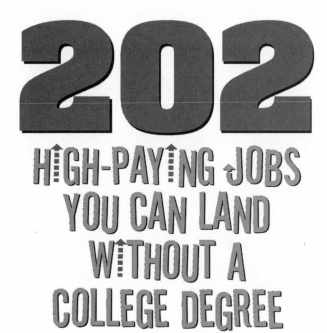

202
HIGH-PAYING JOBS
YOU CAN LAND
WITHOUT A
COLLEGE DEGREE

Other Entrepreneur 202 titles

- *202 Things to Make and Sell for Big Profits*

- *202 Things You Can Buy and Sell for Big Profits*

- *202 Services You Can Sell for Big Profits*

- *202 Ways to Supplement Your Retirement Income*

202

HIGH-PAYING JOBS
YOU CAN LAND
WITHOUT A
COLLEGE DEGREE

JASON R. RICH

EP
Entrepreneur.
Press

Editorial director: Jere L. Calmes
Cover design: Beth Hansen-Winter
Composition and production: Eliot House Productions

This publication is designed to provide accurate and authoritative information in regard to the subject matter covered. It is sold with the understanding that the publisher is not engaged in rendering legal, accounting, or other professional services. If legal advice or other expert assistance is required, the services of a competent professional person should be sought.

Library of Congress Cataloging-in-Publication Data
    Rich, Jason
        202 high-paying jobs you can land without a college degree/By Jason R. Rich.
            p.   cm.
        ISBN 1-59918-016-2 (9871599180188: alk. paper)
        1. Occupations. 2. Job hunting. 3. Vocational guidance. I. Title: Two hundred two high-paying jobs you can land without a college degree. II. Title.
    HF5381.R475 2006
    331.702—dc22   2005033738

Printed in Canada

11 10 09 08 07   10 9 8 7 6 5 4 3 2

CONTENTS

CHAPTER 8

Food Services Jobs _____ 117

CHAPTER 9

High-Tech and Computer Jobs_____ 129

CHAPTER 12

Sales-Oriented Jobs _____ 213

202

High-Paying Jobs You Can Land Without a College Degree

CHAPTER 13

Service-Oriented Jobs _____ 235

ACKNOWLEDGMENTS

First, I'd like to thank Jere Calmes, Jen Dorsey (congratulations on the new baby), and Karen Thomas at Entrepreneur Press for inviting me to work on this book, as well as the new personal finance book series we'll begin working on next.

Also, thanks to my literary agent, Jeff Herman, for introducing me to the folks at Entrepreneur Press.

I'd also like to extend my gratitude to my best friends—Ferras AlQaisi (www.FerrasMusic.com), Mark Giordani, and the whole Bendremer family (Ellen, Sandy, Emily, and Ryan)—and to my family, for their ongoing love and support. A special shout out also goes to my puppy Rusty (www.MyPalRusty.com). He's an adorable Yorkshire Terrier who sits by my side as I work each day.

Finally, I'd like to thank you, the reader, for picking up a copy of this book. I sincerely hope you're able to benefit from the hard work and research I put into this project. Best of luck on your job search efforts! Remember, nothing replaces the need for hard work when it comes to success, but don't be afraid to pursue something you're passionate about as well.

—Jason R. Rich, www.JasonRich.com

PREFACE

When was the last time you asked yourself, "What am I going to do with my life?" Perhaps you haven't been able, for whatever reason, to pursue a college education, but at the same time, you can't afford to get stuck in a miserable dead-end, low-paying job that won't even allow you to maintain a decent quality of life. Well, if you're in this situation, this book is for you! It's full of career-related advice, including 202 ideas for jobs and career paths you can pursue even if you don't have a college education.

This is an idea book that describes many jobs and career opportunities you might not otherwise have considered. Most importantly, once you discover a handful of potential jobs that you believe are worth pursuing, this book offers you resources for obtaining additional information about those opportunities and shows you how to find specific jobs in your area that are available right now.

This book, combined with access to the internet (for additional job-related research) are the tools you'll need to find and land a job that will provide upward mobility and career advancement opportunities in the future. The jobs and career paths described within this book focus on a wide range of industries and fields, so no matter where your interests lie, chances are you'll find opportunities worth pursuing.

In the early part of this book, you'll receive advice on how to find job opportunities, create a resume and cover letter, and perform well in job interviews. You'll also discover how to analyze job offers and ensure you don't end up in a dead-end job that will lead to misery.

So, if you're ready to jumpstart your job search efforts and find exciting new opportunities, then continue reading and make a promise to yourself that you'll invest the time, effort, and resources at your disposal to find and land the best possible job. Then, once you've landed that job and you're gainfully employed, that you'll continue to work hard to expand your knowledge, experience, and skills so that you quickly become qualified for advanced and higher paid positions.

It's no secret that the more hard work and dedication you invest in advancing your skills, knowledge, and experience, the bigger the payoff will be when it comes to landing higher paying jobs.

Ideally, at some point in the future, you might want to consider pursuing a two- or four-year college education, or completing a certificate or degree program, either through a traditional vocational school, college, university, or a distance learning program. But for now, this book will help you find a good paying job based on the education, experience, and skills you can currently showcase to potential employers.

CHAPTER

IDEAS FOR YOUR FUTURE

Nearly everyone understands how important it is to pursue a college education and how earning a college diploma dramatically increases your earning potential and qualifies you for higher paying jobs.

Statistics show that college graduates take home an average annual salary of $45,678, whereas high school graduates earn an average salary of only $24,572. Futhermore, the Employment and Training Administration, a division of the U.S. Department of Labor (www.doleta.gov) reports that a person with a bachelor's degree from an accredited college will earn at least $1 million more over her lifetime than a worker with only a high school diploma.

If you're one of the millions of people who, for whatever reason, can't pursue a college education at this point in your life, this book is for you! Although statistics show that you're at a distadvantage when it comes to earning potential, as you'll soon discover, there are plenty of jobs that allow you to earn a respectable income and offer a wide range of career advancement opportunities, even if you only have a high school diploma or GED.

Jobs that require only a high school diploma or GED are the focus of *202 High-Paying Jobs You Can Land without a College Degree.* This is an idea book for your professional future. It will provide you with detailed overviews of hundreds of job opportunities you can pursue, starting immediately, with little or no training—and no college degree.

It's true, some of the jobs described offer no significant career advancement opportunities (they're dead-end jobs), so they're probably not the best long-term career options. But, these jobs can provide a viable income for several months or years as you plan for your future.

By reading this book, you'll learn about 202 respectable jobs you can pursue without a college education. You'll discover how to find the best opportunities and land a job that's right for you, plus how to make intelligent decisions about your professional future. You'll also learn that having a defined plan for your future will help you pinpoint career advancement opportunities and how pursuing additional training and education throughout your career will dramatically improve your long-term earning potential, plus make you a more attractive candidate for employers.

Even without attending college, if you're willing to take advantage of on-the-job training and other methods for acquiring new skills and knowledge, you'll be well on your way to paving a long-term career path that offers plenty of upward mobility from an earning perspective. Throw into the mix a bit of long-term planning, a touch of creativity, and plenty of hard work, and you'll be able to enjoy a successful career doing whatever you set out to do professionally.

Yes, obtaining a college education can be important for most people. But, it's not critical for achieving long-term success. After all, many highly successful people from all walks of life have had extremely lucrative careers even though they never graduated from college. Granted, this is harder to do these days, but it's still possible. Although you might never become a multi-millionaire, you should be able to find and land a job you'll enjoy, that will also allow you to support yourself and your family.

Based on your interests, the skills you already possess, and your work experience, use this book for ideas to help you pinpoint the types of jobs you're most qualified to fill.

If you have limited work experience, keep your expectations realistic as you begin your job search efforts. Chances are, you'll need to start in an entry-level position, possiblly earning only minimum wage. However, if the job you accept offers career advancement opportunities and you work hard to gain valuable on-the-job training to develop the necessary skill set, you should be able to earn promotions and pay raises in a relatively short amount of time and get on your way toward pursuing a successful career.

Many excellent jobs don't require a college education, but specialized training, certification, a license, or completion of an apprenticeship *is* required. For these jobs, you'll need to make a commitment to obtaining the training you'll need to land the best possible job within that field. As a general rule, the more skills you possess and the more work experience and training you have, the more valuable you are to an employer and the easier it will be to land a new job.

Finding a Job That's Right for You

No matter who you are, there are careers or professions that you can be highly successful in, based on your personality, education, interests, and personal skills. Finding a job you're very good at isn't good enough, however. Ideally, your job should also allow you to exploit most, if not all, of your personal strengths. Your work should involve performing tasks that you enjoy.

Of course, every job will have things about it you don't like; the trick is to make sure that the positives outweigh the negatives by a significant margin. As you start your job search, look for a job you'll be passionate about. Otherwise, waking up every morning and going to work will quickly become a miserable chore.

As you consider the type of work you'll enjoy, also consider what you're looking for in terms of

- Your daily or weekly work schedule.
- The salary and benefits you want and need.
- The work environment.
- The commute to work (including the length of the commute, how long it will take, and the travel costs.)
- The type of coworkers you'll have.
- The on-the-job responsibilities.

- The on-the-job training you'll be eligible to receive.
- The career advancement opportunities that will be available.

By taking a look at the big picture, you'll more easily be able to pinpoint the best possible job opportunities.

Defining Your Skill Set

Once you define the type of job you believe you'd most enjoy, the next step is to be creative and discover job opportunities that will require you to incorporate your strengths and involve your interests.

To help you define yourself and determine what type of career you want to pursue, write down all of your marketable skills and abilities, as well as your interests, hobbies, and the work-related activities that you really enjoy doing. Think about what the ideal work atmosphere would be for you and what specific things you liked and disliked about your previous work experiences. After you have compiled lists of your skills, likes, dislikes, and interests, think about where potential job opportunities might exist.

Your personal and professional skill set can be any knowledge or ability that makes you a more desirable and productive person on the job. Depending on the industry you work in or the type of position you're looking to fill, your skill set goes beyond the core education you received in school. It includes any skills that will ultimately allow you to meet the responsibilities of your job, whether it's working the computerized cash register at a retail store or using a specialized set of tools.

Being fluent in multiple languages, for example, can be an asset that will set you apart from other applicants when applying for a wide range of positions. Other skills employers often look for include: sales, public speaking, management, leadership, typing, bookkeeping, filing, telemarketing, being detail-oriented, and having strong organizational abilities. Basic computer literacy is also an important skill for a wide range of jobs.

Once you know what type of job you're applying for and have a general idea of what the employer is looking for, your cover letter, resume, and employment application provide excellent initial opportunities to quickly showcase your personal and professional skill set.

The Help Wanted ad or job description provided by the potential employer will offer valuable clues regarding the specific skills and training you should already possess and what is of particular importance to an employer. Determine exactly what the employer is looking for before you devise a plan on how to best promote your skill set.

Simply stating you have a skill that's required for a job isn't enough. Within your resume, for example, you'll want to clearly spell out every skill you have that's directly relevant to the job you're applying for, then be able to provide specific examples of how you've already used each skill in a previous work situation. In other words, proof that you possess each skill is essential.

As you list each skill and describe how you've used it on the job, provide specific quantitative and qualitative details that convey the positive results of your abilities. You can later provide written documentation or support materials during a job interview.

Use your resume and employment applications to list all of your relevant skills and to briefly describe how you've used them. In your cover letter, emphasize one or two of your most marketable skills or job qualifications so they stand out, without blatantly repeating information within your resume.

Every marketable skill you possess has a value to an employer. Thus, having more skills than what's specifically spelled out by the employer will make you more desirable. It's your responsibility to demonstrate exactly how your particular combination of skills will make you a valuable asset to a potential employer.

By carefully describing your skill set and customizing it to the job you're applying for, you're more apt to get invited for an interview, at which time you'll be given the opportunity to discuss your skills in person. The interview is your opportunity to describe your skills, how you've used them in the past, and exactly how they could be used in the future to meet the requirements of the job you're applying for.

Your Previous Work Experience

From a potential employer's perspective, your previous work experience defines who you are and helps them determine if you'll be capable of meeting the requirements of the job you're applying for. It also helps a potential employer determine what your value to them will be if you get hired.

Your employer will pay you a salary or hourly wage. Every employer, no matter what type of jobs you pursue, will be looking for employees who offer more value than what they're paying for. In other words, the question on a potential employer's mind will be, "If I will be paying this person $9 per hour will he or she be worth that salary? Or, am I better off hiring someone else who offers more value, in terms of their productivity, skill set, previous work experience, and what they'll be able to accomplish on the job?"

As the job applicant, it's your responsibility to demonstrate your value to potential employers and show them exactly why you deserve to be hired and what the benefits to the employer will be if they hire you as opposed to someone else.

Typically, it's your previous work experiences that have taught you valuable skills and allowed you to showcase your skills on the job. If you can demonstrate that you've met or exceeded the expectations of past employers, you're more apt to be seriously considered for future jobs.

As you begin applying for jobs, completing job applications, and participating in job interviews, make sure you can demonstrate to potential employers exactly why you're worth the salary you're looking to be paid, keeping in mind that potential employers will be looking at your previous work experience as proof you're capable of meeting or exceeding the job's requirements.

Defining Your Interests

It's one thing to be good at your job and another thing entirely to enjoy doing it. As you seek job opportunities, find job openings that involve tasks you enjoy and that best utilize your skills and interests. Try to find a job opportunity you'll enjoy waking up every morning to go to and that will offer you a challenge. You'll be happier in a job where your coworkers are friendly and that offers a positive atmosphere and work environment.

Before you look for jobs, take time to consider not just what skills and experience you can offer to the employer, but what your individual interests, likes, and dislikes are. Describe what the ideal job (dream job) for you would entail, then seek either a job that closely resembles that job or one that offers career advancement opportunities that will eventually lead you to your dream job.

As you define your interests, likes, and dislikes, consider your work habits. Ask yourself questions such as:

- Are you a "people person" who enjoys a lot of interpersonal interaction or do you prefer to work alone at your desk?
- Are you an independent self-starter or do you work better being supervised by superiors?
- Are you satisfied receiving an hourly wage or salary, or would you prefer a compensation package that involves commissions, bonuses, and various types of benefits? What types of benefits are most important to you?
- Do you prefer busy work environments with a lot of hustle and bustle, or do you prefer a small quiet work environment?
- What are your weaknesses?
- What industry or type of company interests you?
- What tasks are you exceptionally good at?

- What tasks do you absolutely hate?
- What type of career advancement opportunities are you looking for in the near future and over the long term? Where would you like your career to be six months from now? What about one year or five years from now? Does your potential employer offer the training or career advancement opportunities you're seeking?
- What type of tasks would you prefer to be doing during your average work day?
- What type of work schedule would you like to have?
- What types of job responsibilities are you most skilled at handling?
- What types of skills do you lack that will prevent you from landing your dream job? How can you start building or expanding upon your skill set?

By answering these questions, you'll have a much better understanding of the types of jobs you should pursue. Knowing about yourself can help you avoid dead-end jobs that you'll hate. There's nothing worse than having to spend eight to ten hours per day in a job where you're miserable and that's leading you nowhere. The frustration, anxiety, and depression that this can cause will definitely impact other aspects of your personal life. Though always focusing on your financial situation is important, it's equally important to focus on your personal and professional wants and needs to achieve long-term success.

The 202 Job Ideas Featured within this Book

The title of this book is self-explanatory. In addition to offering tips and advice for finding and landing the most suitable job, helping you to create a high-impact resume and cover letter, and providing the information you'll need to ace your job interviews, the majority of this book focuses on describing 202 job opportunities and career paths you can pursue without a college education.

Many of the jobs described in this book require a high school diploma. Some also require some type of certification, license, successful completion of an apprenticeship program, and/or on-the-job training. Once you pinpoint the types of jobs that appeal to you, it may be necessary for you to seek additional training and/or prepare for a licensing exam to become qualified for that type of job.

When it comes to additional training or education, you'll have many affordable options, including:

- Apprenticeship programs offered through your employer, professional trade organization, or union
- Attendance at a local community college

- Distance learning programs (correspondence schools)
- Evening and weekend classes at a post-secondary, technical, or vocational school
- Full-time attendance at a post-secondary, technical, or vocational school
- Online training programs
- On-the-job training
- Self-paced home study courses (book, video, or computer software)

It is your decision to obtain the additional training or education you want or need, but you'll quickly discover that the more time and effort you put into building your skill set and obtaining the most education possible, the better jobs you'll be qualified for and the easier it'll be to land those jobs. Plus, you'll be eligible to earn higher wages because you'll be a more valuable employee.

It's important to understand that when an employer offers you a salary, it's not an arbitrary amount of money someone chooses to pay you. Your salary has nothing to do with how much you're liked or disliked by the employer on a personal level. One of the key elements that will determine what you'll be paid, no matter what type of job you pursue, will be how much value you bring to the company you're working for. From the employer's perspective, are you worth more to them than they're paying you? For an employer, deciding how much salary to pay employees is usually a purely financial decision based on the company's bottom line. Keep in mind, the employer wants to hire the best qualified, most productive, and most motivated employees to generate the highest possible profits and pay out the least amount of money in salaries, wages, bonuses, commissions, and benefits.

Once you've pinpointed the types of jobs you're interested in and most qualified for, it's important to research how much someone with your skills, work experience, education, and capabilities is paid for holding the same position in your geographic area. As you'll discover later in this chapter, someone with your exact skill set and work experience, for example, could be paid substantially more in a different city or another part of the country, or by holding the same job, but working for a different employer in a different industry.

Use This Book to Generate Ideas

Within this book, you'll find information about 202 jobs and career paths. The jobs described are extremely diverse and represent many different industries. Some pay minimum wage and offer minimal career advancement opportunities, but most are entry-level positions that, with hard work, training, and dedication on your part, can and will lead to higher paying and rewarding jobs.

In reality, there are many high-paying jobs that do not require a college education. Use this book as an informative resource and idea book. Use it to pinpoint types of jobs that interest you, as well as industries and even specific companies you might be interested in working for. Once you have some general ideas about the types of jobs you're interested in and qualified to pursue, do research to learn about specific opportunities being offered by companies in your area.

Though descriptions of 202 potential jobs and career paths may seem like a lot, it's just a small percentage of the many types of jobs currently available to people without a college degree.

202 High-Paying Jobs You Can Land without a College Degree is full of ideas that will point you toward a successful job or career path. Once you have your ideas, gather more information from the internet, from professional trade associations, from the career gudiance office at your high school, by attending job fairs, by reading the Help Wanted or Careers section of your local newspaper, and by talking to people currently working in the fields that most interest you. You can also read industry magazines and newsletters, attend conferences and conventions, contact schools or training programs that offer education related to your field of interest, and utilize the vast amount of job- and career-related information offered by the U.S. Department of Labor (www.dol.gov).

Every two years, the U.S. Department of Labor's Bureau of Labor Statistics publishes the *Occupational Outlook Handbook.* This 500-plus page book is loaded with information about thousands of jobs in a wide range of industries. The book is available at libraries and through many schools. In a traditional book format, the *Occupational Outlook Handbook* can be purchased online ($68) at http://stats.bls.gov/opub/opborder.htm, or a less expensive CD-ROM edition is available for $22.

The online edition of the *Occupational Outlook Handbook,* however, can be accessed free from any computer that's connected to the internet. Point your web browser to: http://stats.bls.gov, then follow the links for the *Occupational Outlook Handbook* or other topics that interest you.

Avoid Dead-End Jobs

A dead-end job leads nowhere, with no career advancement potential, no higher earning potential, no opportunity to learn new skills, and no way to move your career forward. From day one on the job, you'll be doing the same thing, have the same responsibilities, and receive the same basic pay as you will after one, three, five, or even ten years on the job. For most people, this leads to a tremendous amount of frustration.

There are many entry-level jobs that offer a wide range of career advancement opportunities, but to pursue them, you'll often need additional work experience, on-the-job training, new skills, and perhaps an additional certification or license (which you can earn over time). If you're starting an entry-level position you know has career advancement opportunities, starting your first day on the job, begin working toward your first promotion and pay raise by exceeding (not just meeting) the expectations of your employer.

Determine what it'll take to earn that first promotion and/or pay raise, then do what's necessary to obtain it, keeping it mind, it could take three months, six months, one year, or longer to achieve, depending on what's required by the employer.

The main difference between a job and a career is that a basic job leads nowhere. When you're pursuing a career, you'll have a steady upward path to follow as you work toward specific promotions to climb the corporate ladder.

Always Look for Career Advancement Opportunities

Always be looking toward your future! From the day you start a new job, focus on what it'll take to advance your career and earn promotions and pay raises, then do what's necessary.

Ideally, every six months to one year, you should evaluate where you stand in your job, determine what needs to happen to move your career forward, and determine if you have a future with your current employer. In some situations, it could be in your best interest professionally to seek employment elsewhere, where your skills, experience, and qualifications will be better utilized and rewarded.

Make sure you have a clear understanding of what your employer's expectations are and what the job requirements for the job you're holding are. Using this information, you can exceed expectations, which will make it easier to earn promotions and pay raises faster. If what you need to do to earn a promotion isn't clearly spelled out for you and understood, it'll be much harder to reach your long-term goals.

Make Sure You're Earning What You're Worth

Every employer in every industry strives to hire the most dedicated, hard working, and qualified applicants possible, while offering them the lowest compensation possible. As the employee, it's important to understand what you're worth in today's job market, based on your educations, skills, work experience, and overall qualifications in the industry you work in and your geographic area.

Because salary information is often a carefully guarded secret at most companies, it's important to do research to ensure your overall compensation package is fair and that you're not being taken advantage of by your employer. The best way to do this is by conducting your own research.

Web sites, such as Salary.com (www.salary.com) and the Department of Labor (www.dol.gov) offer free access to salary information for thousands of jobs in any georgraphic area. Many other career-related web sites also profile popular industries and careers and offer related salary information.

As you research salary information and try to determine if you're being paid what you're actually worth in today's job market, keep in mind there's a huge difference between what you're actually worth and what your perceived value is. Everyone thinks they're overworked and underpaid. The question is, what are other people with similar qualifications holding the same type of job in your georgraphic area being paid? When you know the anwser to this question, you'll more easily be able to determine if you're being paid what you're actually worth.

CHAPTER

2

WHERE TO FIND THE BEST JOB OPPORTUNITIES

Once you know what type of job or career path you're interested in pursuing, make sure you're qualified to fill that type of job, in terms of your education, skills, previous work experience, and overall qualifications. Next, start putting together a resume and think about what you'll write in your cover letters. Finally, start seeking specific job opportunities to apply for.

As you'll discover, there are many ways to learn about job openings. Finding a job and applying for it will be a time-consuming process that'll often require a bit of hard work, dedication, and persistence. It's often very competitive to apply for entry-level positions, so you'll need to find innovative ways to stand out from other applicants and showcase yourself to employers.

To ensure your job search efforts will be successful, try two or three of the methods described in this chapter. Don't just rely on the Help Wanted section of your local newspaper or the online career-related web sites.

Career-Related Web Sites

Access to the internet puts the most powerful job search tool at your disposal anytime. If you don't have access to the internet from home, visit a local library or an internet café.

In addition to job listings, many of the career-related web sites offer extensive information about specific jobs, careers, and industries. In addition to the general interest career-related web sites listed in this section, consider visiting the web sites operated by specific companies you'd like to work for (and visiting the Job Openings or Careers areas of those web sites), as well as visiting industry-oriented web sites hosted by professional trade associations.

When it comes to finding online job listings and career-related information, the following career-related web sites are excellent resources:

- Career Builder, www.careerbuilder.com
- Careers.org, www.careers.org
- Craigslist.org, www.craigslist.org (Choose your local city from the main menu, then access the job listings area of the web site.)
- Employment Guide, http://jobs.employmentguide.com/home
- Government Job Search, www.federaljobsearch.com
- JobBank USA, www.jobbankusa.com
- Jobs.net, www.jobs.net
- Monster Board, www.monster.com
- Summer Jobs Web, www.summerjobs.com
- USA Jobs, www.usajobs.opm.gov
- Yahoo! HotJobs, http://hotjobs.yahoo.com

On these career-related web sites, you'll find job listings, informative articles, details about specific jobs and industries, and career-related advice. You'll also have the opportunity to post your resume online, to be viewed by the human resources professionals at companies currently hiring.

Job Fairs

Job fairs offer an excellent opportunity to meet a handful of potential employers at once, in a relatively casual environment. You'll discover career fairs are hosted in virtually every city across America. Some focus specifically on entry-level jobs, whereas others are attended by employers working in specific industries. For example, TechExpo (www.techexpousa.com) hosts job fairs across America that focus on technical, computer-related jobs.

When you attend a job fair, dress as if you're going to a formal job interview. Also, don't forget to bring at least a dozen (or more) copies of your resume. Often, job fairs are attended by human resources professionals looking to hire people immediately. If you're able to make a positive first impression, you could be hired on the spot, or at least be invited to participate in a formal job interview.

Many high schools and colleges host job fairs. Others are advertised in local newspapers or on career-related web sites.

Networking

Networking is an extremely powerful job search tool. Many of the best job openings are never advertised. The way to find out about them is through networking with friends, family members, past coworkers, your school's employment/career guidance office, or even your barber/hairstylist. Word of mouth and personalized introductions are great ways to find job opportunities that aren't advertised.

Let people know what type of job you're looking for and where you'd like to work. Ask people if they know anyone who can help make an introduction for you. Seek referrals and advice from the people you know. You'll often find that someone you know may know someone else who knows of a job opening that's perfect for you.

Another way to network is to attend tradeshows and industry-oriented conferences and introduce yourself to as many people as you can. Explain that you're looking for a job (and what type of job you're looking for) and don't be afraid to ask for referrals or advice. Most employers are more apt to hire someone who comes highly recommended by a current employee, for example, than someone who simply walks in off the street after sending in a resume.

Newspaper Help Wanted Ads

Newspaper Help Wanted ads often list dozens, perhaps hundreds, of entry-level jobs in your immediate geographic area. This is an excellent resource for job leads; however, it's important that you act immediately on each ad of interest. If an ad catches your attention in Sunday's newspaper, respond to it first thing on Monday morning. If you wait until later in the week, that employer will most likely have already received dozens of resumes from qualified applicants, which puts you at a disadvantage.

When responding to a help wanted ad, make sure you're actually qualified for the job before you apply. Also, follow the directions in the ad carefully. If you're instructed to fax or e-mail your resume, don't send it via U.S. mail, and don't call the employer if the ad specifically states "No phone calls, please." If the ad requests additional information, make sure you provide exactly what's requested in the format it's requested in.

Professional Trade Associations and Unions

Professional trade associations and unions are typically nonprofit organizations made up of employers and employees working in a specific industry. These organizations typically offer job placement services, training opportunities, and maintain a database of related job openings. Job listings could be published online, printed in a trade magazine, or available by calling the trade association or union directly.

Trade associations and unions also hold meetings, seminars, tradeshows, and conferences, which provide excellent networking opportunities for job seekers. The training these groups provide can help you become more qualified to fill specific types of jobs and increase your earning potential.

The Career Guidance Office at School

Most high schools, trade schools, vocational schools, and distance learning programs offer a career guidance or job placement office. Here, you'll find information about job openings and resources to help you land a job. You might also receive help putting together your resume or preparing for a job interview, for example. These services and resources are free to current students (and often alumni), so be sure to take full advantage of them as you embark on your job search efforts.

Read Industry Magazines, Newsletters, and Trade Journals

Reading industry-oriented magazines and trade journals offers the job seeker many advantages. Not only will you learn about a specific industry you're interested in and what the latest trends are within that industry, you'll also discover who the key players are and which companies are hiring. Most industry magazines and trade journals publish job listings.

You'll find industry-oriented magazines and trade journals either at large newsstands or libraries. The online editions of these publications can often be found on the web.

What's Next?

Now that you know what *202 High-Paying Jobs You Can Land without a College Degree* offers and how to utilize the information offered in this book, it's time to kick start your job search efforts.

Chapter 3 will help you create a high-impact resume and cover letter, prepare you for your job interviews, and give you insight about how to effectively complete job applications.

As you read the rest of this book, keep an open mind, seek ideas for potential jobs and career paths, and consider which ones you're most suited to fill, based on your interests, skills, education, experience, and overall qualifications. Keep in mind, the 202 job descriptions within this book are only a sampling of the countless jobs available in today's job marketplace.

CHAPTER

3

RESUMES AND COVER LETTERS

202 *High-Paying Jobs You Can Land without a College Degree* is an idea book for your future. In this book, you'll find job descriptions, information about career paths to follow, and discover opportunities you might otherwise overlook as you embark on your job search efforts. Ultimately, for the majority of people in the workforce, pursuing a two- or four-year college degree or obtaining certification in a specific field (at a postsecondary technical school, vocational school, or community college) will allow you to pursue higher paying jobs, have more job stability, and achieve higher levels of success in the future.

For a multitude of reasons, some people simply can't pursue a degree or training beyond a high school diploma or GED. If you're currently in this situation, it becomes even more important to pursue opportunities that offer on-the-job training and career advancement possibilities. Ideally, every job you take should help advance your career, allow you to earn more money, teach you new skills, and provide a broader range of work experience (something all employers seek).

Steps to Finding Your Next Job

As you begin your job search efforts, you'll embark on a process that has many steps. Finding the right job for you will take time, energy, research, and commitment. The primary steps you'll need to complete during your job search efforts (for each job you apply for) include:

- Pinpointing the type of job(s) you want to pursue.
- Choosing an industry that offers the right job opportunities.
- Selecting companies within that industry where you might want to work.
- Determining what information about yourself needs to be conveyed to potential employers to position yourself as the ideal applicant for the job you're seeking.
- Creating a one-page resume that is well-written and successfully showcases all of the information about you that employers want and need to know.
- Utilizing the online career-related web sites, Help Wanted ads in newspapers, networking, attending job fairs, and so on. Research is required to find these job opportunities.
- Customizing your resume for each job opportunity that you are qualified to fill.
- Creating a well-written cover letter to accompany your resume when sending, submitting by mail, e-mail, or dropping it off in person.
- Following up with each potential employer a few days after submitting your resume and cover letter.
- Preparing for an interview, if the potential employer calls and wants you to either come in for an interview or asks you to participate ina phone interview involves practice. This includes how you'll answer interview questions and interact with the interviewer, deciding what you'll wear to the interview if you have a face to face meeting, and researching the company you'll be interviewing with.

- Completing an employment application as you're waiting for the interview to begin is another part of the process. Many of the questions you'll be asked will require information that's already in your resume and/or cover letter. Consistency is important.

- Showcasing your personality in the interview, as well as your skills, experience, and overall qualifications, while asking intelligent questions and engaging in a conversation with the potential employer is recommended.

- Determining what the next step will be once the interview is over is important. Should you follow up with the employer? Do you need to provide the employer with additional materials? Will the employer be in touch with you? If so, in what timeframe? If it becomes you're responsibility to take the next step, make sure you do so in a timely manner.

- Send a handwritten and personalized thank-you note to the person or people who interviewed you within 24 hours is good business practice.

At this point in the job search process, you may be invited for a second or third interview or asked to provide additional materials to the potential employer. If the employer is interested in hiring you, you may then receive a job offer. Make sure you ask for this offer in writing and that you understand what's expected of you and exactly how you'll be compensated. This should all be made clear before accepting the job offer and starting work.

Until you have a firm job offer from an employer, don't stop your job search efforts. Continue submitting resumes and seeking opportunities with other employers. The best case scenario will be that you receive multiple job offers and you will be put in a position to choose which one is best for you and offers the most money.

Creating Your Resume

Chances are, it will be the information you incorporate onto your single-sided, one-page, 8.5-by-11-inch resume that will determine whether an employer has any interest in inviting you to come in for an interview and ultimately hiring you. Within your resume, you must concisely summarize all of the reasons a potential employer should hire you and include examples.

The human resources professional who works for a potential employer will read (or often simply scan) your resume, typically in 30 seconds or less, he or she will be asking themselves a few simple questions, including:

- What position are you applying for?
- What are your skills and qualifications?

- What work experience do you have that directly relates to the job you are applying for?
- Are you worth the salary the job pays?
- What will you bring to the company that other applicants can't or won't?
- Will hiring you benefit the company?
- Will you be able to help the employer solve the problems it is facing?

Your resume is a tool that should help you make a positive first impression on a potential employer. Even if you create the perfect resume, it is not a guarantee that you will receive a job offer. The primary goal of your resume is to pique a potential employer's interest in you. Based on that interest, you ultimately want to be invited to participate in a job interview.

As an applicant, it's important that you adhere to one of the following formats, the most popular of which is the Chronological Resume Format, which for at least 95 percent of all job applicants is the best resume format to use and the most widely accepted.

The Chronological Resume Format

By far, the most popular resume format is the chronological format. Unless you have unusual circumstances surrounding your employment history or you're using the internet and e-mail to submit resumes, it's a good idea to adhere to this format.

The popular chronological resume format describes your work history and education in *reverse chronological order*. Using this resume format, you can easily demonstrate upward or lateral mobility in your career path as you have moved from job to job.

Figure 3.1 is an example of how a chronological resume should be formatted. Of course, you'll have to incorporate your personal information into each section of the resume as it's appropriate.

The Electronic Resume Format

An electronic resume is one that will be sent to a potential employer via e-mail, posted on a career-related web site, such as Monster (www.monster.com), or included in an online resume database.

Many employers accept electronic resumes via their web sites, but they have a pre-defined resume form that must be completed online. This also holds true for the majority of career-related web sites.

When creating an electronic resume, adhere exactly to the formatting specifications provided by the employer or career-related web site. This means offering only the information requested in each field of the online form. You'll discover

FIGURE 3.1: Chronological Format

Your Full Name
Street Address, City, State, Zip
Phone Number/Cellular Number
E-mail Address

Objective: Place a well-written, one- or two-sentence summary of your accomplishments and your career objective here. The information here should be specifically targeted to the job you are applying for. Avoid being generic!

Work Experience
200#–Present—Your Job Title   Employer, Employer's City, State
A one-sentence description of your responsibilities.

- Using three to five bullet points, include short, concisely written accomplishments (listed one at a time). Use specific facts and figures to support your statements.
- List a second accomplishment.
- List a third accomplishment.
- List a fourth accomplishment. Because this is your most recent job, include more information about it. For subsequent jobs, you will list fewer bulleted points. Be sure to list any awards or recognition you received, plus highlight specific skills you used to succeed in each job.

19##–200#—Your Job Title   Employer, Employer's City, State
A one-sentence description of your responsibilities with the company.

- Using two to four bullet points, include short, concisely written accomplishments (listed one at a time). Use specific facts and figures to support your statements.
- List a second accomplishment.

19##–19##—Your Job Title   Employer, Employer's City, State
A one-sentence description of your responsibilities with the company.

- Using two to four bullet points, include short, concisely written accomplishments (listed one at a time). Use specific facts and figures to support your statements.
- List a second accomplishment.

Education
School Name (City, State)
    Highest Degree Earned, Graduation Date   Major
(List each school separately, and include all degrees, honors, credentials, certifications, and licenses earned.)

Certifications and Licenses
This is an optional section of your resume where you can highlight any specialized training, certifications and/or licenses you've earned that relate directly to your field.

Skills: Using one- or two-word phrases, include a short list of five to ten skills that you possess that you know will be utilized in the job you're applying for and that the employer is seeking. This section of your resume is simply a short list, with items separated by commas.

that what information is asked for is exactly the same as what would be incorporated into a traditional, printed, chronological resume, however, the formatting is different.

One difference between an electronic format and a traditional (printed) format is that as you're writing it, you'll want to use *keywords*, as opposed to action words to describe your employment history, skills, and education.

USES OF AN ELECTRONIC RESUME. The internet is probably the most powerful job search tool at your disposal as a job seeker. Using the internet and e-mail, you can find job opportunities, research companies, apply for jobs online, and communicate with potential employers. To do this successfully, you'll want to utilize an electronic resume for three main purposes:

1. To find and apply for jobs online using popular career-related web sites, such as Monster (www.monster.com), HotJobs (http://hotjobs.yahoo.com), or CareerBuilder (www.careerbuilder.com).
2. To apply for and submit your resume directly to employers by visiting the company's web site or sending your resume directly via e-mail. When you do this, your resume and electronic cover letter can either be incorporated into the message of an e-mail or sent as an attachment.
3. To add your resume to one of many online-based resume databases that are used as an applicant search tool by potential employers, headhunters, and employment agencies.

Though you will not have to deal with issues like choosing resume paper, picking the perfect font, or formatting your resume to look perfect on the printed page, there are other issues you will need to contend with when creating an electronic resume.

Keep in mind, there are no standard guidelines to follow when creating an electronic resume, because employers use different computer systems and software. Thus, it is important to adhere to the individual requirements of each employer in terms of formatting, saving, and sending your resume electronically.

When completing an online resume form, be sure you fill in all fields with the appropriate information only. Be mindful of limitations for each field. For example, a field that allows for a job description to be entered may have space for a maximum of only 50 words, so the description you enter needs to provide all of the relevant information (using keywords), but also be written concisely. Because an electronic resume is as important as a traditional one, consider printing out the online form first and then spending time thinking about how you will fill in each field (or answer each question).

Never attempt to be clever or creative by trying to add information that wasn't requested in a specific field. For example, if you are only given space to enter one phone number, but you want to provide a home and cell phone number, don't use the fields for your address to enter the second phone number.

The majority of online resume templates you will come across on the various career-related web sites and sites hosted by individual employers follow the same basic format as a traditional chronological resume; however, you will be prompted to enter each piece of information in separate fields, and you will most likely be limited to the number of fields you can fill to convey your information.

SENDING YOUR RESUME AND COVER LETTER VIA E-MAIL. When sending a resume via e-mail, the message should begin as a cover letter (and contain the same information as a cover letter). You can then either attach the resume file to the e-mail message or paste the resume text within the message (making sure the formatting remains intact).

Always be sure to include your e-mail address as well as your regular mailing address and phone number(s) in all e-mail correspondence. Never assume an employer will receive your message and simply hit Respond or Reply using their e-mail software to contact you.

Tips for Creating an Electronic Resume

It's usually easier to first create a traditional (printed) chronological resume and then edit it accordingly to fit into an electronic format. The following tips will help you create and properly format your electronic resume:

- Avoid using bullets or other symbols. Instead of a bullet, use an asterisk (*) or a dash (-). Instead of using the percentage sign (%) for example, spell out the word percent. (In your resume, write 15 percent, not 15%.)
- Use the spell check feature of the software used to create your electronic resume and then proofread the document carefully. Just as applicant tracking software is designed to pick out keywords from your resume that showcase you as a qualified applicant, the same software packages used by employers can also instantly count the number of typos and spelling errors in your document and report that to an employer as well.
- Avoid using multiple columns, tables, or charts within your document.
- Avoid abbreviations within the text; spell everything out. For example, use the word Director, not Dir. or Vice President as opposed to VP. In terms of degrees, however, it is acceptable to use term like MBA, BA, PhD, and so on.

Keywords are the backbone of any good electronic resume. If you don't incorporate keywords, your resume will not be properly processed by the employer's applicant tracking software. Choosing the right keywords to incorporate into your resume is a skill in itself that takes some creativity and plenty of thought.

For example, each job title, job description, skill, degree, license, or other piece of information you list should be descriptive, self-explanatory, and contain the keywords the potential employer's applicant tracking software is on the lookout for as it evaluates your resume. One excellent resource that can help you select the best keywords to use within your electronic resume is the *Occupational Outlook Handbook* (published by the U.S. Department of Labor, http://stats.bls.gov/oco/home.htm). Additionally, always try to use the same keywords the employer uses in the job description.

Tips for Creating and Formatting Your Resume

These tips will help you create a resume that contains the information employers are looking for.

- Start by writing out answers to the following questions: What are your skills and qualifications? What work experience do you have that directly relates to the job you're applying for? What can you offer to the employer? Specifically, how will hiring you benefit the employer? Can you help solve problems or challenges that the employer is facing? What sets you apart from other people applying for the same job? Answering these questions will help you determine what information to include in your resume.
- The main sections of a resume are the Heading, Job Objectives, Education, Accreditation and Licenses, Skills, Work and Employment Experience, Professional Affiliations, Military Service, References, and Personal Information. Choose what information about yourself should be included under each heading. The actual wording for each resume section can be modified. Also, only include the sections that apply to you.
- In the Heading, include your full name, address, telephone number(s), fax number, pager number, and e-mail address. If you're trying to keep your job search a secret from your currently employer, don't list your work telephone or fax number. Also, make sure that there's an answering machine or voice mail to the number listed on your resume, so a potential employer can reach you any time. Missing a message could result in a missed job opportunity.
- When listing your education, don't include your grades, class rank, or overall average unless this information is extremely impressive and will help to

set you apart from other applicants. The first piece of information listed in the Education section of your resume should describe the highest level of education you've earned or that you're in the process of earning.

- To decide what work experience to include on your resume, start by listing all of your internships, after-school jobs, summer jobs, part-time jobs, full-time jobs, and volunteer/charitable work. Be prepared to provide specific dates of employment, job titles, responsibilities, and accomplishments for each position. How you convey this information in your resume will be critical. Ultimately, you may have to refrain from including some of the less pertinent information in order to conserve space.

- As you sit down to write your resume, use action words, which are usually verbs that make your accomplishments sound even better, without stretching the truth. What your resume says about you, and more importantly, how it's said, will make your resume a powerful job search tool.

- Choose a resume format that best organizes your information for an employer. Using a chronological format is the most popular. Your employment experience is listed in reverse chronological order, with your most recent job listed first.

- Keep your resume short and to the point. Make sure all of the information is well organized and is stated as succinctly as possible. Remove words and phrases that are redundant.

- Print your resume on good quality, white, off-white, or cream-colored paper. Use 24- or 28-pound bond paper made of 100 percent cotton stock. Your finished resume should be neat and well balanced on the page. It should be inviting to the reader and not look cluttered.

- Before distributing your resume to potential employers, proofread it carefully. Even the smallest spelling or grammatical error will not be tolerated and could result in your missing out on a job opportunity.

Spending extra time on your resume is an excellent investment in your future. Pay careful attention to detail, and make sure that your resume promotes you in the best possible way. To assist in formatting and designing your resume, consider using specialized resume creation software. Since the design and formatting of a resume is so important, consider reading one of the many books available that explain and demonstrate the resume creation process.

WARNING! There is no room for false information on your resume or in your cover letters! Most employers will check all past employment, references, and other information you provide. Some employers even conduct full background checks on applicants. If it's discovered that you've lied or stretched the truth, you will not be hired.

A Cover Letter Introduces You to an Employer

If you already understand the format of a typical business letter and know what you are trying to convey in your cover letters, creating this document is relatively easy. Whether you are creating a cover letter that will be printed out, then hand-delivered, mailed, or faxed (as opposed to e-mailed), the content and format of the cover letter is the same.

As a general rule, never submit your resume to a potential employer unless it is accompanied by a personalized and custom-written cover letter. This is an important companion document to your resume. A cover letter serves as your initial introduction to a potential employer. It should get the recipient interested and even excited to read your resume.

Your cover letter and resume should summarize your accomplishments, education, and skills, using plain English. These documents must incorporate perfect spelling and grammar and be written in a formal business style.

Just as your resume should be one, 8.5-by-11-inch page in length, your cover letter should also be kept to less than one page in length. The shorter the better, because most people do not have time to read long letters.

Make Sure Your Resume and Cover Letter Work Together

A cover letter is designed to accompany your resume. Create these documents with synergy in mind when it comes to appearance and content. If you are creating a printed resume and cover letter (as opposed to an electronic resume for use with the internet), always use the same paper, fonts, and typestyles when creating both documents.

Virtually all employers put great value on an applicant with strong written and verbal communication skills. After all, a resume is typically a series of bulleted lists and short sentences, but a cover letter represents an actual writing sample.

Unless you impress an employer with your cover letter first, many HR professionals will not bother to read your resume. Thus, there is a chance your cover letter will be your *only* opportunity to convince a potential employer you are a viable job candidate. Both the wording and the overall appearance of your cover letter should nicely complement your resume.

The Purpose of a Cover Letter

Your cover letter should not duplicate too much information that is in your resume. Instead, you ideally want to use a cover letter to:

- Introduce yourself
- State exactly what job you are applying for
- Seize the attention of the reader
- Pique the reader's interest
- Convey information about yourself that is *not* in your resume
- Briefly demonstrate your skills/accomplishments
- Convince the reader to review your resume
- Ask the reader for an action to be taken

If you want your cover letter and resume to stand out, it needs to look professional, as if you have put considerable thought and attention into the appearance of these documents. First impressions, in this case, are extremely important.

Though the reader of your cover letter will, of course, be looking at the letter's content and meaning, your writing style, spelling, punctuation and the format of your document will all evaluated. What you say in your cover letter is important, but you should also think carefully about how you want to say it, and make sure that your overall presentation is professional and visually appealing. Each cover letter should be custom written for the job you are applying for and personalized using the name and title of the recipient.

Strategies for Formatting a Cover Letter

Before sending your cover letter and resume to anyone, call the recipient's office and ask for his/her full name and title. Obtaining the correct spelling of the recipient's name, along with the company's name is important.

It is also critical to confirm the recipient's gender, so you can address the envelope and cover letter to Mr., Ms., Mrs. (insert last name). Refrain from making assumptions.

Before sitting down to write your cover letter, first obtain the following information and make sure it's accurate:

- Recipient's full name
- Recipient's job title
- Company name
- Mailing address
- Phone number
- Exact position you're applying for
- Recipient's fax number (optional)
- Recipient's e-mail address (optional)

In terms of the letter's format, at the top, be sure to list *your* full name, address, phone number(s), and e-mail address. If you have personalized stationery that matches your resume paper, use it. Your contact information should be followed by the recipient's address and the date (using a standard business letter format).

Next add the salutation. The body of the letter will include an opening paragraph, your marketing message, one or two support paragraphs, your formal request for an interview, and finally, closure.

Just as in a verbal conversation (where you begin by saying "hello"), your cover letters should start off with a salutation, such as Dear Mr./Mrs./Ms./Dr. (insert recipient's last name) or Dear Sir or Madam.

Next comes the opening paragraph of your letter. Keep it short and simple. This paragraph should answer the questions: "Who are you?" and "Why are you writing this letter?" Keep this part of your cover letter to no longer than two or three sentences. Be sure to mention specifically what job opening you are applying for, especially if you are responding to an ad.

Following the opening paragraph, use the next paragraph or two within the body of your cover letter to quickly set you apart from the competition. Make sure you convey reasons you are the best applicant for the job you're applying for. Addressing the employer's needs is the primary goal of this portion of the cover letter.

By conducting research about the potential employer (and from the wording of the Help Wanted ad or job description you're responding to), you should have a basic understanding of what the employer's needs are. In your cover letter, describe how you (with your education, skills and experience) can meet those needs and help the company achieve its goals.

Use the next paragraph of your cover letter to answer this question: What is it about the employer that piqued your interest? This is your opportunity to compliment the employer and demonstrate you have done some research about its organization and industry.

The next section of your cover letter should be a request for the reader to take action, such as inviting you in for an interview. Finally, your cover letter should conclude with a formal closure and your signature. Be sure to thank the reader for their interest, time, and consideration.

Formatting Your Cover Letter

All correspondence with a potential employer, with the exception of a thank-you note, should be typed or created on a computer, not handwritten. Figure 3.2 provides a sample showing how you should format your cover letter on a printed page.

FIGURE 3.2: Sample Cover Letter

Your Name
Your Address
Your Phone Number
Your Fax Number (Optional)
Your E-Mail Address (Optional)

Date

Recipient's Full Name
Recipient's Title
Company Name
Address
City, State, Zip Code

Dear (Mr./Mrs./Mrs./Dr.) (Insert Recipient's Last Name):

Opening Paragraph

Support Paragraph #1

Support Paragraph #2

Request For Action Paragraph

Closing Paragraph

Sincerely,

(Your Signature)

(Your Full Name Typed)

COMPLETING APPLICATIONS AND JOB INTERVIEW DOS AND DON'TS

The first time you visit a potential employer, often for an interview, you'll be asked to complete a one- or two-page job application. This is simply a questionnaire that will ask you to reiterate much of the information that's already in your resume and cover letter. At the end of the application, you be asked to sign a statement indicating that all of the information is true.

Job applications are completed by hand. Be prepared by bringing your own pen with black or blue ink (not a pencil). As you answer each question, make sure your handwriting is legible and that whatever you write is grammatically correct. Spelling mistakes won't be tolerated. One reason an employer requires applicants to complete a writing sample is to gauge their written communication skills and penmanship.

The answers you provide to each question on the application should be consistent with information you've already provided in your resume and cover letter. You also want to insure that the information you provide actually answers the question(s) being posed to you.

One excellent strategy is to ask the employer for two blank copies of the employment application. Use the first copy to practice answering each question, then copy the appropriate information onto the second copy once you're comfortable with your responses. It is not acceptable to have information crossed out or written over on the application.

You'll notice that many employment applications will ask you to list referrals or references. Now is the time to provide personal and/or professional references. You do not need to list this information within your resume. Before listing a reference, make sure you've asked that person's permission and that he or she is aware of what job(s) you're applying for.

Personal references can be relatives or friends. Professional references, however, should *not* be related to you. These should be people who will have positive things to say about you, your work ethic, your reliability, and your skills. Past coworkers, past managers or supervisors, or teachers/professors who taught you in school all make excellent professional references. For each reference, provide a full name, describe the relationship to you (how you know the person and/or job title and company), along with phone number and e-mail address.

Job Interview Dos and Don'ts

Assuming your resume does its job and captures the attention of a potential employer, you'll be invited to participate in an in-person or telephone job interview. This is your opportunity to sell yourself to a potential employer by demonstrating through your words, appearance, attitude, and body language that you're the best candidate to fill the job opening. Hiring decisions are made as a result of how you conduct yourself during interviews!

An employer's decision about whether to hire you will be based on your skills, experience, educational background, and how well you represent yourself and perform during your job interview(s).

The following strategies will help you to properly prepare for an interview and make a positive first impression:

- Before the interview, research the company you're interviewing with, the industry you'll be working in, and if possible, try to learn as much as possible about the individual who will be conducting the interview.

- As part of your preparation, participate in mock (pretend) interviews with a friend, relative, or career counselor. Practice answering common interview questions out loud, and compile a list of at least five intelligent questions you can ask the employer during the interview.

- Be sure to get a good night's sleep before the interview. You want to look and feel rested.

- Before your interview, take a shower, shampoo your hair, clean your fingernails, brush your teeth, shave, and apply antiperspirant and deodorant. Your appearance is the very first thing a potential employer is going notice when you arrive for an interview.

- Make sure what you'll be wearing to your interview is clean, wrinkle-free, and fits perfectly. Also, be sure your shoes are shined and coordinate well with your outfit.

- Before arriving at the interview, make several extra copies of your resume, letters of recommendation, and your list of references. Have these extra copies with you at the interview. You'll also want to bring your daily planner, along with your research materials, a pad, and a pen. All of this paperwork will fit nicely in a briefcase or portfolio.

- The morning of your interview, read a local newspaper or watch a morning news program. You'll want to be aware of the day's news events and be able to discuss them with the interviewer. Many interviewers like to start off an interview with general chit-chat. Your goal is to appear knowledgeable about what's happening in the world around you.

- Arrive to your interview at least 15 minutes early and check in with the receptionist. While it's okay for an interviewer to keep you, the applicant, waiting, it's never acceptable for the job seeker (applicant) to show up for an interview even one minute late. Next to being unprepared for the interview, arriving late is the worst mistake you can make.

- From the moment you arrive at the interview location, act professionally. Be polite to everyone, including secretaries and receptionists.

- As the interview gets underway, sit up straight. Listen carefully to the questions posed to you and take a moment to think about each answer. Respond using complete sentences. Words like, "yeah," "nope," and "umm" should not be used as part of your professional vocabulary.

- Throughout the entire interview, in addition to what you say, you will be evaluated based on how you conduct yourself and use body language. Control your nervous habits. If you know what your nervous habits are, they'll be easier to control in stressful situations.
- During the latter part of your interviews, make a point to come right out and ask for the job you're applying for. Explain exactly why you want the job, what you can offer the company, and why you're the best candidate to fill the position.

Anticipate Job Interview Questions

As part of your job interview preparation, determine the types of questions the interviewer will most likely ask. With experience participating in interviews, you'll discover you'll be asked the same questions over and over again. Spend time developing well thought out, complete, and intelligent answers to common questions.

Here are some tips for answering all of the interviewer's questions:

- Avoid talking down to an interviewer or making him/her feel less intelligent than you are.
- Be prepared to answer the same questions multiple times. Make sure your answers are consistent. Never reply, "You already asked me that."
- Don't be evasive, especially if you're asked about negative aspects of your employment history.
- Don't lie or stretch the truth.
- Never apologize for negative information regarding your past.
- Never imply that a question is "stupid."
- Use complete sentences and proper English.

Be Prepared for a Background Check

One of the final steps related to landing a new job will often be allowing your new employer (once you receive a job offer) to conduct a full background check on you. You may also be asked to undergo a drug test. Employers can't afford to allocate resources to training and begin relying on employees who ultimately aren't capable of handling the job or who have something in their backgrounds that could be detrimental to the employer.

If there is something negative in your past, bring it to the attention of employers *before* they discover it for themselves. If you're able to put a positive spin on the situation and convince the employer you're not a risk and won't turn into a liability, chances are you'll still get hired. This is when having several very positive references and letters of recommendation will come in handy.

If, however, you're actively involved with any type of illegal drug use, seriously consider participating in a rehabilitation program before pursuing a new job. Most companies have a zero tolerance policy for drug and alcohol abuse.

Thanks to advances in computer and internet technology, performing background checks and drug tests is easier and cheaper than ever for employers. Never assume that the employer won't discover something about your past.

Have You Considered Self-Employment?

Some of the jobs described within this book, plus countless others, allow for far greater earning potential if you choose to become self-employed. This means you operate your own business and become your own boss. Sure, becoming self-employed requires a lot more risk. If you're cut out for the additional responsibilities, however, the rewards are well worth it.

When you're self-employed, you're responsible for all aspects of your livelihood, which means it'll be up to you to financially support your business until it's fully established. You'll also need to market, advertise, and promote your business, perhaps deal with inventory issues, potentially manage employees, and make countless decisions that will impact your success.

Before launching your own business, do plenty of research and make sure you're prepared. The biggest reasons for the failure of start up businesses is due to lack of planning or funding. Make sure you understand the business you're entering and know who your customers are.

It's always a good idea to work for another company first, learn all you can, gain valuable experience, and then choose to launch your own business. Even if you don't have a college education, there's no reason you can't launch your own business if you have the skills, knowledge, resources, and motivation to pursue it.

Your Job Search Is Ready to Begin!

The first few chapters of this book have provided you with the core information you need to begin your job search efforts. The rest of this book describes 202 potential job opportunities or career paths you can pursue. No matter what direction you choose to follow when seeking jobs, keep in mind that the basic process for finding, applying for, and landing any job is basically the same.

To achieve success, it's important that you be honest with yourself and potential employers, in terms of your skills, education, employment history, experience, licenses, accreditations, and any other details about yourself. Choose job opportunities that you know you're qualified for and always be on the lookout for career advancement opportunities and ways to enhance your skill set and training.

Finally, try to pursue jobs you know you'll enjoy. While earning a paycheck and being able to support yourself (and perhaps your family) is critical, you should also seek opportunities that you'll find rewarding, challenging, and fun on a personal and emotional level. As you'll discover, if you look hard enough, there are plenty of awesome job opportunities available. It's up to you to find the best opportunities for you.

Just as the title of this book promised, here you'll find information about 202 jobs and career paths suitable for someone without a college degree. In the next several chapters, you'll find out about job and career opportunities you might otherwise not have considered. Plus, you'll be provided with additional resources to help you determine if a specific opportunity is right for you, based on your interests, education, skills, experience, and overall qualifications.

Understanding the Job Descriptions within this Book

To help you get the most out of this book, each of the 202 job descriptions offers important information you'll need to consider. In addition to a wide range of potential jobs and career opportunities for each job, you'll also find valuable resources regarding where you can go for more information about that specific job. If you find a job or career you're interested in learning more about, research it, starting with the web site links and contact phone numbers listed within the book.

Here's a rundown of what each job description offers:

- *The job title.* This is the name or description of the job. Keep in mind, some job titles are self-explanatory, whereas others are broad and can apply to jobs in multiple industries.
- *Salary potential.* This is a range of what someone can expect to earn working full time in this job. Often this range is broad because what an individual employer actually pays will depend on a wide range of factors, including an employee's experience, training, skill set, geographic area, competition, state of the economy and the industry you'll be working in. The abundance (or lack thereof) of qualified applicants also impacts what an employer is willing to pay.
- *Training/license/certification required.* For many of the jobs listed within this book, nothing more than a high school diploma or GED is required. Some, however, require specific training, licenses, or certifications. What pre-existing

qualifications employers will look for is listed here. For information on how to obtain the necessary qualifications, such as a specific type of license or certification, be sure to read the For More Information section of the job description. Keep in mind, licensing requirements for many of the job opportunities vary by state. So, be sure to utilize the resources offered to determine what's required in the state where you live or will be working.

- *Other requirements.* Here, you'll learn about some of the other important skills or personality traits employers look for when hiring people to fill this type of job.

- *Career advancement opportunities.* In some cases, the jobs listed within this book are considered entry-level. As a result, they're initially low paying. Most are not dead-end jobs, however. With additional training, on-the-job experience, and hard work, you'll be able to earn promotions and pay raises. If the job has career advancement opportunities, they'll be described here. When looking for a job, always search for jobs with career advancement potential. In this book, if a job has limited career advancement potential, you'll see the word "limited" displayed. This is a tip-off that the job might not be suitable if you're seeking a long-term career with upward mobility potential.

- *Description.* This section of every job description offers valuable information about what the job is all about, what the work environment is like, and what you can expect from this type of job should you choose to pursue it.

- *For more information.* This is perhaps the most valuable section of each job description. It's here you'll discover where to find more information about the specific job or career opportunity profiled. Resources such as professional trade associations, unions, trade/vocational schools, industry magazines/newsletters, online job listings, are listed here. If you're interested in learning more about a specific job, these resources are an excellent place to begin your additional research efforts. Because most people use the internet as a powerful job search tool, the majority of the resources listed in this book include web site addresses. Visiting these web sites is one of the fastest ways to gather pertinent information.

Throughout this book, you'll also read Career Spotlights, which are in-depth profiles of 15 career opportunities, including interviews with people, just like you, who have achieved success working in that specific field. These detailed profiles are designed to help you understand the importance of pursuing career advancement opportunities and seeking opportunities beyond the entry-level position you're initially hired to fill. It's these advancement opportunities and promotions that will lead to greater job stability and offer you higher earning potential.

CHAPTER

ARTS, ENTERTAINMENT, AND SPORTS JOBS

This chapter focuses on jobs that involve arts, entertainment, and sports. Whether you have musical abilities, a flare for the dramatic, a passion for sports, or want to focus your career on something that involves a lot of creativity, check out this section for job ideas worth pursuing.

Actor

> **AT A GLANCE**
>
> **SALARY POTENTIAL:** Varies dramatically.
>
> **TRAINING/LICENSE/CERTIFICATION REQUIRED:** None, but experience in school plays or with local, non-professional theater groups is strongly recommended.
>
> **OTHER REQUIREMENTS:** A professional head shot (8-by-10-inch photograph) and a resume. Working as an actor requires extensive memorization of dialogue and stage direction.
>
> **CAREER ADVANCEMENT OPPORTUNITIES:** There are many types of acting jobs, ranging from local community/dinner theater, to starring on Broadway, in TV commercials, on a network television series, or in a movie (where the income potential can be in the millions).

First, becoming a professional actor requires talent, the right look, and an incredible amount of motivation and dedication. Ultimately, you'll need to hire an agent and/or manager to send you out on auditions. However, as you break into the business, you'll need to attend countless open casting calls (referred to as "cattle calls") and meet with casting directors.

The best way to get started is to participate in school plays or to work with a local theater group to gain valuable experience. Taking professional acting classes (from a reputable acting coach/teacher) is also highly recommended, but not required.

As a professional actor, you'll seldom have a steady income (except when you're working). Once you reach a certain level, you may need to join a union. You must be able to deal well with rejection at auditions and casting calls. Acting allows people with an outgoing personality to showcase their creativity and talent in front of an audience.

For More Information

- American Federation of Television & Radio Artists (AFTRA). A professional trade organization, (212) 532-0800 or (323) 634-8100, www.aftra.org.
- *Back Stage* and *Back Stage West*. Weekly newspapers for actors, (800) 562-2706, www.backstage.com, $132 (12-month subscription, with single issues available at major newsstands).

- *Ross Reports Television & Film.* Monthly publication for actors, (800) 562-2706, www.backstage.com/backstage/rossreports/directories.jsp, $109 (12-month subscription, with single issues available at major newsstands. This publication offers a detailed list of agents and casting directors in Los Angeles and New York.
- Screen Actors Guild (SAG). This is a professional trade organization. The web site offers an abundance of career-related information for actors and those looking to break into show business, (323) 954-1600 or (212) 944-1030, www.sag.org.

Artisan/Crafter

AT A GLANCE

SALARY POTENTIAL: Varies.

TRAINING/LICENSE/CERTIFICATION REQUIRED: None.

OTHER REQUIREMENTS: Artistic and/or crafting abilities.

CAREER ADVANCEMENT OPPORTUNITIES: Many artisans and crafters are self-employed and earn money by selling their handmade crafts to local merchants, as well as at fairs, flea markets, and online (using eBay.com, for example). More established artisans sell their work through upscale galleries and/or are affiliated with museums.

If you have a passion for crafting or creating some type of art (such as knitting, pottery, jewelry, painting, drawing, stained glass, or sculpture, for example), and your work is good enough to exhibit and sell, there are many ways to supplement your income or develop a business based on your hobby. For many hobbyists, selling their art offers a secondary income, generated on weekends and during free time.

For More Information

- *American Style* magazine. This is an industry-oriented trade magazine; subscriptions are $24.99 per year, (800) 272-3893, http://americanstyle.com.
- Craft Marketer. Strategies for building a successful crafts business can be found on www.craftmarketer.com.

- Festival Network Online. A nationwide listing of craft shows, art fairs, music festivals, and events are offered on this site, www.festivalnet.com/events2.html.
- National Association of Crafters & Artists. This is a professional trade organization offering information and resources for crafters, www.nationalaac.org.
- National Craft Association. This is a professional trade organization offering information and resources for crafters, (800) 715-9594, www.craftassoc.com.

Artist

AT A GLANCE

SALARY POTENTIAL: Varies.

TRAINING/LICENSE/CERTIFICATION REQUIRED: None.

OTHER REQUIREMENTS: Graduation from art school is recommended, but not required. Natural talent and artistic ability is a must.

CAREER ADVANCEMENT OPPORTUNITIES: Aside from displaying and selling your work at galleries and art exhibits, depending on the type of art you create, there are countless job opportunities available in corporate America, at advertising agencies, graphic design firms, publishing companies, or animation companies. You can also work in a wide range of traditional companies, developing product packaging and marketing materials, for example. Career opportunities vary greatly.

Whether you're a painter, sculptor, or illustrator, there is a wide range of career opportunities available. More than half of all professional artists are self-employed. Fine artists typically display and sell their work through museums and art galleries, while other types of illustrators, for example, work for traditional companies.

Most artists work from studios, located either in their homes or within commercial buildings. To land a job as a professional artist, skill is far more important than education. Earning a Bachelor of Fine Arts (BFA) or a Master of Fine Arts (MFA) will help you land certain types of jobs, however. There are more than 200 postsecondary schools in the United States that offer programs in art and design.

As an artist who is first starting out, you'll probably want to create a portfolio of your best work. A portfolio allows you to showcase your work in an organized way. It's used by artists, graphic designers, photographers, and others working in highly creative fields where the end product of their work is more important than their credentials.

For More Information

- ArtDeadline. This is an online resource for artists looking for employment and/or exhibiting opportunities, http://artdeadline.com.
- eLance. This is an online service for promoting yourself as a freelance artist/illustrator or graphic designer, www.eLance.com.
- National Association of Schools of Art and Design. A listing of art and design schools in America can be found at http://nasad.arts-accredit.org.

Calligrapher

> ### AT A GLANCE
>
> SALARY POTENTIAL: Varies. Calligraphers typically charge by the character, word, line, or project.
>
> TRAINING/LICENSE/CERTIFICATION REQUIRED: None.
>
> OTHER REQUIREMENTS: Ability to write in calligraphy using a fountain pen or other fine writing instrument and use creativity to create professional look-ing invitations and announcements.
>
> CAREER ADVANCEMENT OPPORTUNITIES: Create wedding and event invitations from home or an office, working full or part time.

Creating handwritten, personalized wedding invitations, baby announcements, dedications, proclamations, personalized stationery, business cards, or other spe-cial announcements for clients can be a lucrative, full-time or part-time business that requires minimal training and low start-up costs. You can be self-employed or work for a printing or stationery company.

For More Information

- Asian Brush Art Supplies. Supplies for Asian calligraphy can be purchased from this web site, www.asianbrushart.com/supplies.html.

- Calligraphy Center. Learn about calligraphy classes and instruction from this site, www.calligraphycentre.com/begin.html.
- Calligraphy On Demand. This is an online resource for calligraphy supplies and services, www.calligraphyondemand.com.
- Fountain Pen Hospital. This company is a calligraphy supplies wholesaler, www.fountainpenhospital.com.
- Graphò. From this site, you can learn about calligraphy training from The International Calligraphy Correspondence Program, http://catalog.com/gallery/grapho.html.

Clown or Street Performer

AT A GLANCE

SALARY POTENTIAL: Varies. A street performer works exclusively for tips, whereas a professional clown (who appears at birthday parties and events) might be paid per performance. A clown employed by a circus, for example, will typically be paid a salary.

TRAINING/LICENSE/CERTIFICATION REQUIRED: To become a street performer, a local license is required. Contact your local city hall. A small, annual fee will be required. Professional clowns are often graduates of clown or improvisational acting schools.

OTHER REQUIREMENTS: The ability to entertain. A street performer can be an amateur or professional musician, singer, juggler, puppeteer, mime, clown, or skilled at providing other types of entertainment outdoors, at popular parks and tourist attractions. Street performers must adhere to all local laws and guidelines whenever they perform in public areas.

CAREER ADVANCEMENT OPPORTUNITIES: Limited.

If you've ever visited the South Street Seaport in New York City, Faneuil Hall Marketplace in Boston, The Third Street Promenade in Santa Monica, California, or other popular, outdoor tourist destinations, chances are, you've seen street performers entertaining crowds.

This is an excellent full- or part-time job for someone with a unique talent who enjoys performing and entertaining people in an informal environment. Though you're financial compensation is based exclusively on tips, many street performers work year-round, visiting and performing at popular tourist attractions in various cities throughout America. Musician and singers, for example, also generate revenue by selling their self-produced CDs and merchandise at their performances.

Becoming a professional clown can be a self-taught profession; however, there are several clown, comedy, and improvisational acting schools across the country that can prepare you for a career entertaining people of all ages. Clowns are hired to work at birthday parties and special events, work as street performers, and appear in circuses. In addition to having a flare for physical comedy and a willingness to dress in a goofy outfit, the ability to juggle, create balloon animals, performing magic tricks, and make people laugh are all valuable skills for this position.

For More Information

- California Clown School. One of several schools located in the United States that teaches clowning, www.californiaclownschool.com.
- Cirque Du Soliel. Learn about casting opportunities with the world famous Cirque du Soliel shows presented throughout the world, www.cirquedu soleil.com/CirqueDuSoleil/en/jobs/onstage/default.htm.
- Clowning Around. An online store offering a wide range of products used by clowns, ranging from juggling supplies to wigs, www.clowningaround .net/webstore.
- Feld Entertainment. Producer of the Ringling Brothers, Barnum & Bailey Circus and other live entertainment shows. Learn about career opportunities as a performer from this web site, www.feldentertainment.com/pa.htm.
- Mooseburger Camp. Learn about this world-famous clown school, www .mooseburger.com.

Coach, Umpire, Referee

> ### AT A GLANCE
>
> SALARY POTENTIAL: Varies, based on the education, experience, sport, and qualifications. Some coaches, umpires, and referees are paid a salary, whereas others are paid by the hour, by the game (match or competition), or by the season.

TRAINING/LICENSE/CERTIFICATION REQUIRED: This varies greatly, depending on the level and type of sport. Professional coaches at the college and professional level typically receive on-the-job experience working at lower levels before moving up. Public high school and college-level coaches typically possess a teaching degree or specialized certification, but this varies by state. To become a professional umpire or referee, graduating from an accredited umpire or referee school is necessary. To be a professional baseball umpire, for example, applicants must graduate from one of two programs accredited by the Professional Baseball Umpires Corporation.

OTHER REQUIREMENTS: A passion for sports and an extensive knowledge of the sport you'll be working in are necessary. The ability to motivate, instruct, train, and manage athletes and entire teams is also important. Many elementary school, middle school, and high school coaches are accredited teachers who work full-time teaching a traditional subject and supplement their income by coaching a team on a part-time basis. On the college and professional level, coaching is considered a full-time job.

CAREER ADVANCEMENT OPPORTUNITIES: Coach, umpire, and referee jobs are available through schools, camps, amateur leagues, and professional leagues.

The job of a coach, umpire, and referee differs dramatically, yet all require training, extensive knowledge of a specific sport, and experience. The training and job requirements for a Little League coach will differ dramatically from what's required of a high school or college-level baseball coach or a baseball coach working for an major league baseball team, for example. All of these jobs, however, require a passion and dedication to the sport, a flexible work schedule and the ability to work well with others in a highly competitive and often stressful environment.

For More Information

- C.O.A.C.H. An online resource for coaches. The web site includes job listings and plenty of "how-to" information, www.coachhelp.com.
- CoachingJob.Net, Online job listings and career information for coaches at all levels and for all sports can be found at www.coachingjob.net.
- JobsInSports.com. Online job listings and career information for coaches at all levels and for all sports can be found at www.jobsinsports.com.

- National Association of Sports Officials. This is a professional organization offering information for people working in professional sports, www.naso.org.
- National High School Athletics Association. This is a professional organization offering information for coaches working at the high school level, www.hscoaches.org.

Cosmetologist

> **AT A GLANCE**
>
> **SALARY POTENTIAL:** $15,000 to $40,000 (or more), plus tips. Income is based on skills, experience, and the type of place of employment. Working at an upscale spa or salon offers greater earning potential.
>
> **TRAINING/LICENSE/CERTIFICATION REQUIRED:** Depending on the specialty, a state-issued license may be required. Qualifications for a license vary by state. Typically, graduating from a state-licensed cosmetology school is required.
>
> **OTHER REQUIREMENTS:** Creativity and the ability to interact well with people are important skills when working in this field.
>
> **CAREER ADVANCEMENT OPPORTUNITIES:** Varies, based on specialty and training.

Like so many fields, cosmetology encompasses a wide range of specialties in the beauty field. Hairdressers, hair stylists, manicurists, pedicurists, shampooers, and skin care professionals all fall into this category.

Barbershops, beauty salons, day spas, nail salons, and resorts are some of the places that hire cosmetologists. About half of the people working in this field are self-employed. These people rent space at local salons, for example, but are responsible for finding and catering to their own clients. One benefit to this type of work is a flexible schedule.

Cosmetology schools offer daytime, nighttime, or weekend programs. The programs last between nine and 24 months. Becoming a nail technician (manicurist or pedicurist), however, requires significantly less training, while working as a shampooer requires no training or license.

For hairstylists, upon completing cosmetology school, participating in an apprentice program is typically required.

For More Information

- Beauty Schools Directory. A listing of licensed beauty schools and detailed career-related information is offered at www.beautyschoolsdirectory.com/faq/find.php.
- National Accrediting Commission of Cosmetology Arts and Sciences. This is a professional trade organization offering information about cosmetology training programs and licensed schools, www.naccas.org.
- National Cosmetology Association. This is a professional trade organization offering career-related resources, www.salonprofessionals.org.
- Vocational Information Center. This web site offers links to a wide range of resources of interest to cosmetologists and those interested in entering this field. Includes a list of Cosmetology State Boards (to obtain information about licensing), http://www.khake.com/page76.html.

Disc Jockey/DJ

AT A GLANCE

SALARY POTENTIAL: Varies.

TRAINING/LICENSE/CERTIFICATION REQUIRED: None.

OTHER REQUIREMENTS: A passion and knowledge of music, as well as an outgoing personality and a flexible work schedule.

CAREER ADVANCEMENT OPPORTUNITIES: Disc jockeys are hired to entertain parties, weddings, bar/bat mitzvahs, graduation celebrations, retirement parties, corporate parties, and other types of functions. They're also hired by radio stations and nightclubs.

The job of a disc jockey is to play music at a wide range of parties and functions, entertain guests and often work as a master of ceremonies at functions. Many disc jockeys are self-employed or work for an agency. Those who are self-employed must have their own equipment, sound systems, and an extensive music libraries. This job requires working nights and weekends. Nightclubs also hire disc jockeys.

Radio stations hire disc jockeys to play music on the radio and entertain listeners. The best way to break into this type of work is to land an internship at a radio station while you're in school, plus study broadcasting in college or through a technical school. Radio disc jockeys must have a professional sounding voice and extremely outgoing personality. Top-notch vocal skills are a must.

For More Information
- Contact a disc jockey agency in your area.
- Contact local radio stations and inquire about internship/volunteer opportunities.
- National Broadcasters Training Network. Details about training programs for disc jockeys, as well as extensive career-related information is available at www.learn-by-doing.com.

Disney Imagineer®

> **AT A GLANCE**
>
> **SALARY POTENTIAL:** Varies.
>
> **TRAINING/LICENSE/CERTIFICATION REQUIRED:** Varies.
>
> **OTHER REQUIREMENTS:** In addition to being an expert in a specific field, the core requirements for this type of job include an abundance of creativity and ability to work in a team-oriented environment.
>
> **CAREER ADVANCEMENT OPPORTUNITIES:** There are virtually unlimited career advancement opportunities within the Walt Disney Company, particularly for successful Imagineers.

According to the Walt Disney Company web site, a Disney Imagineer is, "the master planning, creative development, design, engineering, production, project management, and research and development arm of The Walt Disney Company and its affiliates. Representing more than 150 disciplines; its talented corps of Imagineers is responsible for the creation of Disney resorts, theme parks and attractions, hotels, water parks, real estate developments, regional entertainment venues, cruise ships and new media technology projects."

The job requires the blending of creativity and innovative technological advancements. Job opportunities are available in Glendale, California; Anaheim,

California; and Orlando, Florida. The job requirements for Disney Imagineers are extremely diverse. Some require specialized education or training.

For More Information

- Entertainment Careers. This web site offers jobs listings available within the entertainment industry, including various divisions of the Walt Disney Company, www.entertainmentcareers.net.
- The Walt Disney Company. http://corporate.disney.go/careers/who_ima gineering.html. From this corporate web site, you'll learn more about Disney Imagineers. For job listings within the Walt Disney Company, point your web browser to http://jobsearch.disneycareers.newjobs.com.

Exotic Dancer

> **AT A GLANCE**
>
> **SALARY POTENTIAL:** Varies (based mainly on tips).
>
> **TRAINING/LICENSE/CERTIFICATION REQUIRED:** None, but participating in basic dance and movement classes will be beneficial.
>
> **OTHER REQUIREMENTS:** The ability to dance, an outgoing personality, and a nice body.
>
> **CAREER ADVANCEMENT OPPORTUNITIES:** Limited (in terms of jobs that are legal).

A female or male exotic dancer can work for an adult-oriented strip club, dance club, or an outcall service that provides entertainment to bachelor or bachelorette parties, for example. This type of job is legal in most states and requires some level of partial or total nudity. Exotic dancers mainly rely on tips for their income. Career advancement opportunities include working in the adult film industry, escorting, or prostitution (which this book is in no way endorsing). Many people have moral and ethical objections to this type of work. If it's something you choose to pursue, make sure you have a good understanding of what you're getting into.

Some people find lucrative work as a dancer or hostess working overseas, in a country like Japan. In the United States, gentleman's clubs hire exotic dancers to provide entertainment for clientele.

For More Information

- Adult Employment. Online job listings for exotic dancers. Contact local clubs for job opportunities, www.adultemployment.com.
- Dance.com. Online listings for legitimate dancing jobs, www.dance.com.
- Exotic Dancer Superstore. An online resource for job listings and career-related information for exotic dancing, stripping, and related fields, www.exotic dancer.com.
- Exotic Dancing and Hosting Jobs in Japan, www.geocities.com/dancejapan agent.

Fashion Model

AT A GLANCE

SALARY POTENTIAL: Varies greatly. Minimum wage to thousands of dollars per day.

TRAINING/LICENSE/CERTIFICATION REQUIRED: None.

OTHER REQUIREMENTS: Depending on the type of modeling you do, especially runway modeling, in addition to being attractive, you must be within a certain height and weight range. Obtaining some form of modeling training is useful, but not always required.

CAREER ADVANCEMENT OPPORTUNITIES: Models are hired for photo shoots (to appear in magazines, catalogs, and newspapers), as well as for fashion shows, trade shows, conventions, and events.

Landing a job as a fashion model requires a certain look. You must be attractive, outgoing, and photogenic. To break into this highly competitive field, you'll need to create a photographic portfolio (a collection of photos taken by a professional photographer), plus you'll need to work with a legitimate modeling agency. It is the modeling agency that books you for modeling jobs, either with photographers or other types of clients, such as advertising agencies or fashion designers. There is no pre-defined age minimum or educational requirement for modeling.

Beware! Millions of people have tried to break into modeling and have fallen victim to a wide range of scams. Make sure the photographer(s), modeling school(s), and agent(s) you work with have a good reputation and are legitimate.

Most of the top modeling agencies, like Elite, Wilhelmina, Ford, IMG, Q Model Management, and Next have offices in New York and Los Angeles, with satellite offices in other major cities.

For More Information

- Barbizon Modeling School. One of many national schools for modeling, www.modelingschools.com.
- John Robert Powers Acting and Modeling School. A national school for modeling, www.jrpowersphila.com.
- Modeling Job Bank. Online listings for modeling jobs, www.modelingjob bank.com.
- Models.com. Online resources for up-and-coming models, www.models.com.
- Check your local Yellow Pages for modeling agencies and modeling schools in your area.

 CAREER SPOTLIGHT

Floral Designer

> AT A GLANCE
>
> SALARY POTENTIAL: $20,000 to $35,000 per year.
>
> TRAINING/LICENSE/CERTIFICATION REQUIRED: The majority of floral designers are trained on the job. Employers look for people who know about flowers and who have a flare for design and creativity. There are, however, formal floral design training programs offered by vocational schools. These programs typically last under one year. Two to four-year programs in floriculture, horticulture, floral design, or ornamental horticulture are offered by community and junior colleges, colleges, and universities.
>
> OTHER REQUIREMENTS: Creativity, time management, and good verbal communication skills are necessary.
>
> CAREER ADVANCEMENT OPPORTUNITIES: Limited.

Floral designers work for florists and flower delivery services. Their job involves cutting and arranging live, dried, or artificial flowers and foliage into designs, according to the customer's order. Floral designers create customized arrangements for clients by trimming flowers and arranging bouquets, sprays, wreaths, dish gardens, and terrariums.

To customize an appropriate arrangement, the floral designer needs to think in terms of the occasion, the customer's budget, the types of flowers available (or requested by the client), and the time the arrangement needs to be delivered to the recipient.

If the floral designer is employed by a florist that's affiliated with a network, such as FTD or 1-800-FLOWERS, he or she will be required to create and deliver specialized arrangements based on specific guidelines and products offered through the network. At times, however, the floral designer will need to tap his or her own creativity and flower arranging skills to create original arrangements for clients.

A skilled floral designer knows how to create gorgeous flower arrangements, bouquets, corsages, garlands, wreaths, and baskets for parties, banquets, weddings, birthdays, funerals, and other occasions. This is a $20 billion per year industry that continues to grow, so there are plenty of job opportunities.

Here's My Story

Allison is a 31-year-old, divorced woman from Connecticut who has always enjoyed gardening. When she needed to obtain a full-time job to support herself, she decided to transform her love for flowers into a career. She started by applying for an entry-level job working at a local florist. Once she landed the job, she began learning the skills needed to be a floral designer through on-the-job training, watching her coworkers, and by gaining hands-on experience.

"As a teenager, I held a variety of traditional retail-oriented jobs, which made it easier for me to apply for a job with a local florist. Initially, I started doing very basic tasks, like greeting customers and taking phone orders. As time went on, I started learning the art of floral design, plus learned all about buying flowers wholesale for the shop. I discovered how the business was run on a day-to-day basis," said Allison.

"Once it was clear to me that I really enjoyed this type of work and that my favorite aspect of the job was actually creating the floral arrangements, I sought out training from a floral design school," she added. "My employer actually helped pay the tuition. I was able to attend classes and continue working, so I, along with my employer, benefited."

According to Allison, "Working as a floral designer is all about creativity, however, the job also entails a lot of repetitive and mundane tasks. I would recommend this type of work to someone who appreciates the beauty of flowers and loves being creative. This job is rewarding because what I create makes the recipients happy and brings beauty and pleasure into their lives."

For More Information

- 1-800-Flowers. Career opportunities at 1-800-Flowers can be found at www.1800flowers.com/about/employment.asp.
- American Institute of Floral Designers, www.aifd.org. This organization offers an accreditation examination to its members which indicates professional achievement in floral design. For a listing of accredited floral design schools recognized by the American Institute of Floral Designers, point your web browser to www.aifd.org/edpartnerslist.htm.
- FTD. Learn about career opportunities at FTD from this web site, www.ftd.com/528/content/jobposting.epl.
- *Make People Smile: Grow Your Future In The Flower Design Industry*. Download a free, informative, 24-page brochure outlining career opportunities as a floral designer, www.safnow.org/Public/career%20brochure.pdf.
- PCDI Home Study Courses. Learn about one of many online-based home study courses in floral design, www.pcdicourses.com/html/programs_fl.php.
- Society of American Florists. This is a professional trade association for florists and floral designers. The web site offers a wide range of resources and career-related information, plus online training opportunities, (703) 836-8700, www.safnow.org.
- Wholesale Florist & Floral Supplies Association. This is a professional trade association for florists and floral designers. The web site offers a wide range of resources and career-related information, www.wffsa.org.
- Online job listings can be found at general interest career-related web sites, like Monster (www.monster.com) or Yahoo! Hot Jobs (http://hotjobs.yahoo.com).

Golf Instructor and Golf Industry Jobs

> AT A GLANCE
>
> SALARY POTENTIAL: Varies.

> **TRAINING/LICENSE/CERTIFICATION REQUIRED:** PGA training and/or other certification is recommended and required by most golf courses and related employers. The related field of PGA Professional Golf Management (PGM) is a program currently taught at 17 PGA accredited universities.
>
> **OTHER REQUIREMENTS:** An intimate knowledge of golf is required for any type of job relating to this sport. Proficiency playing the game is also necessary.
>
> **CAREER ADVANCEMENT OPPORTUNITIES:** A wide range of jobs are available to certified golf instructors and others with expertise in various aspects of the golf industry.

Within the United States, there are over 18,000 golf courses in addition to thousands of other golf-related businesses that hire golf pros and instructors. Product manufacturers, teaching centers, country clubs, upscale hotels, resorts, and other golf-related businesses all offer career opportunities for trained golf instructors. As a result of these many opportunities, over 500,000 people are employed in golf-related jobs. For some jobs within this field, a four-year college degree is a prerequisite. Many employers, however, require only a certification for instructing jobs.

For More Information
- E-Golf Jobs. Online job listings for people interested in breaking into the golf industry, www.golfcourse-jobs.com.
- Golfing Jobs. Online job listings and career-related information is offered at www.golfingjobs.net.
- NRPG. Information about a distance learning program for golf instructors can be found at (800) 643-0612, www.usntagolf.com.
- PGA. The official web site of the PGA. Online job listings offered through the PGA can be found at http://careernet.pgalinks.com/helpwanted/emp center/. For information about training with the PGA, call (800) 477-6465 ext. 8559, www.pga.com.
- San Diego Golf Academy. Information about a golf training program for instructors is available from this web site, (800) 342-7342, www.sdga golf.com.
- The Golf Institute. Information about instruction and certification programs for golf instructors can be found at www.golfinstitute.net.

Graphic Designer

AT A GLANCE

SALARY POTENTIAL: Varies.

TRAINING/LICENSE/CERTIFICATION REQUIRED: Graphic design is taught at professional and vocational schools, as well as in traditional colleges and universities. More than 200 schools across the United States offer post-secondary
art and design programs.

OTHER REQUIREMENTS: Graphic designers must be creative, artistic, and able
to create designs using computer-based tools, as well as traditional art
materials. Communication and problem-solving skills are also useful for this
type of work.

CAREER ADVANCEMENT OPPORTUNITIES: Graphic designers are in high demand
in a wide range of industries, including advertising agencies, printing companies, and publishers. Graphic designers also achieve success as web site
designers or working with web masters in the design of sites.

Any time you see an advertisement, sign, logo, magazine, product packaging, newspaper, web site, book, computer animation, or almost any other form of visual communication material, chances are a graphic designer had something to do with the conception of the overall look of that piece. A graphic designer's job, for example, is to make ordinary text and images look creative and highly visual, using colors, fonts, typestyles, graphic elements, and a wide range of other techniques.

In a nutshell, graphic designers develop visual solutions to communications problems in virtually all forms of media. Graphic designers work in a wide range of industries and play an important role in all forms of visual communication.

While pursuing an education in graphic design is definitely helpful, a graphic designer must have at least some level of natural artistic ability. Some designers utilize that natural ability and are self-taught. Ultimately, it'll be samples of your work that get you jobs.

For More Information
- About.com. Information about graphic design careers and where to find job listings online can be found here, http://jobsearch.about.com/od/graphic designjobs.

- American Institute of Graphic Arts. Information about careers in graphic design and related fields can be found at www.aiga.org.
- eLance. This is an online service offering job listings for freelance graphic designers, www.eLance.com.
- National Association of Schools of Art and Design. A listing of accredited schools offering degree programs in art and design, including graphic design, http://nasad.arts-accredit.org.

 CAREER SPOTLIGHT

Hairstylist

> ### AT A GLANCE
>
> SALARY POTENTIAL: Varies, based on your skill, experience, and employer.
>
> TRAINING/LICENSE/CERTIFICATION REQUIRED: Certification and training is required. Licensing requirements vary by state. Training from an accredited barber or cosmetology school can last between nine and 24 months. Participating in an apprenticeship program is also often required.
>
> OTHER REQUIREMENTS: Creativity, top-notch people skills, and the ability to engage clients in discussions on a wide range of topics are useful skills for hairstylists. This job requires being on your feet for extended periods, plus staying on top of the latest hairstyle trends.
>
> CAREER ADVANCEMENT OPPORTUNITIES: Hairstylists are primarily employed by salons; however, there are other career opportunities available in related fields.

A hairstylist does a lot more than just cut hair. He or she evaluates the client's face, body, and hair, then creates a style that brings out their best features using a wide range of cutting and styling tools and techniques. A full service hairstylist will shampoo, cut, color, and style hair, plus perform scalp treatments, straighten hair, or curl it as needed. When necessary, they'll utilize hair extensions to create the look and style the client wants to achieve.

Working as a hairstylist in a salon typically means being on the job at least 40 hours per week and having a flexible schedule to accommodate the needs of regular clients. Thus, working evenings and weekends is sometimes required.

While salon jobs are the most common, hairstylists also work on the sets of television shows and movies, help prepare models for fashion shows, and work on location for rich and famous clients. Some hairstylists are self-employed and choose to open their own salons or rent space in existing salons, which gives them greater control over their earning potential. In addition to having the hair styling skills needed for this job, the ability to successfully build professional, long-term relationships with clients is essential for repeat business.

Here's My Story

When Melissa graduated from high school, she knew she wanted to pursue a job as a hairstylist. She'd always been interested in hair and fashion. Instead of going to college, Melissa registered as a full-time student at a cosmetology school in her city and completed her training. With the help of her school's job placement office, she landed an entry-level job at a small salon, where she worked as an apprentice until she earned her full license and certification as a professional hair stylist.

"After cosmetology school, I took a job at a small hair salon, because I wanted to learn everything I could about the business. Initially, the salary was very low and the hours were long. But I learned enough, plus gained enough professional experience to eventually seek out a job at a more up-scale and expensive salon. This immediately boosted my earning potential," said Melissa.

"I really enjoy the creativity involved with working with a new client and helping her or him create a new look. When I do a great job, you can see it in her eyes when she looks in the mirror for the first time and discover a new person looking back. A great hairstyle gives someone so much extra self-esteem," added Melissa.

"I find myself working at least 45-hours per week. Now that I've begun building up my core group of clients whom I see every one, two or three weeks, I do my best to accommodate their schedules. Thus, I sometimes need to work until 9:00 P.M. at night or come in early on a Saturday morning," explained Melissa.

"When you're looking for your first salon job, find a place that offers a great work atmosphere. You spend a lot of time in the same room with your coworkers, so it's important that everyone gets along. You can also learn a great deal from the more experienced stylists you work with. In addition to all of the training, one of the most important things a hairstylist can do is stay up-to-date on all of the latest trends. I personally read at least five to ten entertainment, fashion and style magazines every month," she added.

Professional hair care is a $56 billion per year industry that continues to grow and employ over two million beauty professionals nationwide. "I am very proud to be a part of this industry. It's something I'd always dreamed about. Sure, certain aspects of the job haven't lived up to expectations, but overall, this is a fun, challenging and rewarding career."

For More Information

- National Accrediting Commission of Cosmetology Arts & Sciences. This professional trade association offers career-related information, plus information on licensing and certification, www.naccas.org.
- National Cosmetology Association. This is a professional trade association that offers career-related information, plus information on licensing and certification for people working in the salon industry, www.salonprofes sionals.org.
- StyleCareer.com. This web site explores the many career opportunities available to skilled hairstylists. Plenty of free information is provided, www.stylecareer.com/stylist.html.
- Online job listings can be found at general interest career-related web sites, like Monster (www.monster.com) or Yahoo! Hot Jobs, http://hotjobs .yahoo.com.

Illustrator (also see Graphic Artist)

AT A GLANCE

SALARY POTENTIAL: Varies.

TRAINING/LICENSE/CERTIFICATION REQUIRED: While natural artistic ability is a requirement that can't necessarily be taught in school, there are over 200 professional and vocational schools, as well as traditional colleges and universities, that offer art and design certificate and degree programs. Earning a Bachelor of Fine Arts (BFA) or a Master of Fine Arts (MFA) will help you land certain types of jobs in this field.

OTHER REQUIREMENTS: Creativity and problem-solving skills are necessary. Illustrators must be able to communicate using visuals.

> CAREER ADVANCEMENT OPPORTUNITIES: There are a wide range of career advancement opportunities in many industries for talented illustrators. In this field, employers will base hiring decisions on the quality of your work and experience over your education and training.

The job of an illustrator is to create artwork, drawings, or other visuals for use in a wide range of media. This includes creating original pictures for books, magazines, and other publications, and for commercial products such as textiles, wrapping paper, stationery, greeting cards, and product packaging.

Like a graphic artist, some of work performed by an illustrator is done using computers in addition to or instead of traditional art supplies. Many employers that would hire a graphic artist also have a need for illustrators, including publishers, advertising agencies, manufacturers, and web site design firms.

For More Information

- ArtDeadline. This is an online resource for artists looking for employment and/or exhibiting opportunities, http://artdeadline.com.
- eLance. This is an online service for promoting yourself as a freelance artist/illustrator or graphic designer, www.eLance.com.
- National Association of Schools of Art and Design. This web site offers a listing of art and design schools in the United States, http://nasad.arts-accredit.org.

Interior Designer

> AT A GLANCE
>
> SALARY POTENTIAL: Varies, based on your skill, experience, and employer.
>
> TRAINING/LICENSE/CERTIFICATION REQUIRED: Certificate and degree programs are available through a wide range of vocational schools, colleges, and universities.
>
> OTHER REQUIREMENTS: Creativity, organizational skills, an eye for color and the ability to implement the ideas of clients, as well as your own ideas, are all necessary for this job.

> CAREER ADVANCEMENT OPPORTUNITIES: An interior designer can be self-employed or work for a wide range of companies in various industries, including furniture, flooring, and home improvement stores and manufacturers.

An interior designer's goal is to transform an inside space, such as a home, apartment, condo, office, hotel, retail store, theater, or restaurant into a highly functional, visually attractive, safe, and well-organized space. This includes coordinating and placing furniture and fixtures, wall coverings, lighting, and a wide range of other interior design elements. The job also involves coming up with your own creative ideas, implementing ideas and demands from clients, and working with contractors and other professionals to bring those ideas into fruition on time and within a pre-defined budget.

The job involves working extensively with clients in person and on the phone, working with suppliers and contractors, being extremely detail oriented, and having the ability to solve problems while utilizing your artistic and creative abilities. Part of this job involves designing spaces that conform to federal, state, and local laws, including building codes. When designing public areas, the work must meet accessibility standards for the disabled and elderly.

For More Information

- About.com. Career-related information for interior designers can be found at http://interiordec.about.com/od/careerinfo.
- Interior Design Schools. This web site offers a listing of schools offering Interior Design programs, along with useful career-related information, www.interior-design-school.net/careers.htm.
- Westwood College. This is one of many schools that offers a distance learning program that results in a bachelor's degree in Interior Design, www.westwood-college.net.

Jeweler/Jewelry Repair Technician

AT A GLANCE

SALARY POTENTIAL: Varies.

TRAINING/LICENSE/CERTIFICATION REQUIRED: Completion of a six-month to one-year program taught at a trade school, technical school, or through distance learning will prepare you for a career working in a jewelry store. This will involve training in sales, repair, polishing, and basic jewelry design. If you plan to pursue college, you can obtain a Bachelor of Fine Arts or Master of Fine Arts in jewelry design.

OTHER REQUIREMENTS: Good eyesight, hand-eye coordination, creativity, attention to detail, the ability to work with small tools, and patience are all needed to work as a jeweler.

CAREER ADVANCEMENT OPPORTUNITIES: Careers in jewelry can involve design, manufacturing, repair, sales, and a wide range of related tasks. With additional training, you can become a gemologist.

With only a few months of training, you can become qualified to pursue a career in the jewelry industry. These jobs involve working hands-on with jewelry, but also typically involve sales (often on a commission or salary plus commission basis). There are many specialties in this field, each of which offers a different set of core skills, including designing, creating, repairing, or selling jewelry.

For More Information
- About.com. Career-related information about the jewelry field can be found here, http://jewelry.about.com/od/jewelrycareers.
- Careers 'n Jewelry. This web site offers job listings plus career-related information for someone looking to enter this field, www.careersnjewelry.com.
- Gemological Institute of America. This is an organization offering career-related information and a wide range of resources for anyone interested in jewelry. Information about training programs is also offered, www.gia.com.
- Manufacturing Jewelers and Suppliers of America. This is a professional trade organization for jewelers. Includes information about the MJSA Jewelry Academy, (800) 444-6572, http:// mjsa.polygon.net.

Musician

> **AT A GLANCE**
>
> SALARY POTENTIAL: Varies.
>
> TRAINING/LICENSE/CERTIFICATION REQUIRED: A license or certification is not required, however, training can be obtained through private or group instruction or from accredited music schools.
>
> OTHER REQUIREMENTS: The ability to play a music instrument, either solo or as part of a band or orchestra.
>
> CAREER ADVANCEMENT OPPORTUNITIES: A wide range of career opportunities is available to musicians. An accomplished musician can also become a music director, composer, or arranger.

Musicians can perform concerts at clubs, resorts, hotels, cruise ships, upscale restaurants, and other venues, be part of a band or orchestra, perform at weddings and other functions, and/or work in recording studios. Accomplished musicians can also teach music, write and publish songs, work in music stores, or hold a wide range of other music-related jobs.

Some musicians are self-taught, whereas others receive many years of training. The skill level and training you'll require will vary greatly based on the instrument you play and the type of job(s) you pursue. It's important to understand that competition for musician jobs is often fierce. An audition is almost always required to land a job. The majority of jobs are available in major cities, including New York City, Los Angeles, and Nashville.

For More Information

- Berklee College of Music. An accredited, undergraduate music school in Boston that focuses on contemporary music, (800) BERKLEE, www.berklee.edu.
- Music Careers. Information about career opportunities for musicians in the music industry can be found at www.music-careers.com.

- National Association of Music Education. Career-related information for musicians is offered at this web site. Job information is broken up by careers in a wide range of music-related fields, www.menc.org/industry/job/careers/careers.html.
- National Association of Schools of Music. Information for musicians interested in obtaining training can be found at http://nasm.arts-accredit.org.

Nail Technician/Manicurist

AT A GLANCE

SALARY POTENTIAL: $15,000 to $30,000 per year.

TRAINING/LICENSE/CERTIFICATION REQUIRED: Completion of a certification program and a license is required. Certification requires between 150 and 300 hours of training. It can be completed in ten weeks or less. Tuition is typically under $3,000, with financial aid and financing available.

OTHER REQUIREMENTS: Good people skills are required.

CAREER ADVANCEMENT OPPORTUNITIES: Limited.

The job of a nail technical or manicurist is to offer manicure and pedicure services to customers. Employers include beauty salons, nail salons, spas, and resorts. Nail technicians must be proficient using a wide variety of products, including nail enamel, polish remover, cuticle remover, and aromatherapy, plus a variety of tools, such as manual or electric files, buffers, cuticle pushers, and nippers.

For More Information

- Beauty Schools Directory. A listing of schools throughout American that offer training and certification as a nail technician or manicurist can be found at www.beautyschoolsdirectory.com.
- BeautyTech. Career-related information is offered at www.beautytech.com/nailtech/index.htm.
- Online job listings can be found at the general interest career-related web sites, such as Monster (www.monster.com) or Yahoo! Hot Jobs (http://hotjobs.yahoo.com).

- Loraine's Academy, Inc. This is a Florida-based training program for nail technicians and manicurists, (888) 393-5015, www.lorainesacademy.com.
- *Nails* Magazine. An industry trade magazine for nail professionals. It's worth reading to learn more about this industry, www.nailsmag.com.
- Nailsplash.com. Job listings and career-related information is offered at www.nailsplash.com/careers.html.
- National Cosmetology Association. This is a professional trade organization for salon workers, www.salonprofessionals.org.

Party/Event Planner

AT A GLANCE

SALARY POTENTIAL: Varies. Pay can be by-the-hour or by the project.

TRAINING/LICENSE/CERTIFICATION REQUIRED: None. To become a bridal consultant or wedding planner, certification can be obtained.

OTHER REQUIREMENTS: In addition to being extremely outgoing and social, a party or event planner should be detail-oriented, well-organized, able to juggle many tasks simultaneously, and have top-notch communication skills. The job involves meeting deadlines and being extremely reliable.

CAREER ADVANCEMENT OPPORTUNITIES: Many event and party planners are self-employed, but some work for hotels, resorts, restaurants and function halls. A wide range of career opportunities is available in this field. If working in a corporate environment is more appealing, a related job could involve meeting, convention, or conference planning.

An event or party planner is hired to assist the host in managing all details for a party, such as hiring and coordinating caterers, entertainment, decorations, preparing the guest list, sending out invitations, managing RSVPs, negotiating with vendors, and ensuring that everything happens in a timely manner.

The job involves working under tight deadlines, multitasking, and being able to oversee others while managing your own responsibilities. Being able to work well with clients, understanding their needs, and meeting their expectations is critical.

The job typically involves working nights and weekends, plus being on call to handle last-minute emergencies. Some party planners specialize in specific types of parties, such as weddings, bar mitzvahs, anniversary parties, corporate events, or children's parties.

For More Information

- Association of Bridal Consultants. This is a professional trade association for bridal consultants and wedding planners, (203) 355-0464, www.bridal assn.com.
- Event Planners Association. This is a professional trade association for event planners. This web site offers a wide range of resources www.event plannersassociation.com.
- FabJobs.com. Career-related information about how to become an event planner can be found here, www.fabjob.com/eventplanner1.asp.
- Online job listings can be found at the general interest career-related web sites, such as Monster (www.monster.com) or Yahoo! Hot Jobs (http://hot jobs.yahoo.com).

CAREER SPOTLIGHT

Photographer

> **AT A GLANCE**
>
> **SALARY POTENTIAL:** $15,000 to $50,000 (or more) per year.
>
> **TRAINING/LICENSE/CERTIFICATION REQUIRED:** None, however, attending some type of photography school, or apprenticing (or interning) with a professional photographer to gain on-the-job experience is extremely helpful.
>
> **OTHER REQUIREMENTS:** A flare for capturing visual images, the ability to use camera equipment (both digital and traditional film cameras), and for some jobs, excellent communication and people skills are required.
>
> **CAREER ADVANCEMENT OPPORTUNITIES:** There is a wide range of jobs available for professional photographers. Some photographers shoot portraits,

weddings, special events, concerts, celebrity events, headshots, fashion models, commercial products, or have some other type of specialty. Photo-journalism for a newspaper or magazine can also provide lucrative work. Working as a photographer for an advertising agency requires a very different set of skills than those needed by a wedding photographer or a member of the paparazzi.

There's a saying that a picture is worth a thousand words. Well, it's the photographer's job to communicate through his or her photographic images. A photographer is someone who takes photographs for a living. Depending on your skills and interests, there is a wide range of fields you can break into as a professional photographer. Most photographers own their own equipment and specialize in either digital photography or traditional film photography. Of course, many photographers use both types of cameras. In addition to being highly proficient using your camera equipment, a good photographer is extremely creative and is able to capture images that are truly artistic.

Many professional photographers start out as hobbyists, then pursue some type of formal training or an apprenticeship to learn how to pursue photography as a career. Because there are so many different opportunities for photographers, it's important to choose an area of interest, whether it's shooting weddings, photojournalism, or commercial photography, for example.

Thanks to ever-evolving technology, photographers who specialize in digital photography must also learn how to edit their images using a computer and specialized software. It's important to understand that while shooting photos is a job, it's also an art form that requires a combination of skill and artistic ability.

Because many jobs in this field involve working with people, it's important for the photographer to have the skills necessary to put the person or people they're shooting at ease, because many people are uncomfortable in front of the camera. This skill is needed for many types of photography, whether it's shooting portraits, weddings, corporate events, parties, fashion models, or celebrities.

If you're interested in becoming a portrait photographer, one way to do this is to land a job working at a one-hour portrait studio, like the Picture People or Glamour Shots, which are retail businesses found in malls.

Because there are so many job opportunities for professional photographers that are vastly different from each other, there are no set rules for breaking into this field or obtaining the training that's necessary. This is why working as an intern or apprentice for an established photographer becomes important. Most photographers ultimately land jobs based on their reputations and the quality of their work. Photographers put together portfolios, which are a sampling of their best work and that serves as their calling cards, helping them land new business.

Here's My Story

Alexandra is a mother of two. As a teenager and young adult, she worked as a fashion model and actress, appearing in numerous television shows and movies, and was photographed for dozens of catalogs and magazines. During her years of modeling, she developed a strong interest in what happens behind the camera. Several years later, when she retired from acting and got married, she decided to take up photography as a hobby.

It wasn't long before she was asked to shoot headshots for her actor friends and even shoot a few of their weddings. "What started out as a hobby transformed slowly into a wedding photography and portrait business. At first, I only charged friends enough to cover my expenses, but I kept getting requests to do more and more work. In less than a year, I was being booked almost every weekend and I was earning a good living as a photographer," recalled Alexandra.

After hiring several photographers to help with the wedding photography aspect of her business, Alexandra continued to get hired through friends and word-of-mouth for other projects, such as shooting products for catalogs and even working as the official photographer of a high-rated network television show.

"At first it was strange to be working behind the cameras, after spending so many years posing in front of them. My work as an actress and model, however, allowed me to become friendly with many well-known professional photographers who have acted as my mentors," said Alexandra.

"I shoot using only digital cameras and I'm self-employed, which means I need to purchase all of my own equipment. At first, I invested in one high-end camera. I then built a small studio in my garage and needed lights and backdrops. When I started shooting weddings and working on the sets of television shows, I needed to purchase additional lenses, a second camera and other related equipment. Over the years, as my business has expanded, I've constantly had to invest in newer, higher-end photography equipment. Despite the fact this is now my business, I still consider it a hobby. It's something I truly love," added Alexandra.

For someone interested in becoming a photographer, Alexandra said, "I recommend teaming up with one or more established photographers and working as their assistant for at least several months. There's so much to learn. Sure, you can teach yourself a lot about photography, read books, and take classes, but there's no substitute for getting hands-on experience working with someone who is a skilled photographer. When choosing with whom to work, choose a photographer who specialized in the type of photography work you ultimately want to do. Just make sure that you'll have an opportunity to learn by doing, not just watching."

For More Information

- Brooks Institute of Photography. This is one of many accredited photography schools where you can learn how to become a professional photographer and earn an associate's degree in as little as 18 months, http://brooks photo.college-info.org.
- eLance. This web site offers job listings for freelance photographers, www.elance.com.
- New England School of Photography. Learn about one of the country's leading photography schools, located in Boston. The school offers a two-year professional photography program, www.nesop.com/main.htm.
- *Photo District News*. This is a professional trade magazine and web site specifically for professional photographers, www.pdnonline.com/pdn/about_us/ad_opps.jsp.
- *Photographer's Market*. Published annually and available from bookstores ($24.99/Writer's Digest Books), *Photographer's Market* is a directory of newspapers, magazines, stock photo agencies, and other outlets where professional photographers can sell their work.
- Photography Schools. This web site offers a comprehensive list and details about more than 600 photography schools and educational programs, www.photographyschools.com.

Radio (Voice Over) Announcer

> **AT A GLANCE**
>
> **SALARY POTENTIAL:** Varies.
>
> **TRAINING/LICENSE/CERTIFICATION REQUIRED:** None, although training is available at a handful of broadcasting schools nationwide.
>
> **OTHER REQUIREMENTS:** A pleasant speaking voice, good diction, a strong vocabulary, the ability to read scripts aloud, and an upbeat personality are

useful skills. Being able to think fast on your feet is also an important skill for broadcasters.

CAREER ADVANCEMENT OPPORTUNITIES: Radio announcers and voice-over actors are employed by radio stations, advertising agencies, recording studios, and animation production companies.

Every time you listen to the radio and hear a disc jockey speak, or hear an advertisement with an announcer on TV, but don't see the speaker, you're hearing the work of a radio announcer or voice-over actor. Jobs that involve using your voice as your primary communication tool often require some training at a broadcasting or other type of trade school. Employers often require a demo tape showcasing your talents. Working with a legitimate talent agent who will send you on auditions for voice-over or radio announcer jobs is helpful.

For More Information

- Interactive Voices. Online job listings for voice-over actors and announcers can be found at www.interactivevoices.com/for-voice-talents.htm.
- Radio Connection. Information about an on-the-job mentoring program that involves working at a local radio station in your area can be found at www.radioconnection.com.
- Radio Mentor. Information about an on-the-job mentoring program which involves working at a local radio station in your area is offered at this web site, www.radiomentors.org.
- Voice 1-2-3. Online job listings for voice-over actors and announcers can be found on this site, http://voice123.com/s/voice_over_jobs.html.

Resume Writer

AT A GLANCE

SALARY POTENTIAL: Varies. This type of work typically involves being self-employed and getting paid by the job.

TRAINING/LICENSE/CERTIFICATION REQUIRED: None.

> OTHER REQUIREMENTS: A strong knowledge of human resources and top-notch writing skills are critical. Computer skills and proficiency using a word processor and the internet are also required.
>
> CAREER ADVANCEMENT OPPORTUNITIES: With additional training, resume writers can pursue jobs as career counselors, personal coaches, or as human resources professionals.

A resume writer is someone who understands all of the popular resume formats, knows what it takes to create an attention-getting, well-written resume, and who works with job seekers to assist them in creating their custom resumes. Most resume writers are self-employed and have a human resources backgrounds or experience working as professional writers. Others work for resume writing services, employment agencies, or job placement offices.

The job entails finding job seekers who need help creating their resumes, working with those clients to pinpoint what content should be included in their resumes, then creating professional-quality resumes that are customized and error-free. While a resume writer works with the client, he or she must determine what resume format will work best based on each client's needs, then structure each resume so that it showcases the applicant's work history, experience, education, and skills in a way that will get attention from prospective employers.

Some resume writers utilize off-the-shelf resume creation software and also work as career counselors or advisors to clients. Other services offered by resume writers include writing custom cover letters and performing company or industry research on behalf of their clients.

A resume writer must be able to communicate well with their clients, be able to market their services to potential clients, and provide timely service.

For More Information

- eLance. Online job listings for freelance writers and other professionals can be found at www.elance.com.
- National Resume Writers' Association. This is a professional trade association for resume writers. The organization offers a certification program for resume writers, as well as training and career-related resources, http://www.nrwaweb.com/certification/certification_home.htm.
- ResumePro. Career-related information and online resources for professional resume writers can be found at this web site, http://resumepro.com/resume_links.html.

Singer

> ### AT A GLANCE
>
> SALARY POTENTIAL: Varies.
>
> TRAINING/LICENSE/CERTIFICATION REQUIRED: None, although most professional singers work with a skilled vocal coach on a regular basis. Schools like Berklee College of Music in Boston (www.berklee.edu) offer formal training and a college degree for singers interested in pursuing music and performing as a career.
>
> OTHER REQUIREMENTS: A pleasant singing voice and the ability to perform in front of audiences.
>
> CAREER ADVANCEMENT OPPORTUNITIES: Job opportunities for talented singers are extensive. Singers can perform at special events (such as weddings or corporate events), at restaurants or clubs, aboard cruise ships, in concerts, at theme parks, in musical theater productions, or in a recording studio. Singers can also perform commercial jingles for advertisements. One of the most lucrative, but difficult gigs to get as a singer is to land a recording contract with a major record label, although jobs working as a studio singer or background singer for a well-known recording artist are often difficult to land.

If you have a good singing voice and enjoy performing, there is a wide range of opportunities to pursue. Working as a singer, musician, actor, or in a related field and earning enough money to support yourself can be challenging, because these fields are extremely competitive. Many singers pursue other jobs while performing on the side, until they become fully established. Depending on the type of singing jobs you want to pursue, working with a booking agent and/or manager can be beneficial.

It's important to understand that few singers are able to maintain steady, full-time employment. Singers who also play one or more instruments tend to have higher earning potential. Though there are many regional, national, and televised talent competitions designed to "discover" new talent, not all of them are legitimate, so be careful as you enter into this type of situation or begin working with someone offering you a deal that's too good to be true. To truly understand the music industry, it's important to read industry trade magazines, such as *Billboard*, as well as books, such as Donald S. Passman's *All You Need to Know About the Music Business* (Simon & Schuster).

The best way to determine if you have singing talent and to learn about the music industry is to begin working with a reputable vocal coach on a regular basis. A vocal coach will help you improve your singing technique, strengthen your voice, and teach you about the music industry.

For More Information

- Career Overview. Information about career options for singers are described in detail at this web site, http://careeroverview.com/music-careers.html.
- ShowBizltd. This is one of many web sites that offer job listings for singers, musicians, actors, and performers, www.showbizltd.com/music.cfm.
- Vocalist.org. This web site offers a humorous, but informative overview of the many types of singing careers someone can pursue, www.vocalist.org.uk/singing_careers.html.

Ski/Snowboard Instructor

AT A GLANCE

SALARY POTENTIAL: Varies.

TRAINING/LICENSE/CERTIFICATION REQUIRED: Virtually all ski resorts hire certified instructors and then provide on-the-job training, although certification isn't always required. Being an excellent downhill skier or snowboarder is also a requirement.

OTHER REQUIREMENTS: None.

CAREER ADVANCEMENT OPPORTUNITIES: Limited.

Ski instructors work at ski resorts and slopes teaching people to ski, either in private or through group lessons. Though this isn't necessarily a high-paying career, for people who love to downhill ski and are good at the sport, the biggest perk of the job is unlimited access to the slopes when not teaching. For most ski instructors, this is a seasonal job. However, some instructors "follow the snow" and work at ski resorts all over the world during different times of the year.

In addition to being good at the sport, instructors must be outgoing, able to teach kids, teens, and adults, and be in good physical condition.

For More Information

- CoolWorks. Job openings available at ski resorts worldwide can be found at www.coolworks.com/ski-resort-jobs.
- If You Ski. Job openings available at ski resorts worldwide can be found at this web site www.ifyouski.com/jobs/.
- Job Monkey. Information about career opportunities as a ski instructor can be found at www.jobmonkey.com/ski/html/intructor_jobs.html.
- Professional Ski Instructors of America. This professional trade association offers information about training and certification, plus a vast amount of information about pursuing jobs at ski resorts, (303) 987-9390, www.psia.org.
- Contact ski resorts directly to learn about career opportunities.

Sound/Recording Engineer

AT A GLANCE

SALARY POTENTIAL: Varies.

TRAINING/LICENSE/CERTIFICATION REQUIRED: Training can be obtained at a vocational or technical trade school, broadcasting school, or at various accredited colleges. Some recording engineers, however, start off as unpaid interns and learn the trade working on the job.

OTHER REQUIREMENTS: In addition to having a passion for music and audio, sound engineers must be proficient using a wide range of computer and audio equipment.

CAREER ADVANCEMENT OPPORTUNITIES: Sound recording engineers are hired by radio stations, recording studios, record labels, advertising agencies, and TV stations, along with audio and video production houses.

A recording engineer is someone who works in a recording studio, TV, or radio station, for example, and actually operates the equipment on behalf of the producer and talent. In some cases, the audio engineer also works as the producer. Because most recording is now done digitally, developing a strong knowledge of the latest recording technology and software is critical.

The best way to break into this field is to complete a program at an accredited broadcasting school or a college/university that offers an audio engineering program. These skills, however, can be self-taught or obtained on the job working as an apprentice or intern.

For More Information

- Berklee School of Music. An accredited four-year college offering a degree in music production, www.berklee.edu.
- Career Connection. A self-paced training program for recording engineers that involves an internship at a studio near where you live, www.recording connection.com.
- Columbia School of Broadcasting. An accredited professional trade school that offers a training program for recording engineers, http://columbia schoolbroadcast.com.
- Connecticut School of Broadcasting. An accredited professional trade school that offers an eight-week training program, www.800tvradio.com.
- Recording Industry Association of America. This is a professional trade association for people working in the recording industry. Here, you'll find information about jobs, training programs, plus a wide range of useful resources, www.riaa.com.
- Contact a local radio station or recording studio in your area to learn about internship and apprenticeship opportunities.

Stand-Up Comedian

AT A GLANCE

SALARY POTENTIAL: Varies.

TRAINING/LICENSE/CERTIFICATION REQUIRED: None. Many comedians train by attending acting and improvisational comedy classes.

OTHER REQUIREMENTS: An awesome sense of humor and the ability to stand up on stage and tell jokes in an entertaining way is essential.

CAREER ADVANCEMENT OPPORTUNITIES: Limited. Most stand-up comedians tour the country performing at comedy clubs and other venues. The best stand-up comedians make television appearances and eventually star on television

> sitcoms or host morning radio programs. Others land jobs as comedy writers for television or movies.

A stand-up comedian is a performer with an awesome sense of humor. Anyone who has seen a show at a comedy club knows that the job involves standing up alone on a stage and entertaining audiences with jokes and comical stories. Some stand-up comedians also perform impersonations. The job typically involves extensive travel because touring and appearing at comedy clubs across the country and around the world is a big part of the job for those who become established.

The best way to break into this field is to prepare a comedy act and sign up to perform at open mike nights held at comedy clubs. If you're good enough, you'll eventually get hired to perform for pay at those clubs. In addition to working in comedy clubs, comedians are also hired by cruise ships, resorts, and to perform at parties and special events.

Stand-up comedians typically work nights, holidays, and weekends. It's very difficult for people breaking into this field to earn a full-time living.

For More Information

- Hollywood Web. Job listings and audition opportunities for comedians are listed on this web site, www.hollywoodweb.com/jobs/view.php/3.html.
- Stand-Up Comedy FAQ. Written by professional comedians, this document offers a vast amount of information for someone interested in becoming a stand-up comedian, www.faqs.org/faqs/comedy-faq/standup, http://members.aol.com/comedyfaq/faq.html.
- Contact comedy clubs in your area about audition opportunities, workshops, and open mike nights.

Surfing Instructor

> AT A GLANCE
>
> SALARY POTENTIAL: Varies. Instructors are typically paid by the hour.
>
> TRAINING/LICENSE/CERTIFICATION REQUIRED: None.
>
> OTHER REQUIREMENTS: Being highly skilled at the sport, plus the ability to teach others is important.

> CAREER ADVANCEMENT OPPORTUNITIES: Limited. Surf instructors can also partic-
> ipate in competitions or work at surf shops or equipment manufacturers.

Surfing instructors are highly skilled surfers who are able to earn an income working for a surfing school, surf shop, or at a resort teaching people how to surf. In
addition to traditional surfing, instructors are also hired by resorts to teach kite
surfing and other related sports. The job involves spending a lot of time at the
beach, typically starting very early in the morning. Most surf instructor jobs are
seasonal.

For More Information

- Eastern Surfing Association. The largest association of amateur and professional surfers in America hosts this web site, www.surfesa.org.
- International Surfing Association. This is an association of amateur and professional surfers. Here, you'll find a vast amount of information about this
  popular sport, www.isasurf.org.
- Professional Air Sports Association. Information about becoming a professional kite surfing instructor is offered at www.professionalairsports.org/
  beckitsurin.html.
- To find surfing instructor jobs, contact surf shops and resorts in the beach
  communities where you want to work.

Swimming Instructor

AT A GLANCE

SALARY POTENTIAL: $10 to $50 per hour.

TRAINING/LICENSE/CERTIFICATION REQUIRED: Certification from The Red Cross is
typically required.

OTHER REQUIREMENTS: Being a good swimmer and able to teach others is
necessary. An outgoing personality and patience are also useful. Knowledge
of basic first aid and CPR is often sought by employers.

CAREER ADVANCEMENT OPPORTUNITIES: Limited. Swimming instructors can also
work as swimming team coaches at schools, colleges, and universities.

Swimming instructors are employed by resorts, public pools, schools, camps and private pool owners. The job typically involves instructing kids, teens and/or adults on how to swim. Swimming instructors work at beaches, as well as at indoor and outdoor pools. The job has many of the same requirements as that of a certified lifeguard, although job responsibilities between these two jobs may differ.

For More Information

- Camp Resource. This web site offers online job listings for openings available at camps, www.campresource.com.
- Club Swim. Online job listings for swimming instructors can be found at www.clubswim.com/swimming-instructor-jobs.asp.
- Los Angeles Trade Tech. This school offers an aquatic certificate program for people interested in becoming swimming instructors, life guards, or work in related jobs, http://wellness.lattc.cc.ca.us/aquatics/aqua.cert.html.
- Swimming Jobs. Online job listings for swim instructors can be found at this web site, www.swimmingjobs.com.
- The Red Cross. Information about certification and training programs offered to swimming instructors can be found at www.redcross.org/services/hss/resources/upswim.html.

Talent Manager

AT A GLANCE

SALARY POTENTIAL: Varies. Talent managers represent actors, models, singers, and other types of performers. They typically earn a commission of between 10 and 20 percent of what their clients earn.

TRAINING/LICENSE/CERTIFICATION REQUIRED: None. Most people working in the entertainment industry break in by first participating in internship programs or working their way up from minimum wage positions. Courses in talent management and music business, for example, are offered at some specialized colleges, such as Berklee School of Music in Boston.

OTHER REQUIREMENTS: Talent managers need to understand the entertainment industry from a business and legal standpoint, have connections that can be utilized to get their clients work, and be well-organized, detail-oriented, and able to multi-task.

CAREER ADVANCEMENT OPPORTUNITIES: Talent managers can be self-employed or work for a talent management company. A successful manager can also pursue other executive-level positions within the entertainment industry.

A talent manager represents one or more clients in the entertainment industry and is responsible for overseeing their careers. For smaller, less established clients, a talent manager will also often work as a booking agent (helping the client find work), business manager (overseeing the client's finances), and as a publicist (helping the client get media attention). The manager's job is also to negotiate business deals and assist clients in handling the day-to-day aspects of their entertainment-related jobs.

Some talent managers first pursue four-year business degrees or become lawyers, whereas others learn the business by working for a talent management company as an intern or by starting off in an entry-level position. Jobs in the entertainment industry are often difficult to land. The work requires long hours, travel, and can involve a significant amount of stress.

Talent managers often specialize in working with actors, singers, musicians, models, professional athletes, or other specific types of entertainers.

For More Information
- *Daily Variety*. This is a daily trade magazine covering the entertainment industry, www.variety.com.
- ShowBiz Jobs. Online listings for jobs in the entertainment industry can be found at www.showbizjobs.com.
- *The Hollywood Reporter*. This is a daily trade magazine covering the entertainment industry, www.hollywoodreporter.com.
- *The Ross Report*. This is a monthly publication that lists many of the talent management companies in New York and Los Angeles. This list could be a source of leads for potential jobs or internships, www.backstage.com/backstage/rossreports/directories.jsp.

Tattoo Designer/Artist

AT A GLANCE

SALARY POTENTIAL: Varies.

TRAINING/LICENSE/CERTIFICATION REQUIRED: None, although most tattoo artists participate in a two-year apprenticeship program.

OTHER REQUIREMENTS: Artistic ability.

CAREER ADVANCEMENT OPPORTUNITIES: Limited.

A tattoo artist typically works at a tattoo parlor and is an artist who creates graphic images for people's skin. The job requires artistic ability which can be self-taught and natural or learned from an art school. The skills needed to actually tattoo people's skin can be learned through an apprenticeship program and on-the-job training.

For More Information
- Academy of Tattoo. DVD training programs for tattoo artists and those interested in pursuing this type of work can be ordered from this web site, www.academyoftattoo.com.
- Tattoo Artist Group. This is a talent management company that represents tattoo artists worldwide, www.tattooartistgroup.com.
- Tattoo Now. Information of interest to tattoo artists, and well as online job listings, can be found at this web site, www.tattoonow.com.
- TattooArtist.org. This web site is an informative resource offering a vast amount of information about tattoos as an art form and the artists who create them, www.tattooartists.org.
- The World's Only Tattoo School. This school offers a two-week training program to become a tattoo artist, www.tattoo-school.com.
- Online job listings can be found at the general interest career-related web sites, such as Monster (www.monster.com) or Yahoo! Hot Jobs (http://hotjobs.yahoo.com).

Tennis Instructor

AT A GLANCE

SALARY POTENTIAL: $15 to $150 per hour.

TRAINING/LICENSE/CERTIFICATION REQUIRED: Certification from the U.S. Professional Tennis Association (USPTA) and/or the U.S. Professional Tennis Registry (USPTR) is typically necessary to land a job at a tennis instructor at a sports club, tennis club, resort, college/university, camp, or country club.

OTHER REQUIREMENTS: In addition to being highly skilled at playing tennis, an upbeat and outgoing personality, patience, and the ability to instruct others are all job requirements.

CAREER ADVANCEMENT OPPORTUNITIES: Tennis instructors and coaches are employed by a wide range of organizations and companies.

A tennis instructor is someone who is not only highly skilled at playing the sport of tennis, but has also obtained the necessary skills and certification to teach others. Many types of employers hire skilled tennis instructors or tennis coaches. The work involves working directly with students, either in a group or one-on-one situation. Patience and an outgoing personality are important. Depending on the employer, working as a tennis instructor may only provide seasonal employment.

For More Information

- About.com. This web site offers an informative article about how to break into this field and the types of jobs available to tennis instructors throughout the world, http://tennis.about.com/od/jobsandtennisindustry/a/beteachpro1.htm.
- MySummerCamps. This web site offers online job listings for openings at summer camps worldwide, http://mysummercamps.com.
- U.S. Professional Tennis Association. This is a professional trade association offering certification programs for tennis instructors, plus online job listings and other resources, (713) 97-USPTA, www.uspta.com.

- U.S. Professional Tennis Registry. This is a professional trade association offering certification programs for tennis instructors, and includes online job listings and other resources, (800) 421-6289, www.ptrtennis.org.
- Contact the human resources department at any tennis club, athletic club, country club, resort, or camp, for example, that hires tennis instructors.

TV/Film Crew Production Assistant

AT A GLANCE

SALARY POTENTIAL: Minimum wage to $30,000 per year.

TRAINING/LICENSE/CERTIFICATION REQUIRED: Education focusing on motion picture or television production is helpful, but not required.

OTHER REQUIREMENTS: A production assistant working in the entertainment industry must be prepared to work extremely long hours for relatively low pay. You must be able to follow directions, meet deadlines, focus on details, and multitask. This can be a high-pressure job that involves performing repetitive or mundane tasks.

CAREER ADVANCEMENT OPPORTUNITIES: Production assistants who prove themselves can often earn promotions working within the entertainment industry.

A production assistant is considered an entry-level position on a television or motion picture production crew. These people work mainly as assistants to directors, producers, talent, and other crew members. The work involves handling a wide range of often repetitive and mundane tasks, but requires organization, the ability to multitask and meet deadlines. Long hours and a flexible work schedule are required.

Working as a production assistant is one step up from working as an unpaid intern on a production crew. Those who demonstrate a responsible work ethic and competence can earn promotions that lead to more responsibilities and higher wages. Most producers, for example, start off as production assistants as they kick off their careers in the entertainment industry.

Television and motion picture studios, production offices and independent production companies hire production assistants. Most production assistants go from project to project because few TV shows or movies involve year-round employment or job stability. Most of the production assistant jobs can be found in Los Angeles or New York.

For More Information

- *Daily Variety.* This daily trade newsmagazine for the entertainment industry offers online job listings. If you're interested in working in the entertainment field, reading *Daily Variety* and/or *The Hollywood Reporter* is a must, http://www.variety.com/index.asp?layout=variety_careers.
- FilmStaff.com. One of many online services that list job openings in television and movie production, www.filmstaff.com.
- ShowBiz Jobs. Online job listings for a wide range of jobs in all facets of the entertainment industry can be found here. This web site offers nationwide job listings, with an emphasis on New York and Los Angeles-based opportunities, www.showbizjobs.com/dsp_jobsearch.cfm.
- *The Hollywood Reporter.* This is a daily trade newsmagazine covering the entertainment industry, www.hollywoodreporter.com.
- Contact the human resources department of the major television and motion picture studios and production companies in Los Angeles, New York, or the city where you live. Job listings can also be found on the web sites for these companies.

TV or Movie Extra

AT A GLANCE

SALARY POTENTIAL: Minimum wage to $200 per day.

TRAINING/LICENSE/CERTIFICATION REQUIRED: None.

OTHER REQUIREMENTS: Extras must be able to follow directions, show up to the set on time, and be prepared for a significant amount of waiting. Patience is definitely required. In most situations, casting agents who hire extras for specific projects seek people with a specific look or who fit into a specific age group.

CAREER ADVANCEMENT OPPORTUNITIES: Limited, although extras are hired to appear in TV shows, movies, commercials, and music videos.

Being an extra is a fun way to get a taste of what working in the television or motion picture industry is all about. As the job title suggests, extras are used when filming TV shows or movies to create crowds or add realistic ambience. Extras have no lines and often don't even get their faces shown. Extras are hired by the day by production companies filming TV shows, movies, commercials, and music videos. The job requires you to submit a photo to a casting agent or extra casting service and then show up for jobs on time.

Though working as an extra will provide a great preview into what it's like working in the entertainment industry, it typically won't lead to traditional acting roles with speaking parts that offer significantly higher pay.

Most TV extras are employed by production companies shooting in Los Angeles or New York. Before seeking work as an extra, have a professional head shot taken of yourself and be prepared to provide casting agents with 8-by-10-inch, black and white prints of your headshot. Photo studios, like the Picture People or Glamour Shots, found at most local malls, can create the headshot for you somewhat inexpensively.

Once you have your photos, contact several casting agencies that specialize in extras to learn about their casting and hiring practices. It is not necessary to join an acting union to pursue extra work. Having a flexible schedule, however, is required. When working with a casting agent, production company, or major studio as an extra, you'll be required to supply two forms of government-issued identification, such as a valid driver's license (or passport), plus your social security card.

When trying to break into this field, beware of the many scams that are out there. Make sure you work only with well-respected and legitimate companies.

For More Information

- Central Casting. This is one of the entertainment industry's most established and respected casting agents that specializes in placing extras in television shows, movies, commercials, and music videos. The company is based in Los Angeles, (818) 562-2755, www.entertainmentpartners.com/products_and_services/services/central_casting/.
- Extra Extra Casting. This web site offers information and extra casting opportunities in New York and Los Angeles, www.extraextracastings.com/index.htm.
- Seeing Stars. This informative web site offers the information you'll need to land work as an extra in the entertainment industrywww.seeing-stars.com/ShowBiz/ExtraWork.shtml.

- Showbiz Ltd. Information on how to become an extra can be found here, www.showbizltd.com.

Writer

> **AT A GLANCE**
>
> **SALARY POTENTIAL:** Varies.
>
> **TRAINING/LICENSE/CERTIFICATION REQUIRED:** None. A college degree or the completion of college-level writing or journalism courses is often helpful.
>
> **OTHER REQUIREMENTS:** Creativity, self-discipline, dedication, organizational skills and the ability to type (using a word processor) are all useful skills for any type of writer or journalist.
>
> **CAREER ADVANCEMENT OPPORTUNITIES:** There are a wide range of job opportunities for writers, working in the newspaper, magazine, radio, television, theater, and publishing fields. Writers are also employed by advertising agencies, public relations firms, marketing companies, web site design firms, and in a wide range of other fields. Writers can specialize in journalism, fiction, poetry, songwriting, playwriting, technical writing, or business writing.

Writers are expert communicators who utilize words as their primary form of communication. Writers are employed in a wide range of fields and come from varying backgrounds. While it's possible to attend college to study writing and journalism, some writers have the natural ability to write and focus on other areas of interest in terms of their education. First, a writer must possess a strong vocabulary. They must also be creative and self-motivated, since much of the work involves sitting in front of a computer using a word processor or writing freehand using a pen and paper.

Like being an actor, musician, or artist, working as a writer involves mastering an art form, which in this case revolves around the use of words. Depending on the type of writing you do, the job itself can be highly technical. It typically involves hard work, plenty of focus, and a strong knowledge of whatever it is you're hired to write about. Depending on the type of writing you do and your employer, this can be a full- or part-time job opportunity.

For More Information

- eLance. This web site offers online job listings for freelance writers, www
.elance.com.
- iHire Publishing, Online job listings for writers can be found here, www.ihire
publishing.com.
- Mediabistro. This web site offers online job listings for journalists and writers for newspapers, magazines, and web sites, www.mediabistro.com.
- *Publishers Weekly*. This is a weekly trade magazine covering the book publishing industry. The magazine's web site also offers news, job listings, and
a wide range of career-related resources for writers and authors, www.pub
lishersweekly.com.
- The Write Jobs. This web site offers job listings for writers www.write
jobs.com/jobs.
- *Writer's Digest. Writer's Digest* is a monthly magazine for professional and
amateur writers. The magazine's web site offers a variety of news, information, and tools for writers, www.writersdigest.com.
- WritersMarket.com. This is a comprehensive directory of book publishers,
newspapers, and magazines that hire writers. A printed edition of *Writer's
Market* can be found at most major bookstores, www.writersmarket.com.

ADVENTURE-ORIENTED JOBS

Jobs that involve a lot of action, danger, or excitement are featured in this section. Learn what it takes to become a police officer or fire fighter, for example. Plus, discover the many career opportunities offered by the United States military.

Boat Captain/Skipper

> **AT A GLANCE**
>
> **SALARY POTENTIAL:** Varies.
>
> **TRAINING/LICENSE/CERTIFICATION REQUIRED:** Varies by state and type of vessel.
>
> **OTHER REQUIREMENTS:** Experience with boats and navigation is required. Employers look for people who are responsible, detail oriented, and passionate about their work.
>
> **CAREER ADVANCEMENT OPPORTUNITIES:** Limited.

There is a wide range of job opportunities for boat captains, which include working for boat charter companies, yacht delivery companies, boat manufacturers, resorts and marinas. Job responsibilities and training vary greatly, based on a wide range of factors, such as the type and size of vessel you'll be captaining.

This is a great career option for someone who has a passion for boating and the sea. You must be responsible, have leadership abilities, be able to make decisions, and possess excellent training in your areas of expertise. The ability to successful manage a crew is also required.

For More Information

- Crew File. Information and job listings for captains, skippers, and crew personnel, www.crewfile.com.
- BoatLinks.com. An online listing of marine jobs, www.boatlinks.com.

Firefighting Occupations

> **AT A GLANCE**
>
> **SALARY POTENTIAL:** Some firefighters are volunteers, whereas others earn anywhere from $9 to $30 per hour or an annual salary of between $25,000 and $80,000 (plus benefits), depending on geographic location, experience, training, and rank.

> TRAINING/LICENSE/CERTIFICATION REQUIRED: A firefighter must pass a written exam as well as a physical exam in most states. Several weeks or months of on-the-job training and/or training at a fire department's training center or academy is also required. Many fire departments have apprenticeship programs which must be completed. Some colleges and universities offer two- and four-year degrees in fire engineering and fire science.
>
> OTHER REQUIREMENTS: In addition to the training provided, a firefighter must be brave, healthy, physically fit, well-coordinated, able to take direction, and able to work well in a stressful environment.
>
> CAREER ADVANCEMENT OPPORTUNITIES: Promotion and career advancement opportunities include becoming a fire chief, deputy chief, assistant fire chief, battalion chief, fire captain, fire lieutenant, or fire inspector.

The job of a firefighter is to help put out fires and deal with other emergencies. This means being able and willing to rapidly respond to emergencies. The work hours are long. Many firefighters report working more than 50 hours per week, with some shifts lasting 24 hours. Firefighters, like police officers, are often looked upon as local heroes because of their work, dedication, and bravery. Firefighter jobs are open to people over age 18, however, competition is often fierce to land a job, even if you successfully pass the exams and training.

For More Information
- Firefighter Career Opportunities. This web site offers resources, training materials, and job listings for firefighters, www.pjpinfo.com/ffa.htm.
- International Association of Firefighters. A professional trade organization offering training and career-related information, www.iaff.org.
- National Fire Academy. Information about accredited training programs and two- and four-year degree programs can be found here, www.usfa.fema.gov/nfa/index.htm.
- U.S. Fire Administration. This is the branch of the federal government that oversees firefighters. It's a great resource for people looking to learn more about careers in firefighting, www.usfa.fema.gov.

Lifeguard

> ## AT A GLANCE
>
> SALARY POTENTIAL: Minimum wage to $25 per hour (or more)
>
> TRAINING/LICENSE/CERTIFICATION REQUIRED: Certification from the American Red Cross (Lifeguard Training Class) is typically required for most lifeguard jobs at hotels, resorts, beaches, swimming pools, and waterparks
>
> OTHER REQUIREMENTS: The minimum age is 15 to take the American Red Cross Lifeguard Training class.
>
> CAREER ADVANCEMENT OPPORTUNITIES: Higher paying jobs are available to lifeguards who complete a separate Water Safety Instructor certification through the Red Cross. Other credentials that can lead to higher paying jobs include the Red Cross Head Lifeguard and Professional Rescuer courses.

You've probably seen the television show *Baywatch* and thought about what life would be like working as a Los Angeles County lifeguard. In addition to working along LA's famous beaches, lifeguards are employed at other beaches, lakes, swimming pools, and water parks across the United States. Lifeguard jobs typically involve watching swimmers and helping to ensure their safety while in the water, as well as enforcing rules, regulations, and local laws. Many lifeguard jobs are seasonal and are held by students.

For More Information

- American Red Cross. Information about lifeguard certification programs is offered at www.redcross.org/services/hss/aquatics/visibilityitems.html.
- eHow.com. Information on how to become a lifeguard and obtain the appropriate certification through the American Red Cross is offered at this informative web site, www.ehow.com/how_16979_become-lifeguard.html.
- Waterparks.com. Career and job opportunities available at waterparks throughout the country can be found here, www.waterparks.com/careers.asp.
- Yahoo! HotJobs. Online job listings for lifeguards are offered at this general interest job-related web site http://hotjobs.yahoo.com/jobseeker/job search/search_results.html?keywords_all=Lifeguard.

U.S. Military Jobs

AT A GLANCE

SALARY POTENTIAL: Varies.

TRAINING/LICENSE/CERTIFICATION REQUIRED: Provided by the military.

OTHER REQUIREMENTS: The willingness to dedicate yourself to supporting The United States of America, while receiving specialized training that can ultimately translate into higher paying jobs in the civilian workforce.

CAREER ADVANCEMENT OPPORTUNITIES: There is a wide range of career paths within the various branches of the U.S. military. The skills you learn through specialized training while active in the military can also help you launch a successful career later and/or provide the money you need for a two- or four-year college education.

The various branches of the United States military all offer a wide range of training programs that will provide you with specialized skills to ultimately launch a successful career as a civilian. The military offers over 4,100 different job opportunities. Long-term career opportunities are also available within the military. To learn about all of your options, contact a local recruiting center for the branch of the military you're interested in serving with.

For More Information

- U.S. Air Force. Get information about the U.S. Air Force, www.airforce.com.
- U.S. Army. Get information about the U.S. Army, (800) GO-ARMY, www.goarmy.com.
- U.S. Coast Guard. Get information about the U.S. Coast Guard, www.uscg .mil/jobs.
- U.S. Marine Corps. Get information about the U.S. Marine Corps, (800) MARINES, www.usmc.mil.
- U.S. Military. Discover opportunities in all branches of the U.S. military, www.todaysmilitary.com or www.military.com.

Police Officer/Law Enforcement Officer

> ### AT A GLANCE
>
> SALARY POTENTIAL: $40,000 to $79,000 per year.
>
> TRAINING/LICENSE/CERTIFICATION REQUIRED: Police officers must be at least 20 years old (in most states), have a high school diploma (or GED), and be in top physical and mental health to qualify for police academy training, which lasts 12 to 14 weeks. Upon graduation, an officer becomes eligible for a position with a local, state, or federal police agency.
>
> OTHER REQUIREMENTS: Work as a police officer requires dealing with extremely stressful and often dangerous situations.
>
> CAREER ADVANCEMENT OPPORTUNITIES: A wide range of career opportunities exist in police departments at the local, state, and federal level. With additional training and experience, promotions to corporal, sergeant, lieutenant, or captain are possible. Police officers can also become detectives, sheriffs, state troopers, FBI agents, DEA agents, U.S. marshals, INS agents, or work in a wide range of other jobs.

The job of a police officer working in a town or city involves maintaining the peace and safety of residents, confronting and arresting criminals, and handling a wide range of responsibilities. The job is both stressful and dangerous, but can be extremely rewarding. Most police officers work more than 40 hours per week (often with paid overtime). A flexible work schedule is important, because working nights and/or weekends may be required.

For More Information

- All Criminal Justice Schools. This is a valuable site for prospective police officers. Here you'll find an abundance of career-related information, including details about criminal justice schools and training programs, www.allcriminaljusticeschools.com/faqs/police.php.
- Officer.com. This is an informative web site for police officers and those interested in careers in law enforcement. Online job listings are provided, www.officer.com.

- PoliceEmployment.com. Information about careers in law enforcement, plus online job listings are offered at this web site, www.policeemployment.com.
- RehiredBadge.com. Online job listings for police officers can be found here, http://rehiredbadge.com.

Private Investigator

> ### AT A GLANCE
>
> SALARY POTENTIAL: $20,000 to $80,000 (or more) per year.
>
> TRAINING/LICENSE/CERTIFICATION REQUIRED: While most private investigators have some law enforcement training and/or experience, there are no formal training requirements to enter this field. Some states require private investigators to be licensed, but requirements vary by state. Training to become a private investigator is available from trade schools. Tuition starts at under $1,000.
>
> OTHER REQUIREMENTS: The ability to perform research, conduct interviews, handle surveillance, perform background checks, analyze financial information, and perform other related tasks on behalf of clients in a timely, responsible, and legal manner is required. Computer literacy, along with excellent communication and organization skills are necessary.
>
> CAREER ADVANCEMENT OPPORTUNITIES: Private investigator work is utilized in the private sector, as well as the legal, financial, and corporate sectors, so many different types of work are available, depending on your training and specialty.

The work of a private investigator varies as greatly as the issues clients are facing. Private investigators are hired to find missing people, investigate cheating spouses, perform detailed background checks on people, find lost or stolen items, investigate insurance claims, and for a wide range of other tasks. The job involves surveillance, research, using the vast resources available on the internet, and working directly with people. A private investigator must have a flexible work schedule, be extremely responsible, and always work within the confines of the law.

Some private investigators are self-employed, whereas others work for private investigation agencies, insurance companies, corporations, law firms, accounting firms, or other companies requiring the ongoing need for the services offered by private investigators. Depending on the type of investigative work being done, the job can involve some level of danger and stress.

It's important for a private investigator to be able to work with his or her clients to define their exact needs and determine the best course of action for attaining the desired objective in a timely manner. Compensation for this type of work can be based on an annual salary, an hourly wage, or a per-project basis.

For More Information

- Criminal Justice Degree Information. Details about multiple training programs are offered at this web site, www.criminaljustice-degrees.com/index.cfm.
- IHireSecurity.com. Online job listings for private investigators are offered at www.ihiresecurity.com.
- National Association of Legal Investigators. This is a professional trade association for private investigators. The web site offers a comprehensive list of resources used by investigators, along with information about training programs, (800) 266-6254, www.nalionline.org.
- Professional Career Development Institute. Information about traditional and online training programs are offered at www.pcdi.com/courses/jr.

FINANCE JOBS

here are literally thousands of job opportunities that involve crunching numbers, working with spreadsheets, developing budgets, and bookkeeping. This section offers descriptions of jobs and career paths involving money, finance, and mathematics that do not require a college degree.

Bank Teller

> **AT A GLANCE**
>
> **SALARY POTENTIAL:** $22,000 to $32,000 (for entry-level positions).
>
> **TRAINING/LICENSE/CERTIFICATION REQUIRED:** High school diploma or GED.
>
> **OTHER REQUIREMENTS:** Good mathematical and interpersonal skills are important.
>
> **CAREER ADVANCEMENT OPPORTUNITIES:** There are several levels of bank tellers. With training and experience, these jobs can lead to becoming a head teller or to other, more lucrative positions working at a bank or financial institution.

Working at a bank, credit union, or financial institution, a bank teller interacts with customers and handles their basic banking needs, such as processing deposits and withdrawals, cashing checks, and accepting loan payments. A bank teller might also sell savings bonds, traveler's checks, and handle other routine transactions. This job requires superior attention to detail, the ability to carefully follow directions and handle repetitive tasks, and a willingness to continuously offer a high level of customer service.

Flexible hours are often required, because many banks remain open for extended hours on weekdays and on weekends. Approximately one in three bank tellers works part-time.

For More Information

- BankJobs.com. An online service that lists job opportunities at banks and financial institutions, www.bankjobs.com.
- Edcomm Group Bank Teller Training. A distance learning program that offers bank teller certification and education, (888) 433-2666, www.teller-training .com.
- iHireBanking.com. An online service that lists job opportunities at banks and financial institutions, www.ihirebanking.com.
- JobsInTheMoney.com. An online service that lists job opportunities at banks and financial institutions, www.jobsinthemoney.com.

Bill, Debt, or Account Collector

> ### AT A GLANCE
>
> **SALARY POTENTIAL:** $25,000 and up, based on performance. Compensation usually involves a base salary, plus a small percentage of the funds collected. According to Salary.com, in May 2005, the annual compensation (including base salary and commissions) for an entry-level collector averaged $28,179.
>
> **TRAINING/LICENSE/CERTIFICATION REQUIRED:** No certification or licensing is required, however, training is available.
>
> **OTHER REQUIREMENTS:** Attention to detail, record-keeping skills, telephone skills, persistence, and the ability to deal well with difficult, upset, and financially desperate people is required.
>
> **CAREER ADVANCEMENT OPPORTUNITIES:** The industry employs over 450,000 collectors and is expected to grow 21 to 35 percent between 2002 and 2012.

Anyone who has ever been late making a payment knows exactly what bill collectors do. They attempt to collect on overdue or delinquent accounts. This typically means having to track people down, make contact with them, then convince them to promptly pay their outstanding debts.

Bill collectors are employed by a wide range of companies, as well as third-party collection agencies and law firms. They have a variety of responsibilities, based on the types of debt being collected. Collectors must always adhere to strict legal guidelines in terms of the techniques used to meet the responsibilities of their job. This includes understanding and working within the limits of the Federal Trade Commission's Fair Debt Collection Practices Act (www.ftc.gov/os/statutes/fdcpa/fdcpact.htm). The job involves a lot of tedious telephone work, often working from a call center or office environment.

For More Information
- American Collectors Association, Inc. A professional trade association for bill collectors, (952) 926–6547, www.acainternational.org.
- Phoenix Resource Group. Offers debt collection training on CD-ROM, (925) 980-5529, www.e-prg.com/education/quickstart.html.

Bookkeeper

> **AT A GLANCE**
>
> **SALARY POTENTIAL:** Starting salary $33,000 to $45,000 per year.
>
> **TRAINING/LICENSE/CERTIFICATION REQUIRED:** Completing a bookkeeping certification program is recommended, but not required. Training is offered at hundreds of colleges, universities, and vocational schools.
>
> **OTHER REQUIREMENTS:** Bookkeepers must be good at math, understand financial statements, and have a good understanding of business finance principles. Computer literacy and being proficient using business-oriented financial software applications, such as QuickBooks and Microsoft Excel, is also useful.
>
> **CAREER ADVANCEMENT OPPORTUNITIES:** The U.S. Bureau of Labor predicts 59,000 new job opportunities for bookkeepers will be created by 2012. With additional training, bookkeepers can train to hold a wide range of financial jobs, such as an accountant, certified financial planner, or auditing clerk.

The bookkeeper at a company is responsible for maintaining and recording financial business transactions, such as accounts payable and accounts receivable, as well as balancing ledgers. Often, this job involves preparing financial information for accountants or other finance personnel. In the United States alone, more than two million bookkeepers are employed in the private sector as well as in government. This can be a full- or part-time job.

For More Information

- American Institute of Professional Bookkeepers. A professional trade association for bookkeepers. This site contains information about obtaining certification as a bookkeeper, www.aipb.org.
- BookkeeperJobs.com. Online job listings for bookkeepers can be found here, www.bookkeeperjobs.com.
- BookkeeperList.com. Another site where online job listings for bookkeepers can be found, www.bookkeeperlist.com/hireabookkeeper.shtml.
- Thomson Education. Training opportunities for bookkeepers are described at this web site, http://educationdirectcourses.com/html/career_diploma/Bookkeeping.php.

Brokerage Clerk

> ### AT A GLANCE
>
> SALARY POTENTIAL: Varies.
>
> TRAINING/LICENSE/CERTIFICATION REQUIRED: At least a high school diploma or GED is required. Some brokerage firms require people in this position to have a bachelor's degree. A Series 7 license is optional, but recommended.
>
> OTHER REQUIREMENTS: To be successful in this job, careful attention to detail is important and people skills are definitely beneficial, because you'll be working with licensed brokers and potential clients. Computer literacy is required.
>
> CAREER ADVANCEMENT OPPORTUNITIES: With additional training, a broker's assistant or brokerage clerk can become a fully licensed broker.

The job title brokerage clerk means different things at different companies. In some cases, this position involves working as a sales assistant, doing clerical and sales work, whereas in other situations, the job will involve working with computers to record and manage data pertaining to securities transactions. This job could also involve working directly with clients at a brokerage firm.

Depending on your job responsibilities, you may find yourself working in a traditional office environment (within a brokerage firm) or actually working on trading floors under the direct supervision of a broker.

By obtaining a Series 7 license as a brokerage assistant, you'll be able to make recommendations to clients (still working under the supervision of a licensed broker), plus your earning potential will improve dramatically.

A Series 7 license qualifies you to sell investment products. You will need a Series 3 license, however, to sell commodities. To obtain this license, specialized training is required to help you develop a solid understanding of stocks, bonds, and options, along with related regulations and laws.

For More Information

- American Investment Training. Learn about a home-study course to prepare you for the Series 7 exam, www.aitraining.com/series7.htm.

- Closers.net. Online job listings and career information for brokerage assistants can be found at www.closers.net.
- Professional Education Corporation. Learn about a training program to prepare you to take the Series 7 exam from this web site, www.pecu.com.
- Total Series 7. Learn about online multimedia training and instruction opportunities for obtaining a Series 7 license. This training will prepare you for the Series 7 exam, www.totalseries7.com.

Financial Investor

AT A GLANCE

SALARY POTENTIAL: Unlimited and varied.

TRAINING/LICENSE/CERTIFICATION REQUIRED: None to invest your own money. To invest other people's money, however, requires extensive training and a license.

OTHER REQUIREMENTS: In addition to having some of your own money to invest, it's important to develop a strong understanding of whatever it is you choose to invest in, whether it's individual stocks, mutual funds, precious metals, businesses, real estate, or other types of investments.

CAREER ADVANCEMENT OPPORTUNITIES: For the individual investor, the opportunities are limitless.

The job of a financial investor can involve helping other people manage their money and assets, or it could involve actually working on Wall Street or at an investment brokerage firm. These career paths all require extensive education and licensing. For the purpose of this book, a financial investor refers to someone who invests his or her own money in hopes of generating more money and building up assets or portfolio.

You can begin investing money in the stock market or in mutual funds with a small amount of start-up capital. You can conduct your own stock trades online through a discount brokerage firm, or you can pursue larger investment opportunities in businesses or real estate, for example. The time commitment involved with managing your own investments or starting your own investment portfolio can be minimal. Plus, you can control the amount of money you choose to invest and the level of risk you're willing to accept in order to achieve your financial goals.

Many people choose to manage their own investments, including their retirement account(s) as a hobby or as a way to supplement their incomes. The core knowledge required can be obtained from reading books or attending seminars. Many investors also learn from experience. Keep in mind, investing your money often involves risk. It's vitally important to understand exactly how an investment opportunity works before getting involved with it.

If you're looking to help others manage their money, consider pursuing a career as an accountant, certified financial planner, or stock broker.

For More Information

- BusinessWeek Online. Personal investing information from *BusinessWeek* magazine can be found at www.businessweek.com/investor.
- Charles Schwab. One of many popular discount brokerage firms that individual, novice investors can utilize to manage their finances and invest in the stock market or mutual funds, (866) 855-9102, www.schwab.com.
- Fidelity Investments. One of many popular discount brokerage firms that individual, novice investors can utilize to manage their finances and invest in the stock market or mutual funds, (800) 343-3548, www.fidelity.com.
- Morningstar. Mutual fund news and information can be found at this web site, www.morningstar.com.
- The Motley Fool. This is a web site chock full of information for personal investors, including novices, www.fool.com.

 CAREER SPOTLIGHT

Certified Financial Planner (CFP)

> **AT A GLANCE**
>
> **SALARY POTENTIAL:** Varies.
>
> **TRAINING/LICENSE/CERTIFICATION REQUIRED:** According to the Certified Financial Planner Board of Standards web site, "There are more than 285 academic

programs at colleges and universities across the country from which to choose. These programs include credit and non-credit certificate programs, plus undergraduate and graduate degree programs. They use various delivery formats and schedules, including classroom instruction, self-study, and online delivery."

OTHER REQUIREMENTS: A CFP must possess mathematical skills and a broad knowledge about personal finance issues. In addition, a good CFP will have excellent people skills and be able to interact well with clients.

CAREER ADVANCEMENT OPPORTUNITIES: A CFP can be self-employed or work for a variety of financial businesses, such as accounting or investment management firms.

According to the CFP Board, "Financial planning is the process of determining how an individual can meet life goals through the proper management of his or her financial resources. Examples of life goals include a comfortable retirement, buying a home, saving for a child's education or starting a business. A financial planner is someone who uses the financial planning process to help clients figure out how to meet their life goals. A financial planner can take a big-picture view of a client's financial situation and make financial planning recommendations based on the client's needs in areas such as budgeting and saving, taxes, investments, insurance and retirement planning. Or, the planner may work with a client on a single financial issue but within the context of that client's overall situation."

A CFP can work with the client on a variety of objectives. For example, the CFP Board reports, "A financial planner helps a client analyze either all or selected areas of his or her finances and develops a 'plan' bringing together all of the client's financial goals, or provides advice on specific areas as needed. A plan does not necessarily have to be a written document; it can also be financial recommendations or alternatives presented by the financial planner. This big-picture approach to a client's financial goals sets the planner apart from other financial advisers, who may have been trained to focus on a particular area of a client's financial life."

CFPs are financial planners who have undergone rigorous training and who have pledged to meet or exceed the core requirements of the CFP Board of Standards. According to the organization's web site, "Certified Financial Planner certificants are individuals who have met CFP Board's education, examination and experience requirements, have agreed to adhere to high standards of ethical conduct and who complete CFP Board's biennial certification requirements. A CFP practitioner is a financial professional authorized to use the CFP certification marks and who has identified himself or herself to the CFP Board as being actively engaged in providing financial planning services."

Of all the jobs and career opportunities described within this book, becoming a CFP requires the most training and education, yet the job opportunities and income potential can be well worth the investment.

Here's My Story

Kevin is a certified financial planner who pursued his financial planning degree via a distance learning program, then held several jobs working for various financial companies. He currently has his own practice and works with a select group of clients, helping them to manage all aspects of their personal financials.

"After graduating from high school, I didn't immediately have the resources to attend a traditional college or university on a full-time basis. Instead, I continued to live with my parents for several years while I worked part-time and attended classes part-time via a combination of distance learning and online training. I ultimately graduated with a degree in financial planning, then contacted The CFP Board and worked on becoming a CFP," explained Kevin.

"I have always been good at math and finance. I look at it as a challenge to assist people in successfully overcoming various financial obstacles. It's also rewarding when you've worked with a client to achieve a specific financial goal and they eventually achieve that goal, in part, because they followed my advice," he added.

As a self-employed CFP, Kevin works from a small office. He has a flexible work schedule and the educational background and certification that have allowed him to pursue a lucrative career. "Becoming a CFP wasn't easy and it certainly isn't something to pursue if you're looking for overnight success. This is something you have to work long and hard for, but the rewards can be worth it," said Kevin.

For More Information

- Certified Financial Planner Board of Standards. This is a professional trade association comprised of certified financial planners. The group offers certification, training, and a wide range of resources for people working in this field, www.cfp.com.
- Closers.net. Online job listings for certified financial planners and others working in the personal finance field, www.closers.net.

- Kaplan University. One of many accredited schools that offers a degree program in financial planning, www.financial-planner-courses.com/index.cfm.
- Your Career as a Certified Financial Planner. This web site, sponsored by the CFP Board, offers career-related information and resources, including a free, downloadable eBook, www.cfp.net/become/career.asp.
- Online job listings can be found at the general interest career-related web sites, such as Monster (www.monster.com) or Yahoo! Hot Jobs (http://hot jobs.yahoo.com).

Fund Raiser

AT A GLANCE

SALARY POTENTIAL: Varies.

TRAINING/LICENSE/CERTIFICATION REQUIRED: A working knowledge of how non-profit organizations operate as well as fund raising techniques is needed.

OTHER REQUIREMENTS: Extremely strong verbal, written, and interpersonal communications are needed for this type of job.

CAREER ADVANCEMENT OPPORTUNITIES: For a skilled fund raiser, there are a wide range of opportunities available working for nonprofit and charitable organizations.

A fund raiser is someone who is hired to raise money for an organization, typically a political campaign, a nonprofit organization, religious organization, charity, or business (such as a hospital). The requirements for this type of job can be as simple as coordinating a bake sale or silent audition at a fund-raising dinner, or as complex as launching a nationwide fund-raising campaign utilizing direct mail, telemarketing, a telethon, or a walk-a-thon.

Some fund raisers are volunteers; whereas others are paid a salary. Some receive a percentage of the money they raise for the organization that hires them. A truly skilled fund raiser will have a strong networking pool comprised of high-income people interested in donating their money to worthwhile causes. College-level programs are available; however, many people learn the skills needed for this type of job through volunteer work and on-the-job training.

For More Information

- Association of Fundraising Professionals. A professional trade organization for fundraisers and people working in the nonprofit field, www.afpnet.org/jobs.
- ExecSearches.com. Online job listings for experienced fund raisers interested in working for nonprofits, www.execsearches.com/exec/default.asp.
- On Philanthropy. Online job listings for fund raisers. This web site also offers some excellent career-related information, www.dotorgjobs.com/rt/dojhome.

Medical Coding and Billing Clerk

> ### AT A GLANCE
>
> **SALARY POTENTIAL:** $20,000 to $36,000 per year.
>
> **TRAINING/LICENSE/CERTIFICATION REQUIRED:** A high school diploma or GED is required. Certification can be obtained from a postsecondary vocational school or distance learning program in as little as three months.
>
> **OTHER REQUIREMENTS:** Basic computer literacy skills are necessary.
>
> **CAREER ADVANCEMENT OPPORTUNITIES:** Limited.

The job of a medical coding and billing clerk is to compile accurate records of charges for services rendered by doctors (and other medical professionals), calculate the patient's outstanding balances, and prepare invoices for the patient and/or insurance companies. The job involves maintaining detailed financial records for bookkeepers and accountants, typically using a computer equipped with specialized billing software.

This is considered an entry-level, data-entry position. On-the-job training is typically provided by the employer. The work can involve completing highly repetitive and mundane tasks with minimal interaction with coworkers.

For More Information

- American Academy of Professional Coders. This is a professional trade association for medical coding and billing clerks, (800) 626-2633, www.aapc.com.

- Health Careers Center. Information about career opportunities as a medical coding and billing clerk is offered at this web site. This site also offers visitors a free, downloadable brochure that provides detailed information for someone interested in entering this field, www.mshealthcareers.com/careers/medicalcoding.htm.
- For online job listings, refer to any of the general interest career-related web sites, such as Monster (www.monster.com) or Yahoo! HotJobs (http://hotjobs.yahoo.com)

 CAREER SPOTLIGHT

Mortgage Broker/Loan Officer

> ### AT A GLANCE
>
> SALARY POTENTIAL: $20,000 to $500,000 (or more). This job is almost entirely based on sales commissions. Sixty percent of all full-time mortgage brokers earn more than $80,000 per year.
>
> TRAINING/LICENSE/CERTIFICATION REQUIRED: As long as you're employed by a licensed mortgage broker, no license is required. On-the-job training is often provided by the employer, however, most mortgage brokers entering this type of job say the training isn't adequate due to the technical nature of the work. Thus, many people working as mortgage brokers participate in training programs on their own and arrange to apprentice for a short time with someone more experienced. Loan officer training can be obtained through traditional classroom instruction or by using a self-paced, distance learning program. There are DVD training programs, for example, offering 20 hours or more of instruction.
>
> OTHER REQUIREMENTS: Working as a loan officer is mainly a sales job, so having strong sales and telemarketing skills is extremely beneficial. It's also important to have friendly personality and patience when working with clients. Due to the technical complexity of the work, being able to perform basic mathematical calculations and handle extremely detail-oriented paperwork is critical.

> Being self-motivated and not afraid of rejection are also helpful for the sales aspect of this job.
>
> CAREER ADVANCEMENT OPPORTUNITIES: Loan officers working for a mortgage broker can specialize in brokering the financing for new home/condo purchases or refinances. Similar work can also be done for commercial properties. This is more complex, but offers higher commissions.

A loan officer who works for a mortgage broker assists people in obtaining the financing for their new homes or condo purchases and can assist with coordinating the refinancing of existing mortgages or obtaining second mortgages. Loan officers can also work on financing pertaining to commercial properties.

This is a highly technical job, but one that requires no formal training or licensing, as long as you're working for a licensed mortgage broker in the state(s) where you're doing business. Because this job is almost entirely based on sales commissions, the earning potential is virtually unlimited. Experienced mortgage brokers can earn upwards of $500,000 to $1,000,000 or more per year, whereas people first entering the field tend to struggle financially for several months as they receive on-the-job training and learn the complexities of this business. Ideally, someone breaking into this field should expect it to take up to three or four months of hard work before they start closing deals and earning commissions.

In addition to the sales aspect of this job, working as a mortgage broker/loan officer requires completing tremendous amounts of paperwork (either manually or using a computer) for each loan that's being processed. As the loan officer, you'll be working directly with clients, as well as many departments within your company that assist with the processing of the loan. Interacting with real estate appraisers and attorneys on a regular basis is also part of the job.

Ideally, a loan officer will have multiple loans in the pipeline at any given time and they'll always be soliciting new business. As a result, the job requires a strong attention to detail and the ability to juggle many tasks at once. Some of the work is highly repetitive and tedious, whereas some aspects are always new and pose different sets of challenges.

Most loan officers can set their own work schedules, however, to successfully accommodate clients, it's often necessary to be on call nights and weekends. To stay in touch with clients, loan officers use telephones, cell phones, fax, e-mail, and in-person meetings. This is a highly competitive business where clients base their decisions on the lowest rates and quality of customer service offered. Providing top-notch service will often result in repeat business and referrals.

Of all the jobs and career opportunities described in this book, becoming a mortgage broker loan officer offers one of the highest income potentials with the least amount of training and education. To be successful, however, long hours of hard work and dedication are definitely required. Working as a loan officer for a mortgage broker is different than working as a loan officer for a bank or another type of financial institution.

Here's My Story

Tristan is a loan officer working for one of the nation's largest mortgage broker-age firms. He works part time from a traditional office and part time from his home (staying connected to his work via the internet, fax, and telephone). Like so many mortgage broker loan officers, Tristan was lured to this field by the high income potential and flexible schedule.

"Prior to working as a mortgage broker loan officer, I held a variety of sales and telemarketing jobs. This experience has proved to be extremely valuable. Before accepting a job, I spoke with many mortgage brokers who worked for a variety of different companies. This allowed me to learn how different companies worked, in terms of commissions, support, and training. What I discovered from these people and ultimately first-hand was that the training that most mortgage brokerage firms offer isn't adequate to successfully learn and do the job. Yet, you're expected to immediately start generating business," explained Tristan. "In addition to finding an experienced broker in my firm who was willing to take me under his wing, I purchased a DVD training program and immediately began reading a handful of books about mortgage and mortgage brokering. This sup-plemented my training and turned out to be extremely necessary."

In terms of advice for potential loan officers, Tristan explained, "When choos-ing what mortgage brokerage firm to work for, you need to understand how their compensation package works. I recommend finding a company that will offer new employees a draw plus commissions for at least the first few months. This insures you'll have money to pay your bills as you're learning the ropes. Also, determine what type of office support you'll receive and how much work you're required to do on behalf of each client," added Tristan.

"The people who do really well at this type of job are highly skilled sales peo-ple who aren't afraid to network. Potential clients will almost always shop around for the best rates, however, they also want to work with someone they can trust and who will explain the whole process to them as it is happening. Clients who are applying for a mortgage or refinancing their existing mortgage will have many questions. As the mortgage broker, you need to be able to answer their questions quickly, accurately and honestly," said Tristan.

Many loan officers who are first starting out are intimidated by the amount of paperwork and the complexity of the mortgage application process. "This job has a definite learning curve. It's important to have people you can get answers from within your company and avoid getting frustrated when you hit some type of snag. When you start doing this type of work, know that it will take you up to six months or longer to learn what you need to know and feel totally comfortable meeting all of the job's responsibilities. Try to find an employer that offers as much support as possible. Later, once you have the knowledge and experience necessary, you can always switch employers and seek out a company that offers higher commissions but less support for its brokers," concluded Tristan. "When you get started, definitely plan to immerse yourself in some training materials that you purchase on your own. To start finding leads for new business quickly, I recommend networking and purchasing leads from a firm that sells qualified leads. You can find these companies on the internet or seek out a referral from another loan officer."

For More Information

- Broker Jobs. Online job listings for loan officers can be found here, www.brokerjobs.com.
- Loan Officer School. This company offers a variety of training materials for loan officers working for mortgage brokers, including self-paced DVD, VHS, and online courses. The company also offers a comprehensive two-day, live training seminar that's presented periodically in various cities throughout the country, (866) 623-1250, www.loanofficerschool.com.
- Mortgage Board. Online job listings for loan officers can be found here, www.mortgageboard.net.
- Mortgage Magazine. This is an industry trade magazine specifically for loan officers at mortgage brokers. Both the publication and the web site are excellent information resources for people working in this field, www.mortgagemag.com.
- National Mortgage Leads. This is one of many companies that sells qualified client leads to loan officers looking for new business, www.national-mortgage-leads.com.
- Referralsoft. This company offers a complete marketing and referral management system for mortgage brokers, www.referralsoft.com.

- The Lead Tree. One of many companies that sells qualified client leads to loan officers looking for new business, www.theleadtree.com.
- Online job listings can be found at the general interest career-related web sites, such as Monster (www.monster.com) or Yahoo! Hot Jobs (http://hotjobs.yahoo.com). Because this is a commission-based sales job, many mortgage brokerage firms are always hiring new loan officers. Check your local Yellow Pages for a listing of potential employers.

Payroll Clerk

> ### AT A GLANCE
>
> SALARY POTENTIAL: $25,000 to $35,000 per year.
>
> TRAINING/LICENSE/CERTIFICATION REQUIRED: No training or certification is required, however, certification at as Certified Payroll Professional (CPP) can be obtained from a postsecondary vocational school, which will improve your chances for landing a job. On-the-job training is typically offered.
>
> OTHER REQUIREMENTS: Computer and data entry experience is required.
>
> CAREER ADVANCEMENT OPPORTUNITIES: Payroll clerks are employed by companies of all sizes and in all industries. With additional training, opportunities in bookkeeping and accounting can be pursued.

The job of a payroll clerk with a company is to ensure that all of the employees get paid on time and receive the correct amount of money. The job involves basic bookkeeping, reviewing timecards, handling a wide range of clerical tasks, working with the company's accounting department to prepare tax and withholding statements for employees, coordinating with an outsourced payroll service, and interacting with all employees. Computer and data entry skills are typically required for this type of job. Working as a payroll clerk can be a part-time or full-time job, depending on the employer. Temporary employment agencies can also help with job placement for payroll clerks.

For More Information
- American Payroll Association. This is a professional trade association for people working in the payroll field. The web site offers information about

certification, education programs, and online job listings, www.american payroll.org.

- Independent Payroll Providers Association. This is a professional trade association for people working in the payroll field, www.ippa.net.
- Payroll Clerk Job Listings for Federal Government Agencies. This web site lists job openings available for payroll clerks within various federal government agencies nationwide, http://federalgovernmentjobs.us/job-search/payroll-clerk-0544.html.
- Online job listings can be found at the general interest career-related web sites, like such as Monster (www.monster.com) or Yahoo! Hot Jobs (http://hotjobs.yahoo.com).

Real Estate Appraiser

> **AT A GLANCE**
>
> SALARY POTENTIAL: Varies. Release estate appraisers are typically paid a flat fee per job. Entry-level appraisers can earn anywhere from $1,500 to $3,000 or more per month.
>
> TRAINING/LICENSE/CERTIFICATION REQUIRED: Specialized training and a license is required to pursue this type of career. Licensing requirements vary by state.
>
> OTHER REQUIREMENTS: A flexible work schedule is required, although most appraisers work a 40-hour week.
>
> CAREER ADVANCEMENT OPPORTUNITIES: Limited.

A real estate appraiser is someone who estimates the value of real estate, such as a home, apartment, condo, lot of land, or commercial property. Most real estate appraisers are self-employed and work on their own or as independent contractors for real estate businesses, including mortgage companies and other financial institutions.

The job involves visiting and analyzing properties, taking measurements, completing standardized forms, and comparing each property to similar recently sold properties in the geographic area to calculate the approximate value of each property in the current real estate market.

Training for this type of career can be done relatively quickly, allowing some-one to launch a lucrative career within a few weeks or months. On-the-job train-ing can be obtained if you work for a real estate appraisal firm or work as an apprentice for an already-licensed appraiser.

For More Information

- California Occupational Guide. Detailed career-related information is offered here. (The information does not apply only to California residents.), www.calmis.cahwnet.gov/file/occguide/REALAPPR.HTM.
- IHireRealEstate.com. Online job listings for licensed real estate appraisers can be found at www.ihirerealestate.com.
- National Association of Real Estate Appraisers. This is a professional trade association for real estate appraisers. At this web site, you'll find career-related information, details about training programs, and a wide range of other resources, www.iami.org.
- Online-Education.net. Information about online training programs for real estate appraisers can be found here. This training will prepare you to take your state's licensing exam, www.online-education.net/real-estate-appraisal-license.html.
- PCDI Home Study Courses. Information about a distance learning pro-gram to become a real estate appraiser is provided at this web site, www.pcdicourses.com/html/programs_rr.php?code=GL4-CPC20501-RealEstateAppraisal.
- The American Society of Appraisers. This is a professional trade association for real estate appraisers. The web site offers an abundance of useful information and resources for people interested in this career, www.appraisers.org.

Real Estate Investor

AT A GLANCE

SALARY POTENTIAL: Varies.

TRAINING/LICENSE/CERTIFICATION REQUIRED: None.

OTHER REQUIREMENTS: Knowledge of finance and real estate are essential.

CAREER ADVANCEMENT OPPORTUNITIES: Limited.

A real estate investor can be a multi-millionaire who invests in large properties, such as housing complexes, apartment buildings, or shopping malls, or it can be an individual who buys and sells one or two investment properties at a time. There are several ways ordinary people can invest in real estate. For example, someone can purchase a home that needs to be fixed up, complete the renovations and then resell the property for a significant profit. This is called "flipping" a property. A small real estate investor can also purchase one or more homes, condos, or apartments and rent them, thus becoming an investor and a landlord.

There are many ways for everyday people to obtain the necessary financing to purchase investment properties. With good credit, it's sometimes possible to buy property with no money down. Like any type of investment, investing in real estate involves some risk. It's important to first acquire the necessary knowledge you'll need to make intelligent investment decisions.

Real estate investing courses are offered across the country. There are also countless books and home study courses you can utilize. For many, investing in real estate begins as a part-time job for generating additional income.

For More Information

- Cash Flow Property. This is an online listing of foreclosed properties that may be of interest to small-time real estate investors, http://cashflowproperty.net.
- Creative Real Estate Online. This web site contains links to training programs, resources, and a vast amount of information for prospective real estate investors, www.creonline.com.
- ForeclosureNet. This is an online listing of foreclosed properties that may be of interested to small-time real estate investors, www.foreclosurenet.net.
- Real Estate Investing. A wealth of free information for real estate investors is offered at this web site, www.real-estate-investing-i.com.
- REI Depot. This web site contains links to training programs, resources, and a vast amount of information for prospective real estate investors, www.rei depot.com.
- REI Town. This web site contains links to training programs, resources, and a vast amount of information for perspective real estate investors, www .reitown.com.

CHAPTER

FOOD SERVICES JOBS

Whether you're looking to pursue a job in fast food or have
bigger aspirations for a career that somehow involves preparing
or serving food and beverages, this section covers everything
you'll need to know to find exciting job opportunities.

Baker

> **AT A GLANCE**
>
> SALARY POTENTIAL: $25,000 to $30,000 per year.
>
> TRAINING/LICENSE/CERTIFICATION REQUIRED: On-the-job training is provided by employers who hire entry-level bakers as apprentices or trainees. Many apprentice bakers first participate in a vocational school or distance learning program and earn a certificate in baking.
>
> OTHER REQUIREMENTS: Bakers need to acquire skills in baking, icing, and decorating. Modern food plants use computerized baking equipment, so basic computer skills are important.
>
> CAREER ADVANCEMENT OPPORTUNITIES: With additional training, bakers can become chefs and ultimately land higher paying, more skill-intensive jobs in food preparation.

Bakers are different than chefs or line cooks. They're responsible for mixing ingredients in accordance with recipes to produce breads, pastries, and other baked items. Bakers are hired by supermarkets, bakeries, resorts, hotels, restaurants, and by high-volume manufacturing facilities.

For More Information

- Culinary Schools Directory. This web site includes a listing of schools offering certificates in baking, www.culinary-schools-info.com.
- hCareers. Online job listings for bakers and other restaurant jobs, www.restaurantjobs.hcareers.com/seeker.
- iHireChefs. Online job listings for bakers and chefs, www.ihirechefs.com.

Bartender

> **AT A GLANCE**
>
> SALARY POTENTIAL: Minimum wage to $20 per hour, plus tips. Tips represent a large portion of a bartender's income.

> TRAINING/LICENSE/CERTIFICATION REQUIRED: On-the-job training is sometimes offered, however, most bartenders learn their skills by participating in a bartending program at vocational schools.
>
> OTHER REQUIREMENTS: Excellent multi-tasking and interpersonal skills are important. Working late-night hours and weekends is typically necessary.
>
> CAREER ADVANCEMENT OPPORTUNITIES: Jobs for experienced bartenders are available in a wide range of environments. Working for a catering company that services events, at a bar, hotel lounge, nightclub, or for a fine dining restaurant, will generate the highest tips.

Bartenders work in restaurants, lounges, bars, nightclubs, and at catered events filling drink orders. This includes knowing how to prepare a wide range of mixed alcoholic beverages quickly and accurately. Knowledge of local laws relating to alcohol consumption is also required. Depending on where you work, a bartender may deal only with a restaurant's waiters and waitresses, or there may be extensive interaction with customers. Many bartenders work part time and/or at night.

For More Information

- ABC Bartending Schools. Learn about accredited training that's offered in over a dozen U.S. cities, (800) COCKTAIL, www.abcbartending.com.
- Bartending School Online. This company offers accredited job training online, (800) 9-TENDBAR, www.bartendingschoolonline.com.
- BartendingJobs.com. An online career-related web site for bartenders that includes job listings, www.bartendingjobs.com.
- Professionals Bartending School. Training information and online job listings are offered at (800) 736-1001, www.barbook.com.

Butcher (Meat, Poultry, and/or Fish Cutter)

> AT A GLANCE
>
> SALARY POTENTIAL: $15,000 to $40,000 (depending on experience and skills).
>
> TRAINING/LICENSE/CERTIFICATION REQUIRED: On-the-job training is provided. No specialized education or training is necessary. In some states, a license is required.

> OTHER REQUIREMENTS: Good hand-eye coordination and physical strength is necessary.
>
> CAREER ADVANCEMENT OPPORTUNITIES: With experience, butchers can land higher paying jobs at supermarkets and restaurants.

The entry-level job of a butcher working in a meatpacking plant is classified as a "food processing" occupation, which according to the Department of Labor, has a high rate of injury and illness. While meatpacking plant jobs offer a variety of challenges, butchers are also employed by supermarkets, restaurants, institutional food services, and food wholesalers (manufacturers). Working conditions vary dramatically. This job involves working with knives, cleavers, and power tools. Most on-the-job injuries are a result of the improper use of these tools.

For More Information

- The Retail Meat Industry Training Organization. Information about careers as a butcher can be found at this web site, www.retailmeat.org.nz/become/become.php.
- Contact the human resources department at local supermarkets, meat packing plants, and restaurants to learn about job openings.

Caterer

> ### AT A GLANCE
>
> SALARY POTENTIAL: Hourly wages vary, based on the job's responsibilities.
>
> TRAINING/LICENSE/CERTIFICATION REQUIRED: Catering companies hire people with a broad range of skills to handle a variety of functions. For some of these jobs, specific training or certification is required. For example, if you want to be a chef or baker who works for a catering company, you'll need to acquire training at a culinary school. To work as a bartender, training from a bartending school will be necessary. Entry-level jobs at catering companies typically involve serving, which requires little or no training or previous

experience. On-the-job training (and uniforms) are often provided by the employer.

OTHER REQUIREMENTS: This type of work requires a careful attention to detail, a high level of professionalism, and strong people skills. Previous experience as a server, waiter, waitress, host, hostess, or bartender can be beneficial.

CAREER ADVANCEMENT OPPORTUNITIES: There are a wide range of jobs within the food service industry (working for restaurants, bars, lounges, hotels, resorts, cruise ships, etc.) that a job at a catering company can lead to and prepare you for. People experienced in working for a catering company can start their own businesses.

Catering is a $5 billion per year industry. Working for a catering company can involve a wide range of responsibilities, such as cooking, baking, food preparation, serving, hosting, event organizing/planning, bartending, and cleaning up after events. A catering company typically provides the food and beverages to private or corporate parties and special events. Working nights and weekends is typically required, as is having a flexible schedule. Many catering companies pay by the hour and hire employees only when events or parties are booked, so the work may not be steady.

For More Information

- *Catering* Magazine. An industry magazine for catering professions. Subscriptions: $35 per year, www.cateringmagazine.com/home.
- hCareers.com. Online job listings available within the food service industry, www.restaurantjobs.hcareers.com/seeker.
- iHireHospitality.com. Online job listings and career-related information pertaining to the food service industry, www.ihirehospitality.com.
- Information about Catering and Culinary Schools. Learn about training programs available throughout the country, www.education-online-search.com/culinary_schools/catering_schools/catering_schools.shtm.

Chef

> ### AT A GLANCE
>
> SALARY POTENTIAL: Varies dramatically. Executive chefs earn in excess of $40,000 per year. Less trained chefs can earn between $25,000 and $35,000 per year and will be paid either an hourly wage or salary.
>
> TRAINING/LICENSE/CERTIFICATION REQUIRED: Training from a culinary (cooking) school or post high school vocational program is required. Upon completing the training, participating in an apprenticeship program is often necessary, especially to become a Master Chef. There are over 100 schools accredited by the American Culinary Federation that offer certification and /or two- or four-year degrees.
>
> OTHER REQUIREMENTS: As a chef, being able to manage a kitchen staff and oversee all aspects of the kitchen's operation are important. This includes not only preparing foods and cooking, but having a good understanding of safe food handling procedures and how to operate a wide range of kitchen equipment. If you'll be working for a hotel, restaurant, or resort, for example, membership in a union may be required.
>
> CAREER ADVANCEMENT OPPORTUNITIES: After becoming an accomplished chef, career advancement opportunities are plentiful. You can earn the title Executive Chef or Head Chef, which involves managing other chefs and the entire kitchen staff where you work.

A chef is a graduate of a culinary school. This job requires significantly more training than a cook or food preparer, who might work for a fast food restaurant, cafeteria, diner, or within the food court of a mall, for example. Thus, chefs also earn significantly more than other types of food preparers.

Chefs are in demand by restaurants, hotels, resorts, private individuals, catering companies, hospitals, nursing care facilities, schools, and a wide range of companies within the food industry. Working conditions for chefs vary greatly, as do the job's responsibilities, depending on where you work.

Some of the skills chefs must have include the ability to follow instructions (including recipes), a developed sense of taste and smell, the ability to work as part of a larger kitchen staff, and personal cleanliness. Good dexterity and hand-eye coordination are also important. Since you'll be potentially preparing dozens or even hundreds of meals per day, good organizational and time management skills are important.

For More Information

- American Culinary Federation. Learn about training programs, culinary schools, and apprenticeship programs from this web site, www.acf chefs.org.
- Culinary Arts Schools. Information about many Culinary Arts schools located throughout the country can be obtained from this site, www.culin ary-schools-info.com.
- National Restaurant Association. A professional trade association for chefs, www.restaurant.org.
- *Star Chefs*. This is a magazine and web site for chefs. The web site offers job listings and other career-related information, www.starchefs.com.

Cook (Fast Food)

> AT A GLANCE
>
> SALARY POTENTIAL: Minimum wage to $10 per hour.
>
> TRAINING/LICENSE/CERTIFICATION REQUIRED: None.
>
> OTHER REQUIREMENTS: Being able to follow directions and work as part of a team are important in this type of work environment.
>
> CAREER ADVANCEMENT OPPORTUNITIES: Limited (unless you obtain formal training from a cooking or culinary arts school).

Working as a fast food or line cook involves preparing a limited number of items, such as burgers, pizza, tacos, or other items found at your favorite fast food restaurant. To prepare these often pre-cooked foods, you will follow specific recipes and guidelines, utilizing training received from the employer. The job involves working with an assortment of fryers and grills. Fast food cooks can work either full-time or part-time, must wear some type of uniform, and follow strict safety guidelines.

In addition to working at fast food restaurants (like McDonald's, Burger King, Wendy's, or Taco Bell), similar jobs are available at diners, cafeterias, cafes, and other types of institutions that serve food. Jobs in fast food are ideal for students and working moms who need part-time employment.

For More Information

- iSeek Careers. Information about career opportunities as a fast food cook can be found here, www.iseek.org/sv/13000.jsp?id=100079.
- Career Depot. Information about career opportunities as a fast food cook can be found at www.careerdepot.org/Descriptions/job_cook_fast_food.htm.
- Cooking Schools. Learn about cooking and culinary schools, www.cooking-schools.us.
- McDonald's. Job information from one of the country's most popular fast food chains is available on this site, www.mcdonalds.com/usa/work.html.

Food and Beverage Service Worker

> **AT A GLANCE**
>
> **SALARY POTENTIAL:** Minimum wage to $10 per hour (in some cases, food and beverage workers also receive tips).
>
> **TRAINING/LICENSE/CERTIFICATION REQUIRED:** None. On-the-job training is typically provided. This is an entry-level job.
>
> **OTHER REQUIREMENTS:** None.
>
> **CAREER ADVANCEMENT OPPORTUNITIES:** Career advancement is available, with additional training, within the hospitality industry at places like hotels, restaurants, or dining facilities.

Restaurants, coffee shops, bars, and a wide range of other food service establishments hire food and beverage servers. In many cases, this type of job is very similar to that of a waiter, waitress, or bartender. For entry-level positions, it can include bussing (clearing) tables, delivering room service to hotel guests, or working as a dining room or cafeteria attendant or a dishwasher. For these jobs, no formal education or training is required. Most people learn from on-the-job training or through training programs offered by their employers. The higher paying jobs go to people with more experience and training.

For More Information

- hCareers.com. Online job listings for food service workers can be found at www.restaurantjobs.hcareers.com/seeker.

- International Council on Hotel, Restaurant and Institutional Education. Learn about two- and four-year degree programs in food service at www.chrie.org.
- National Restaurant Association. This is a professional trade association for those involved in the restaurant and food service industry, www.restaurant.org.
- WorkZoo. Online job listings for food service workers can be found here, www.workzoo.com/US-jobs/Travel-Food-Service/jobs-11.html.

Restaurant Waiter/Server

AT A GLANCE

SALARY POTENTIAL: Varies. Tips typically comprise a large portion of income.

TRAINING/LICENSE/CERTIFICATION REQUIRED: On-the-job training is provided at most restaurants, although upscale restaurants hire servers with previous experience.

OTHER REQUIREMENTS: Servers must be friendly, attentive, and physically able to stand on their feet for hours at a time, plus carry trays of dishes. The job also requires a flexible work schedule.

CAREER ADVANCEMENT OPPORTUNITIES: With experience, jobs can be sought at upscale restaurants which will generate higher tips and income. Other related jobs include working as a host/hostess, bartender, assistant manager, or manger within a restaurant.

Servers take customer's orders and serve meals. In the United States alone, 12.2 million people work at over 900,000 restaurants, which provides for a tremendous and diverse selection of employment opportunities. Many restaurants offer training, but start off servers as bussers. A busser's job involves setting and clearing tables, plus filling water glasses.

A server's income typically includes a relatively low hourly wage in addition to tips. Thus, it's in a server's best interest to offer a customer the best service possible in hopes of receiving a 15 to 20 percent tip based on the total of the guest's check.

When applying for a restaurant job, determine if servers are allowed to keep their tips or if they're required to pool tips with the entire staff or give a portion to the restaurant's owners. Also, determine what on-the-job training is provided and what your typical work schedule will be, because this all varies greatly from restaurant to restaurant. Also, determine if you're required to wear a uniform and if that uniform is provided and will be laundered by the employer.

Jobs at upscale restaurants are definitely more difficult to land, since the tips generated tend to be much higher. As with many types of jobs, the best way to find openings is through a referral or an introduction from people currently working at the restaurant.

As any experienced server (waiter or waitress) will tell you, this job can be stressful and requires excellent organizational, memory, and verbal communication skills. It's also important to be able to work as a team with other restaurant staff members. Some people pursue work as a server as a part-time job or to generate income in between other jobs. Others pursue this line of work as a long-term career.

In addition to traditional restaurants, coffee shops, cafes, and diners, servers are employed by catering companies, hotels, resorts, cruise ships, and many other hospitality businesses that serve food.

For More Information

- hCareers. Online job listings in the restaurant field are offered at this web site, www.restaurantjobs.hcareers.com/seeker.
- National Restaurant Association. This is a professional trade association for restaurant owners and workers. Online job listings and career advice can also be found at www.restaurant.org.
- Waiter Training. Information about books and training manuals for servers is offered at www.waiter-training.com/order.html.
- Online job listings can be found at the general interest career-related web sites, such as Monster (www.monster.com) or Yahoo! Hot Jobs (http://hot jobs.yahoo.com).

Wine Steward

AT A GLANCE

SALARY POTENTIAL: Varies.

TRAINING/LICENSE/CERTIFICATION REQUIRED: On-the-job training is typically provided by upscale restaurants, however, applicants should become familiar with wines and attend formal wine tastings on their own.

> OTHER REQUIREMENTS: A passion and taste for fine wines.
>
> CAREER ADVANCEMENT OPPORTUNITIES: Wine stewards are employed by fine restaurants, hotels, resorts, cruise ships, wineries, wine shops, and vineyards.

A wine steward is responsible for selecting, requisitioning, storing, selling, and serving wines. The job often includes maintaining inventory and storing wines on racks or shelves (within a climate controlled wine cellar). A wine steward is extremely knowledgeable about wine. The job often entails participation in technical discussions about wines with patrons while assisting them in making their wine selections. When serving a fine wine, a wine steward will often taste the wine prior to serving it.

For More Information

- Restaurant Jobs. This web site offers online job listings for people interested in working within the restaurant and hospitality fields, www.restaurant jobs.hcareers.com/seeker.
- Wine Spectator. This web site is hosted by the publisher of *Wine Spectator*, a leading wine magazine. This is a "must read" for people working in this industry, www.winespectator.com.
- Wine Spectator School. This web site offers information about an online training program for wine stewards and those interested in wine tasting, www.winespectatorschool.com/wineschool.
- WineBusiness. This web site offers online job listings. The company also publishes a magazine for wine enthusiasts and those working in the wine industry, http://winebusiness.com/services/jobsearchbasic.cfm.
- WineSquire.com. This web site offers job listings for wine stewards, plus a wide range of resources for people working in the wine industry, including industry-related news, www.winesquire.com/industry/employment/index.htm.

HIGH-TECH AND COMPUTER JOBS

The world of computers and the internet is always evolving, creating a tremendous number of job opportunities for people who know how to utilize the latest technologies. You're about to discover a wide range of job opportunities that focuses on the use of computers.

Computer Operator/Data Entry Professional/Information Processing Specialist

---

AT A GLANCE

SALARY POTENTIAL: Minimum wage to $10 per hour, or $23,000 to $35,000 per year, based on experience and training.

TRAINING/LICENSE/CERTIFICATION REQUIRED: For data entry and information processing jobs, obtaining a Microsoft Office Specialist Certification or becoming certified with specific software programs can increase your earning potential. Some higher-paying computer operator jobs require a two-year degree or certification in Computer Information Technology.

OTHER REQUIREMENTS: Computer literacy and proficiency using popular operating systems and software applications is important.

CAREER ADVANCEMENT OPPORTUNITIES: With additional training, there are a wide range of higher paying jobs available.

A computer operator is someone who typically works in an office environment and is responsible for managing and utilizing the computer systems on the premises. The work of an information processing worker or data entry personnel involves entering and/or managing data using a computer equipped with specialized software, such as applications in the Microsoft Office suite (Word, Excel, Access, etc.). These are typically entry-level positions. The required skills can be acquired through on-the-job training or by taking computer classes offered through adult education programs, computer superstore, or computer training centers. Self-paced video and online training is also available.

The job of a computer operator may involve basic computer system maintenance, but typically requires the use of a computer or workstation to perform operations using a computer equipped with commercially available software or vertical market software created for the employer, such as word processing, spreadsheet applications, or database management applications.

Computer operators may use stand-alone PCs, networked PCs, mainframe computers, computer workstations, or other types of computer systems. Employers typically look for applicants with some type of training or previous work experience using hardware and software similar to what the employer uses. Computer operators are employed by all types of companies in all industries, including the U.S. federal government.

More advanced (and higher paying) computer-related jobs include: computer programmers, software engineers, computer support specialists, database administrators, computer system analysts, and network operators.

For More Information

- Association of Computer Operations Management. This is a professional trade organization for data entry professionals, www.afcom.com.
- Computer Information Technology at International College. Information about training and certification programs for several different careers in computers and IT can be found at www.internationalcollege.edu/CIT/citcareers.htm.
- Data Center Careers. Online job listings for computer-related jobs can be found at www.datacentercareers.com.
- Harper College. Here you'll find information about an online, 30-hour certification program in Computer Information Systems and other certifications and degrees available, www.harpercollege.edu/bus-ss/cis/qa/operato.htm.
- Microsoft Office Specialist. Learn about earning certification as a Microsoft Office Specialist, which can improve your earning potential when applying for entry-level computer operator positions. According to Microsoft's web site, "The Microsoft Office Specialist certification is the globally recognized standard for validating expertise with the Microsoft Office suite of business productivity programs," www.microsoft.com/learning/mcp/officespecialist/default.asp.

 **CAREER SPOTLIGHT**

Computer Consultant

> ### AT A GLANCE
>
> **SALARY POTENTIAL:** $25 to $150 per hour.
>
> **TRAINING/LICENSE/CERTIFICATION REQUIRED:** As a self-employed computer consultant, certification isn't required, but it's recommended because it gives you added credibility.
>
> **OTHER REQUIREMENTS:** In addition to being technologically savvy and proficient using computers, popular software, and operating systems, a computer

consultant should be detailed-oriented, highly professional, have an outgoing personality, and be deadline oriented. Being able to deal with your client's computer emergencies in a timely manner is essential.

CAREER ADVANCEMENT OPPORTUNITIES: Independent computer consultants can pursue IT jobs working for companies in a wide range of industries.

Most computer consultants are either self-employed or work for a computer consulting firm that caters to a variety of clients. A self-employed computer consultant is responsible for soliciting his or her own clients and building relationships with them to generate ongoing or repeat business. A computer consultant is typically called upon to assist in installing, maintaining, repairing, or upgrading a computer system or network.

Computer consultants typically have areas of expertise and cater to a specific clientele, such as companies in a specific industry that utilize a certain type of network or software. Some computer consultants, however, cater to home computer users, helping them select, install, and maintain their computers, remove viruses, recover lost data, and handle other types of emergencies that arise.

Certification training is available for many types of computer systems, operating systems, and software packages. Possessing a certification means you've acquired the training and knowledge needed to handle a wide range of issues relating to your area of expertise.

As a computer consultant, it's important to stay up-to-date on all of the latest hardware and software and be able to deal with all of the common issues associated with them. Reading computer industry trade publications and periodically attending additional training courses will help give you a competitive edge in this field.

Computer consultants are typically paid by the hour or have ongoing contracts with clients who put them on retainers. Some, however, also sell computer hardware, peripherals, and software, which boosts earning potential.

Here's My Story

Mark is an independent computer consultant living and working out of his home in Boston, Massachusetts. Though he's always been interested in computers and much of his knowledge is self-taught, he has participated in self-paced certification training programs for several types of networking systems.

"I started out as a computer consultant catering to home users. This was several years ago. I charged $35 per hour to help someone choose the right home computer, then I'd assist them in installing it. I'd also offer ongoing training, by the hour, and/or be called upon to upgrade a computer system or fix a problem. Later, I began catering to the more lucrative business market. I slowly built up a client base of about 20 regular corporate and business clients and was responsible for the ongoing maintenance and upgrading of their networks. I'd be on-call if any emergencies arose, and have to deal with a wide range of repair issues," explained Mark.

"Working for the corporate and business clients generated substantially more income, as I charged between $100 and $150 per hour for my services, plus travel time. However, I was literally always on call. Much of my time was spent running from client to client handling scheduled appointments and unscheduled emergencies," added Mark.

"I love this work because it allows me to use computers and the latest technology, which is something that I enjoy, plus it allows me to interact and meet many people. When my schedule became too hectic, I hired several employees who now handle the majority of the on-site appointments, while I manage the business, seek out new clients and negotiate long-term service contracts with our clients. By hiring employees, this created an entirely new set of challenges, since I now had to manage a team of people," said Mark.

"The best advice I can offer to someone interested in being a computer consultant is to start off small and specialize in something. As you build up your client base, you can expand your offerings. It's also important to stay up-to-date on the latest technologies, because your clients will turn to you for advice and recommendations. This business is all about building relationships and creating a strong sense of trust. After all, your clients are entrusting you with their vital and often classified information when they allow you to work on their computers or networks. Word-of-mouth is the easiest and cheapest way to land new clients and generate new business," explained Mark, who has begun using the latest internet-based remote access technology to service clients. This allows him and his employees to work on a client's computer remotely by connecting to it via the internet. This dramatically cuts down on travel time, saving him and his clients money.

"To learn this business, you might want to obtain the necessary training and first take a job with an established computer consulting firm. Later, you can start your own computer consulting business," concluded Mark.

For More Information

- C/Net News. This informative web site offers the latest news about computers and the computer industry, http://news.com.com.

- CBT Direct. This is one of many companies that offers self-paced training programs designed for computer consultants and those working in the IT field, www.cbtdirect.com.
- CompuCert. From this web site you can learn about a wide range of computer and networking certification training programs for computer consultants and IT professionals, www.compucert.com.
- SoloGig.com. This fee-based online service matches qualified computer consultants with potential clients, www.sologig.com/soloist.
- Technical Schools and Computer Training. This web site offers a listing of accredited schools offering certification and training for computer consultants and IT professionals, www.techtrainingdirectory.com.

Computer Programmer

> **AT A GLANCE**
>
> SALARY POTENTIAL: $33,000 to $70,000 or more per year, based on experience, training, and overall qualifications.
>
> TRAINING/LICENSE/CERTIFICATION REQUIRED: Some computer programming jobs require a bachelor's degree, however, a proven knowledge and certification using popular programming languages is more important to employers.
>
> OTHER REQUIREMENTS: Problem-solving skills, patience, and the ability to work long hours on specific projects are all important. Some programmers work alone, whereas others work in teams to create and test programs. Long hours working in front of a computer are the norm. The work involves extensive patience, concentration, and logical thinking.
>
> CAREER ADVANCEMENT OPPORTUNITIES: Limited.

The job of a computer programmer involves the development of computer programs by writing, testing, and maintaining programming code, plus developing the appropriate user documentation. Computer programs tell the computer what to do and allow the user to use the computer for a wide range of applications. There are many programming languages used to create programs that handle a wide range of applications. A few popular programming languages include COBOL, C++, and Java.

In addition to software publishers, companies in all industries hire computer programmers. Some programmers are self-employed and work on a consulting basis.

For More Information

- Association for Computing Machinery. A professional trade organization for programmers, (212) 869-7440, http://www.acm.org.
- Association of Information Technology Professionals. A professional trade organization for programmers, (800) 224-9371, http://www.aitp.org.
- Computer Programming Languages. An online listing of popular computer programming languages and links to resources pertaining to them, http://dir.yahoo.com/Computers_and_Internet/Programming_and_Develop ment/Languages.
- eLance. Online job listings for freelance computer programmers can be found at www.eLance.com.
- GURU. This is an online resource for freelance computer programmers. The site offers online job listings, www.guru.com.
- Institute for Certification of Computer Professionals. This is a professional trade organization for programmers, (800) U-GET-CCP, http://www .iccp.org.

Computer Repair Technician/Computer Service Technician

AT A GLANCE

SALARY POTENTIAL: $10 to $100 per hour, depending on training, experience, and the type of work being done.

TRAINING/LICENSE/CERTIFICATION REQUIRED: Specialized training is available from colleges, vocational/technical schools, and computer training centers.

OTHER REQUIREMENTS: Computer literacy, an understanding of computer hardware (including peripherals, such as printers, disk drives, etc.), and the ability to use basic tools to repair and maintain computer hardware is essential. Knowledge about how to repair related office equipment and problem-solving skills is also valuable.

> CAREER ADVANCEMENT OPPORTUNITIES: Limited, although with training, a wide range of higher paying jobs is available in the computer and IT field.

Computer repair technicians are trained to repair, upgrade, and maintain computer hardware. They're employed by computer (and consumer electronics) retailers, computer manufacturers, large corporations in all industries, and can also work as independent consultants. The training required for this type of work is available from a wide range of vocational and technical schools throughout the country, as well as through distance learning programs.

For More Information

- CollegeSurfing.com. An online directory of colleges and schools that offers computer repair training and certification programs, www.collegesurfing .com/ce/search/technology.
- Computer Technology Industry Association. This is a professional trade association for people working in the computer field, www.comptia.org.
- ComputerRepair.com. An online resource for computer repair technicians. The site includes job listings and career-related information, www.computer repair.com/index.php.
- DICE. An online listing of jobs for computer repair technicians, http:// seeker.dice.com/jobsearch/servlet/JobSearch.

Database Administrator

> AT A GLANCE
>
> SALARY POTENTIAL: $50,000 to $70,000+ per year.
>
> TRAINING/LICENSE/CERTIFICATION REQUIRED: At least a two-year degree resulting in an associate's degree in computer science is often required. An alternative is to obtain certification using one or more common database software applications or database programming languages, such as: Oracle, Sybase, SQL Server, MySQL, Perl, PHP, ODBC, OLE/dB, ADO/RDS,

> JavaScript, VBScript, MFC, ATL, Active Server Pages, ActiveX, Java, EJB, and/or JSP.
>
> OTHER REQUIREMENTS: Database administrators must be competent using the database management software implemented by their employers and have a good understanding of the employers' operational needs to insure the data is organized, stored, and accessible by employees in the most efficient way possible.
>
> CAREER ADVANCEMENT OPPORTUNITIES: With additional training, certifications and experience, there is a wide range of career advancement opportunities in the Information Technologies (IT) field.

Database administrators work with computers (mostly mainframes, networks, and servers) and more specifically, database management systems used by a wide range of companies to manage vast amounts of data. The job of a database administrator is to organize, store, and secure data, identify user requirements, and set up and maintain databases (often using commercially available or custom software). This job is highly computer intensive and requires an understanding of how your employer operates, as well as knowledge about the latest technological and software developments. Though no actual programming is required, a database administrator is considered a technical IT job with varying responsibilities, depending on the employer. This job requires more training and experience than a data entry worker, who simply inputs data into a computer (which is an entry-level position).

For More Information

- Dice. Online job listings for database administrators can be found here, http://seeker.dice.com/jobsearch/servlet/JobSearch?op=1013&FREE_TEXT=database%20administrator.
- Quintessential Careers. This web site offers career information, details about training programs and job listings, www.quintcareers.com/database_positions.html.
- Tech Skills. Information about training and certification programs in the IT field are offered at www.techskills.com.

Search Engine Optimization Specialist

> AT A GLANCE
>
> SALARY POTENTIAL: Varies.
>
> TRAINING/LICENSE/CERTIFICATION REQUIRED: None.
>
> OTHER REQUIREMENTS: Computer literacy, limited computer programming (HTML), and the ability to surf the web are important.
>
> CAREER ADVANCEMENT OPPORTUNITIES: Jobs in online marketing, web site creation, and online advertising are available to people with skills designing, managing, and promoting web sites.

Web surfers around the world rely on internet search engines, such as Yahoo! and Google to find web sites and information. For web site operators, obtaining top listings on the most popular search engines is vital for generating traffic to their sites. Because most search engines list web sites based on different criteria and it's often necessary to register a web site with each search engine separately so it can be easily found by web surfers, the job of the Search Engine Optimizer has recently been created.

Search Engine Optimizers work for web site designers and developers, web site hosting services, and domain registrars and other internet-related companies. By developing a thorough understanding of how each search engine works, how web sites are registered/listed, and handling the task of keeping web site listings up-to-date, a Search Engine Optimizer is often able to insure the web sites he or she represents receive top placement on the popular search engines.

The necessary skills are often self-taught, however, some online marketing and web site development companies offer on-the-job training. This job requires basic knowledge of HTML programming and other web site development techniques.

For More Information

- Rent A Coder. Online job listings for search engine optimization specialists can be found at www.rentacoder.com/RentACoder/misc/BidRequests/Show BidRequest.asp?lngBidRequestId=347136.
- Trend Matrix Software. One of many software packages and online services a search engine optimization specialist can use as a primary tool, www

.trendmx.com/website-promotion-optimization-software/website-promo tion-software.aspx?.

- Online job listings can be found at the general interest career-related web sites, such as Monster (www.monster.com) or Yahoo! Hot Jobs (http://hot jobs.yahoo.com).

Technical Support/Computer Support Specialist

AT A GLANCE

SALARY POTENTIAL: $20,000 to $60,000 per year.

TRAINING/LICENSE/CERTIFICATION REQUIRED: Depending on the type of computer support you'll be offering, certification may be required for specific software applications, operating systems, or hardware.

OTHER REQUIREMENTS: Offering technical support requires proficiency using computers, a large amount of patience, plus excellent verbal communication skills.

CAREER ADVANCEMENT OPPORTUNITIES: In addition to working directly for computer or software companies, tech support people are employed by companies in all industries that utilize computers, computer networks, and software applications.

Technical support or computer support specialists are the people you call when you're having a problem using your computer, a specific software application, a peripheral, or some type of hardware. The job involves troubleshooting and diagnosing problems described by the client or caller and talking the user toward a solution. Many entry-level jobs in this field involve working from a telephone call center and spending many hours per day on the phone answering questions and solving problems.

Computer support specialists who offer in-person service tend to earn more money, but are required to have advanced knowledge of the products and/or software they're supporting. High-tech companies and companies with large IT departments employ technical support and/or computer support specialists.

Some computer support specialists are self-employed and work as consultants for multiple clients.

In addition to having the computer knowledge required for this type of job, the best technical support specialists work well with nontechnically savvy people and are able to answer their questions, pinpoint and diagnose their problems, and offer viable solutions to problems in a timely manner.

Many entry-level telephone tech support jobs are now being filled overseas, however, this is a fast growing field with plenty of opportunities. Pay is determined by the level of technical skill you possess. Upon landing a job in this field, you can pursue more advanced certifications that'll qualify you for more specialized and higher paying jobs.

For More Information

- Association of Computer Support Specialists. This is a professional trade association for people working in this field, www.acss.org.
- Computer Training Schools. At this web site you'll find detailed listings of postsecondary vocational and technical schools offering certification and degree programs for tech support specialists, www.computertraining schools.com.
- NetTemps. One of many temporary employment agencies that deal with high-tech positions, including technical support, for a wide range of companies, www.net-temps.com.
- Technology Ladder. This is an employment agency dealing exclusively in mid- to upper-level high-tech jobs, http://technology.theladders.com/reg/ ladders.
- Online job listings can be found at the general interest career-related web sites, such as Monster (www.monster.com) or Yahoo! Hot Jobs (http://hot jobs.yahoo.com).

Video and Computer Game Tester

> AT A GLANCE
>
> SALARY POTENTIAL: Minimum wage to $12 per hour.

TRAINING/LICENSE/CERTIFICATION REQUIRED: None.

OTHER REQUIREMENTS: The ability to play video and computer games, develop strategies, test game play features, and pinpoint programming errors is required.

CAREER ADVANCEMENT OPPORTUNITIES: Limited.

Video and computer game companies seek highly skilled computer gamers to test products before they ship to retail. This means spending countless hours playing a game before it's released, developing play strategies, and finding and documenting programming errors. Game testers might be hired to work from the software developer's offices or the job can often be done from home.

This is the ideal type of job for someone who loves playing video or computer games and wants to be paid for playing. The job involves spending many hours playing the same game repeatedly, often in a relatively short period of time prior to a game's release. Video and computer game developers and publishers, which are located throughout the country, hire game testers. Related jobs that involve being paid to play games include becoming a game reviewer, technical support specialist (game counselor), or working within a store that sells games.

Before a video or computer game is ever released to the public, a team of dozens, perhaps hundreds of programmers, graphic artists, animators, and other professionals work for months to develop that single game, often at a cost of several million dollars. Thus, before the game is released, it's the job of the game testers to insure that it can be played without the gamer running into technical difficulties or programming errors. These jobs are typically open to anyone who demonstrates proficiency playing computer or video games.

For More Information
- BetaWatcher. This web site offers news and information about computer and video game titles before they're released, www.betawatcher.com.
- GamesTester. Online job listings for game testers can be found here, www.gamestester.com.
- Contact any of the popular video and computer game developers' human resources departments for job opening information. You can also learn about job opportunities by visiting their web sites.

 CAREER SPOTLIGHT

Web Site Designer

AT A GLANCE

SALARY POTENTIAL: $15,000 to $50,000 per year, depending on experience, skills, and the employer.

TRAINING/LICENSE/CERTIFICATION REQUIRED: No formal training or certification is required, however, it is possible to earn certifications using specific types of web site design tools and software packages. These certifications are appealing to employers.

OTHER REQUIREMENTS: First, a web site designer needs to be creative. Taking a wide range of materials, including text, photographs, artwork, video, audio, and other assets, the web site designer must design and program a professional quality web site that serves a specific purpose, such as promoting and/or selling products or services.

CAREER ADVANCEMENT OPPORTUNITIES: Some web site designers are self-employed and work freelance jobs for a variety of clients. Others work in-house for a specific company or are employed by an established web site design firm or internet service provider.

The job title web site designer is a broad one and means different things to different employers. Thus, when seeking this type of work, it's important to develop a good understanding of the job responsibilities and the employer's expectations. Typically, a web site designer is responsible for overseeing the design, creation, launching, and maintenance of one or more web sites. This could mean handling all aspects of a web site's operation single handedly or overseeing a team of programmers, content developers, writers, graphic artists, and others.

In addition to having a thorough understanding of what the employer's needs are in terms of a web site, the web site designer must be proficient using all of the latest web site design tools, programming languages, and software packages. This knowledge can be self-taught or acquired through formal training at a vocational school.

Having the basic programming skills and knowing how to use a wide variety of web site design tools and software is essential. The best web site designers are also extremely creative and develop innovative ways to combine text, graphics, animation, video, audio, photographs, and other assets into a truly interactive experience for the web surfer that successfully promotes the intended messages or offers the functionality required by the employer.

A good web site designer will interact with all divisions and departments within a company, get to know its products or services, then develop one or more web sites to successfully achieve the company's cyberspace goals. The objective of the web site designer is to create the most professional looking web site possible, while keeping the site easy-to-navigate and understand for even the most novice of web surfers.

Many web site designers land jobs by showing portfolios of their work. A web site designer should be able to showcase a sampling of several different web sites to demonstrate to potential employers what they're capable of. Because this job requires both technical competence and creativity, only by seeing one's actual work can a web site designer's skills be evaluated. Being an expert programmer using Flash or HTML, for example, is definitely useful. But unless you can creatively use these skills in a way that generates high-quality and professional looking web sites, an employer probably won't hire you.

Here's My Story

Since his teen years and all through high school, Ryan was a self-proclaimed computer geek. He created web sites as a hobby. For example, he created multiple fan sites for his favorite music groups, actresses, and sports teams. To insure that his web sites were fun to visit, visually appealing, and highly engaging for web surfers, he taught himself how to program using several popular web site programming languages and become proficient using a variety of popular off-the-shelf software packages used by professional web site designers.

When he graduated from high school, Ryan sought a job working for a web site design company. In addition to putting together a traditional resume, he was able to create a portfolio of his best web site design work and showcase it to the interviewer when he was invited for a job interview. "Before my job interviews, I made a point to visit the web sites already in existence for the companies I'd be interviewing with. I then thought about how I would improve upon those web sites if I got hired. During my actual job interviews, I was able to showcase my work, plus demonstrate exactly how I'd apply my skills and knowledge to the company I'd hopefully be working for," recalled Ryan.

Now that he's employed as a web site designer, he explained that his biggest challenge when working with new clients is determining what their needs and wants are. "Most clients come to us because they don't have the first clue about web site design. They don't know what's possible, so they don't know what to ask for. My job is to learn about each client's company and determine how they'd best be able to utilize a web site to enhance their business. The needs of each of our clients vary greatly. I'd have to say that in addition to my programming and web site design skills, being able to communicate with my clients, ascertain their needs and develop a web site that meets those needs is the biggest challenge of my job. It's all about communication," said Ryan.

"Because the internet is evolving so quickly, it's fun for me to stay on top of the latest trends and utilize the latest tools and technology to provide the best possible online presence for my clients. This is one of the few jobs I can think of that requires a high degree of technical skill plus a huge amount of creativity," concluded Ryan.

For More Information

- Computer Training Schools. This web site offers a directory of technical schools, colleges, and universities that offer accredited training programs, www.computertrainingschools.com.
- DICE. Online job listings for web site designers and related technical and IT jobs can be found at www.dice.com.
- eLance. Online job listings for freelance web site designer can be found here, www.elance.com.
- Guide To Technical Schools. This web site offers information about technical schools and other training programs of interest to people pursuing a career as a web site designer, www.my-career-education.com/web-design-schools.htm.
- My Career Education. Learn about training programs and schools and obtain career-related information from this web site, www.my-career-education.com/web-design-schools.htm.
- Westwood College. This is one of many accredited schools that offers an associate's degree in web site design that can be earned in as little as 20 months, http://web.design.westwood-college.org.
- Online job listings can be found at the general interest career-related web sites, such as Monster (www.monster.com) or Yahoo! Hot Jobs (http://hotjobs.yahoo.com).

Webmaster

> ### AT A GLANCE
>
> SALARY POTENTIAL: $15,000 to $100,000 per year, depending on the employer.
>
> TRAINING/LICENSE/CERTIFICATION REQUIRED: None.
>
> OTHER REQUIREMENTS: A webmaster must be computer literate and able to program using popular web site development programming languages, such as HTML and Java, plus utilize software and online web site development tools, such as Flash or Microsoft FrontPage. Being detail and deadline oriented is also important.
>
> CAREER ADVANCEMENT OPPORTUNITIES: There are a wide range of job opportunities in all industries for webmasters.

A webmaster is someone who oversees the creation, maintenance, and ongoing operation of a company's web site. This includes working with an internet service provider (ISP), credit card merchant account provider (if applicable); developing and acquiring web site content; programming; and working with writers, graphic designers, programmers, animators, photographers, and other professionals who provide assets to be incorporated into a web site.

Millions of companies have web sites. The larger companies hire teams of people to create, design, maintain, and promote their sites, which often involves working with various divisions within the company to develop content and promote that content to the web surfing public.

A webmaster is in charge of the entire web site and managing the people responsible for various aspects of the web site's design and maintenance. Thus, in addition to being highly computer literate and proficient using popular web site development tools and programming languages, the job involves managing people, overseeing the creative aspects of the web site's design, and assisting with the creation and acquisition of content. Strong language and writing skills are also helpful.

While many schools offer certificate and degree programs in web site programming and design, formal education is not required to land most webmaster jobs. Instead, employers are looking for people with the best skills and talent, most of which can be self-taught.

For More Information

- Computer Training Schools. This web site offers a directory of technical schools, colleges, and universities that offer accredited webmaster training programs, www.computertrainingschools.com.
- DICE. Online job listings for webmasters and related technical and IT jobs can be found at www.dice.com.
- Guide to Technical Schools. This web site offers information about technical schools and other training programs of interest to people pursuing a career as a webmaster, www.my-career-education.com/web-design-schools.htm.
- My Career Education. Learn about webmaster training programs and schools, and obtain career-related information from this web site, www.my-career-education.com/web-design-schools.htm.
- Webmaster Jobs. Online job listings for webmasters can be found at www.web mastersjob.com.

OFFICE AND SUPPORT JOBS

This chapter describes a handful of jobs suitable for anyone looking for an office support, clerical, or receptionist job. You'll also learn about opportunities in medical offices and law offices. These jobs typically require basic typing skills and computer literacy, along with comfort working in a traditional office environment.

Dental Assistant

> **AT A GLANCE**
>
> **SALARY POTENTIAL:** $11 to $18 per hour.
>
> **TRAINING/LICENSE/CERTIFICATION REQUIRED:** Certification programs are available through a growing number of community colleges, technical institutes, and trade schools. On-the-job training is typically provided by employers. Certification programs typically take less than one year to complete. A license is also required in some states.
>
> **OTHER REQUIREMENTS:** As a dental assistant, you'll be working directly with a dentist and patients. You must be able to follow directions exactly, and be attentive, and well-mannered. Having good people skills is also a plus.
>
> **CAREER ADVANCEMENT OPPORTUNITIES:** With additional training, you could train to become a dental hygienist, which offers higher pay and more challenging work.

As the job title suggests, a dental assistant can often be found within arm's reach of a dentist as he or she works on patients. The job is to assist the dentist during procedures, while helping the patient feel comfortable. Sterilizing and disinfecting instruments, preparing the treatment rooms in between appointments, and taking dental X-rays may also be part of your responsibilities. While working with patients, dental assistants wear gloves, a mask, and protective eyewear. This is typically an entry-level position.

For More Information
- American Dental Assistants Association. A professional trade association offering career-related information, details about training and certification programs, and online employment opportunities, www.dentalassistant.org.
- Commission on Dental Accreditation (American Dental Association). A professional trade association offering information about accreditation programs and career opportunities for dental assistants, www.ada.org.

Dental Hygienist

> **AT A GLANCE**
>
> SALARY POTENTIAL: $22 and $35 per hour.
>
> TRAINING/LICENSE/CERTIFICATION REQUIRED: A state-issued license is required. Graduating from an accredited dental hygiene school and passing both a written and clinical examination is required. A certification or associate's degree in dental hygiene is available from many vocational schools.
>
> OTHER REQUIREMENTS: Dental hygienists must be comfortable working in a medical office, under the supervision of dentists. This job typically requires extensive work with patients.
>
> CAREER ADVANCEMENT OPPORTUNITIES: Limited.

The job of a dental hygienist is to clean a patient's teeth and gums and teach them to practice good oral hygiene. They also often work directly with or under the supervision of a dentist on a wide range of treatments and procedures. Working in a private dental office typically allows for a flexible or part-time work schedule.

For More Information

- American Dental Hygienist's Association. This is a professional trade association offering career-related information on its web site, www.adha.org.
- Commission on Dental Accreditation (American Dental Association). A professional trade association offering information about accreditation programs and career opportunities for dental hygenists, www.ada.org.
- For licensing information and requirements, contact your local State Board of Dental Examiners or an accredited dental hygiene school.

Dispatcher

> **AT A GLANCE**
>
> SALARY POTENTIAL: Varies.

> **TRAINING/LICENSE/CERTIFICATION REQUIRED:** Typically none, but this depends on the type of dispatcher job. Specialized training may be required for certain jobs.
>
> **OTHER REQUIREMENTS:** This job requires being extremely detail-oriented and the ability to multi-task. Some jobs require the ability to work under pressure.
>
> **CAREER ADVANCEMENT OPPORTUNITIES:** Career advancement opportunities involve pursuing managerial or supervisory positions, as well as better paying dispatcher positions.

A dispatcher is someone who schedules and oversees workers/drivers, sends them out on jobs, and oversees a fleet of vehicles, such as trucks, tow-trucks, delivery vehicles, taxis, busses, limos, fire trucks, police vehicles, or ambulances. Dispatchers also keep detailed records of their actions, often using a computer with specialized software. The job requires heavy use of the telephone and two-way radios.

Someone who works as a dispatcher for the police, fire department, or an ambulance service is called a public safety dispatcher. This type of job typically requires more training and/or specific certification.

The dispatcher's job typically requires sitting by a telephone, answering incoming calls, determining the caller's needs, dispatching the appropriate vehicles/drivers, monitoring the whereabouts and progress of dispatched vehicles/drivers, and keeping detailed logs of all activities.

For More Information

- 911 Hot Jobs. Online job listings for public safety dispatchers, www.911hotjobs.com/jobtitle/dispatchertitle.htm.
- Association of Public Safety Communications Officials. A professional trade association offering career-related information, training/certification information and job listings, www.apco911.org.
- National Academies of Emergency Dispatch. Career-related information for safety dispatchers is offered at www.emergencydispatch.org.
- Online job listings can be found at the general interest career-related web sites, such as Monster (www.monster.com) or Yahoo! Hot Jobs (http://hotjobs.yahoo.com).

Human Resource Assistant

AT A GLANCE

SALARY POTENTIAL: Minimum wage to $15 per hour (or more), depending on the employer and the work-related responsibilities.

TRAINING/LICENSE/CERTIFICATION REQUIRED: None.

OTHER REQUIREMENTS: Interpersonal skills, good written and verbal communication skills, plus being detail and deadline oriented are all important for this type of job.

CAREER ADVANCEMENT OPPORTUNITIES: There are a wide range of career opportunities in many different industries for someone with experience as a human resource professional or head hunter. To become a full-fledged human resource professional requires some specialized training, either at a two- or four-year college or a post-secondary school.

A human resource assistant helps a human resource executive find, test, and interview qualified applicants to fill a job opening. Companies in all industries that handle their own hiring in-house have the need for human resource personnel. Similar positions are also available at employment agencies and headhunting firms. To succeed in this job, you must have a good understanding of what's required for the jobs you're looking to fill and be able to find and interview qualified applicants to fill those jobs. The HR assistant's job is to organize and maintain personnel records, track applicants, and schedule and coordinate interviews. Many of the requirements are similar to those required of an office assistant or secretary.

For More Information
- CareerBuilder.com. Online job listings in the HR field can be found at http://human-resources.careerbuilder.com.
- Devry University. This is one of many schools that offer training in the HR field, www.devryeducation.com.
- WetFeet. Career-related information pertaining to the HR field can be found here, http://www.wetfeet.com/asp/careerprofiles_lite.asp?careerpk=17.

Legal or Medical Transcriptionist

> **AT A GLANCE**
>
> **SALARY POTENTIAL:** $10 to $20 per hour.
>
> **TRAINING/LICENSE/CERTIFICATION REQUIRED:** A one-year certification or two-year associate's degree in legal or medical transcription can be obtained from a wide range of vocational schools, community colleges, and distance learning programs.
>
> **OTHER REQUIREMENTS:** This is an office job that requires extreme attention to detail and a working knowledge of the legal or medical field.
>
> **CAREER ADVANCEMENT OPPORTUNITIES:** There is a wide range of career advancement opportunities within this field, however, additional training will be required. Many people in this field are able to telecommute (work from home) and make their own hours. Some are self-employed and independent contractors. Others are employed by transcription services, hospitals, doctors' offices, or law firms.

The job of a transcriptionist is to listen to dictated recordings and transcribe them into reports, correspondence, and other types of text-based materials. This job requires the use of dictating equipment, along with a word processor. Top-notch written communication skills (including the appropriate use of spelling, grammar, and vocabulary) are important. A working knowledge of industry-related vocabulary is also necessary. This job requires self discipline and typically requires little actual interaction with other people because much of the job involves listening to recorded material and typing on a computer.

For More Information
- American Association of Medical Transcription. This is a professional trade association offering career-related information, www.aamt.org.
- Guru.com. Online job listings for transcriptionists can be found here, www.guru.com.
- Legal Transcription Help Blog. This is a blog offering job listings and career-related advice, http://legal-transcription-help.blogspot.com.

Medical Assistant (also see Dental Assistant and Home Healthcare Aide)

AT A GLANCE

SALARY POTENTIAL: $18,000 to $28,000.

TRAINING/LICENSE/CERTIFICATION REQUIRED: The majority of employers look for applicants who have completed a formal certification program in medical assisting, which can be obtained from a vocational-technical high school, postsecondary school, junior college, or community college. There are over 500 accredited medical assisting programs in the United States for obtaining the proper training.

OTHER REQUIREMENTS: This job requires good interpersonal skills, compassion, patience, and the ability to work well in a medical environment (such as a doctor's office or hospital).

CAREER ADVANCEMENT OPPORTUNITIES: Career advancement opportunities are limited without additional training and education.

In a doctor's office, clinic, or hospital, a medical assistant performs routine administrative and clinical tasks. This job is different from being a physician's assistant, which requires more extensive training and involves working directly with patients under the supervision of a doctor. The medical assistant's job often involves answering the phone, scheduling appointments, greeting patients, managing files, taking payment for services rendered, preparing examination rooms, purchasing supplies, and processing insurance forms. What a medical assistant can do from a clinical standpoint varies by state.

For More Information

- Accrediting Bureau of Health Education Schools. This web site offers information about accredited schools and educational institutions that offer medical assisting programs, www.abhes.org.
- American Association of Medical Assistants. This is a professional trade association for people working in the medical assisting field, www.aama-ntl.org.
- EDU Directory. This web site offers information about accredited schools and educational institutions offering medical assisting programs, www.edu-directory.org/Continuing_Medical_Education.html.

- Medical Career Info. This web site offers detailed information about a wide range of careers in the medical field, www.medicalcareerinfo.com.
- Online job listings, refer to any of the general interest career-related web sites, such as Monster (www.monster.com) or Yahoo! HotJobs (http://hot jobs.yahoo.com).

Microsoft Office User Specialist (also see Word Processing Specialist)

AT A GLANCE

SALARY POTENTIAL: Varies.

TRAINING/LICENSE/CERTIFICATION REQUIRED: Training and certification through Microsoft on the use of its popular Office suite of software applications is required. This can be achieved through classroom training or online training by completing a distance learning program.

OTHER REQUIREMENTS: Computer literacy.

CAREER ADVANCEMENT OPPORTUNITIES: Companies in a wide range of industries hire office support personnel to handle a wide range of tasks, including word processing. For companies using computers equipped with Microsoft Office, many employers opt to hire office support personnel who have obtained the Microsoft Office User Specialist certification. This insures proficiency using this popular suite of software applications.

Secretaries, office support personnel, executive assistants, and other positions within a wide range of companies require the use of Microsoft Office as a primary business tool. In addition to having the other skills and experience needed to fulfill the responsibilities of a job, some companies seek people with the Microsoft Office User Specialist certification.

According to Microsoft, "Office Specialist exams provide a valid and reliable measure of technical proficiency and expertise by evaluating your overall comprehension of Office or Microsoft Project programs, your ability to use their advanced features, and your ability to integrate the Office programs with other software programs. Office Specialist exams are administered at Authorized Testing Centers worldwide."

If you're applying for a job in an organization that uses Microsoft Office, having this certification not only makes you more qualified, it can also assist you in commanding a higher salary, based on your pre-existing skills and knowledge.

For More Information

- Computer Training Schools. This web site offers a listing of schools that offer training to obtain the Microsoft Office User Specialist certification, www.computertrainingschools.com.
- Microsoft. This web site discusses specific Microsoft certification options, testing requirements, and explains exactly how to obtain certification and why it's important, http://www.microsoft.com/learning/mcp/officespecialist.
- Microsoft Courseware. This web site discusses how to obtain Microsoft-approved courseware for obtaining certification, www.microsoft.com/learning/mcp/officespecialist/officespecialist_materials.asp.
- Self Test Software. One of many companies that offer self-paced training software for obtaining the Microsoft Office User Specialist certification, www.selftestsoftware.com.

Notary Public

> **AT A GLANCE**
>
> **SALARY POTENTIAL:** Varies. A notary public is often hired as a secretary, office assistant, or in other clerical jobs, but also performs tasks as a notary public as an additional work-related responsibility.
>
> **TRAINING/LICENSE/CERTIFICATION REQUIRED:** A license is required. Requirements vary by state, but the completion of an accredited training program and the passing of a written exam is necessary. Online training is available from the National Notary Association's web site (www.nationalnotary.org).
>
> **OTHER REQUIREMENTS:** A notary public must be comfortable working with a wide range of business and legal documents, be extremely detail-oriented, trustworthy, friendly, and always act highly professionally.
>
> **CAREER ADVANCEMENT OPPORTUNITIES:** Limited.

A notary public is a professional witness, often used when someone needs to sign an official or legal document. Law offices, mortgage brokers, title and settlement companies, real estate offices, brokerage firms, accounting firms, and other types of businesses often have a notary public on staff.

The job entails reviewing documents and contracts, checking the identification of those signing the documents, witnessing the appropriate people signing the documents, and certifying the documents with an official notary public stamp. The job can involve reviewing highly technical and often classified information and overseeing (witnessing) the execution of contracts and legal agreements. The work can be repetitive.

Many notary publics are hired by employers as secretaries, executive assistants, or in other clerical jobs. Employers pay their notaries extra to benefit from the utilization of in-house notary public services.

If you already have skills and work as a secretary, executive assistant, or a related job, becoming a notary public is one way to expand your skill set and quickly boost your earning potential, although the work is often on a part-time basis.

For More Information

- Integrity Notary. This company offers a wide range of services and resources including training and certification information, https://cp4.heritageweb design.com/~integrty.
- National Notary Association. This professional trade association's web site offers a wide range of resources, including details about suppliers, licensing and certification requirements for each state, plus offers details about training programs. For someone looking into a career in this field, contacting this association is a great place to begin, (800) US-NOTARY, www.nationalno tary.org.
- NotaryStudy.com. This web site offers online training and certification programs www.notarystudy.com/index.php.

Office Assistant (also see Microsoft Office Specialist, Receptionist, and Secretary)

> **AT A GLANCE**
>
> **SALARY POTENTIAL:** $20,000 to $30,000 per year.

> TRAINING/LICENSE/CERTIFICATION REQUIRED: None.
>
> OTHER REQUIREMENTS: Typing, filing, telephone, and basic computer skills are a plus. Good communication and organizational skills are useful.
>
> CAREER ADVANCEMENT OPPORTUNITIES: Within an office environment, an Office Assistant is an entry-level position, perhaps one step up from an unpaid intern. Career advancement opportunities include taking on the responsibilities of a secretary, executive assistant, or office manager.

The job of an office assistant is to help an office's basic operations run smoothly. This includes assisting the secretaries and other support staff with typing and filing, answering the telephone, shipping packages, and running errands. This is an entry-level job. This job requires little or no training or formal education. The more office skills you have, however, the more employable you'll be and the more valuable you'll become to your employer.

When applying for an office assistant position, make sure you discuss with the employer what the job's responsibilities will entail, because every employer defines this position differently. In some cases, an office assistant and a receptionist have similar responsibilities. As you're developing your resume for this type of position, focus on the common and in-demand office skills and experience you possess. Office assistant jobs are available with companies of all sizes, in virtually all industries.

For More Information

- Many vocation schools offer a one-year Office Assistant certificate program designed to provide the core skills necessary for this type of work.
- Temporary employment agencies can also assist with job placement for office assistants.
- Online job listings can be found at the general interest career-related web sites, such as Monster (www.monster.com) or Yahoo! Hot Jobs (http://hot jobs.yahoo.com).

CAREER SPOTLIGHT

Paralegal/Certified Legal Assistant

AT A GLANCE

SALARY POTENTIAL: $30,000 to $50,000 per year.

TRAINING/LICENSE/CERTIFICATION REQUIRED: Completion of a certification training program is typically required, though the necessary skills can be learned on the job. Many vocational schools and community colleges offer an associate's degree or certification in this field. Formal training programs are offered at more than 600 colleges and universities throughout the country. There are also 250 paralegal training programs that are approved by the American Bar Association. Ultimately, before practicing as a Certified Legal Assistant, it's necessary to pass a two-day exam.

OTHER REQUIREMENTS: A paralegal works in a law office and must be comfortable interacting with lawyers, clients, and office support personnel, handling a wide range of legal documents, and assisting lawyers with a variety of tasks. Paralegals work under the close supervision of attorneys.

CAREER ADVANCEMENT OPPORTUNITIES: Paralegals can attend law school to become licensed attorneys or work as paralegals at law firms, corporate legal departments, or within various government offices. Many paralegals choose to specialize in one or more areas of the law, such as business, intellectual property, healthcare, international, criminal, or environmental law.

A paralegal or legal assistant has obtained some formal legal training and is qualified to assist a licensed attorney in handling a wide range of tasks. Lawyers often delegate repetitive and time-consuming tasks, such as paperwork or research, to paralegals. People working in this type of job are not qualified to offer legal advice or present cases in court. The job primarily involves helping attorneys prepare for closings, hearings, trials, depositions, and client meetings. Working as a paralegal requires more training and demands higher pay than a legal secretary.

Most paralegals working within a law firm are full time and put in at least 40 hours per week. When helping a lawyer prepare for an important trial, for example, overtime is often required.

Because this job involves working closely with lawyers and clients in a law firm environment, the work itself and the atmosphere can be stressful at times. Being able to work under tight deadlines, multitask, and maintain organization are important skills to master.

Here's My Story

Erica is a 24-year-old living in New Jersey. Upon graduating from high school, she wanted to pursue more than just a run-of-the-mill job. She wanted to obtain the skills necessary to have a long-term career. Having always been fascinated by law, she looked into becoming a paralegal and ultimately registered for a paralegal course at a local community college, where she attended classes part time while also holding down a job as a secretary and receptionist at a medium-sized law firm.

Upon completing the program and earning an associate's degree, Erica already had experience working in a law firm and was quickly promoted by the employer she was working for. "While I was in school, I found it extremely helpful to be surrounded by paralegals and lawyers. They were extremely supportive. When I completed the program, they hired me as a paralegal, which included a significant raise. This was great, because I already knew how the firm operated and I knew everyone. I was able to step into my new position and immediately take on the additional responsibilities," said Erica.

As expected, Erica spends much of her time on the job assisting one of three attorneys. She performs extensive research for cases, helps prepare paperwork, and provides a wide range of support services that a legal secretary isn't capable of handling. "The job offers a lot of hard work and research. I spend a lot of time working in the law library or gathering information online. The work environment varies greatly among law offices, so I recommend finding a place where you fit in, based on your personality, as well as your qualifications. Once you become a paralegal, you'll find much greater job stability than if you work in an entry-level secretarial or receptionist job," added Erica, who hopes to eventually attend law school to become a licensed attorney.

"One piece of advice I can offer is to do your research before pursuing this type of work. Make sure it's something you want to do and will enjoy doing. I recommend speaking to a handful of paralegals first in order to get their perspective on what the job is all about," she concluded.

For More Information

- American Association for Paralegal Education. This web site offers detailed information about training programs for paralegals. A free, downloadable brochure called *How to Choose a Paralegal Education Program*, can be obtained at www.aafpe.org.
- Law Crossing. Online job listings and resources for paralegals can be found at this web site, www.lawcrossing.com.
- National Association of Legal Assistants, Inc. This is a professional trade association for legal assistants and paralegals. The web site offers career-related information and resources of interest to people entering this field, ww.nala.org.
- National Federation of Paralegal Associations. This is a professional trade association for legal assistants and paralegals. The web site offers career-related information and resources of interest to people entering this field, www.paralegals.org.
- Paralegal Classifieds. Online job listings and resources for paralegals can be found at www.paralegalclassifieds.com.
- Standing Committee on Legal Assistance (American Bar Association). This is a professional trade association for legal assistants and paralegals. The web site offers career-related information and resources of interest to people entering this field, www.abanet.org.
- Online job listings can be found at the general interest career-related web sites, such as Monster (www.monster.com) or Yahoo! Hot Jobs (http://hot jobs.yahoo.com).

Pharmacy Technician

> **AT A GLANCE**
>
> SALARY POTENTIAL: $18,000 to $30,000 per year.
>
> TRAINING/LICENSE/CERTIFICATION REQUIRED: Certification is typically required. To obtain certification, you must successfully complete a training program and pass a written exam, called the PTCB National Certification Exam (PTCE), which will reward you with the Certified Pharmacy Technician (CPhT) credential.

> OTHER REQUIREMENTS: Pharmacy technicians are hired by pharmacies, nursing homes, and hospitals. They're often required to have flexible work schedules, including the ability to work nights, weekends, and/or holidays.
>
> CAREER ADVANCEMENT OPPORTUNITIES: Limited.

A pharmacy technician works as an assistant to a licensed pharmacist and is responsible for handling a wide range of routine tasks, such as counting tablets or pills and labeling bottles. They may also work as cashiers, stock shelves, and answer phones. Job responsibilities of a pharmacy technician vary by state and employer. On-the-job training is often provided. Most pharmacy technicians are employed by retail or mail-order pharmacies, however, jobs are also available at hospitals, clinics, and elderly care facilities.

For More Information

- American Society of Health-System Pharmacists. Career-related information, a list of accredited schools that offer certification, and other information is offered at www.ashp.org.
- Pharmacy Technician Certification Board. Information about how to obtain training and certification at as a certified pharmacy technician can be found here, www.ptcb.org.
- PharmacyTechs.net. Information and job listings for pharmacy technicians are offered at this web site, www.pharmacytechs.net/pharmacy-jobs.html.
- RxCareerCenter.com. Online job listings for pharmacy technicians can be found at www.rxcareercenter.com/pharmacy_technician_jobs.cfm.
- Virtual Institute of Pharmacy Technology. This web site offers details about an online-based, self-paced training program for pharmacy technicians, http://pharmacytech.org.

Receptionist

> AT A GLANCE
>
> SALARY POTENTIAL: $15,000 to $40,000 per year.

TRAINING/LICENSE/CERTIFICATION REQUIRED: None.

OTHER REQUIREMENTS: The ability to answer telephones, greet visitors, handle office-related tasks, type, and a friendly personality are all beneficial.

CAREER ADVANCEMENT OPPORTUNITIES: At most companies, a receptionist position is considered entry level. With experience, career advancement could involve a promotion to secretary, office manager, or executive assistant.

When it comes to entry-level, office jobs that require minimal skills, the job of receptionist is one of the most popular. Receptionists are employed by virtually all types of companies to answer telephones, greet visitors, and handle basic office-related tasks. On-the-job training is often provided. A good receptionist will be friendly, outgoing, detail-oriented, and proficient using computers. A receptionist should also be comfortable answering multiple telephone lines, taking messages, and transferring callers to appropriate extensions.

Most receptionists work full time, however, some companies also hire part-time receptionists and allow for people in this position to work flexible hours. Job listings for receptionists can be found in the Help Wanted ads of any newspaper and on general interest career-related web sites. One excellent way to quickly land a job and gain experience as a receptionist is to work through a temporary employment agency.

The on-the-job responsibilities of a receptionist are largely the same in all companies. Thus, it's a good idea to choose a company or industry you're interested in, then find a receptionist position in that field. To obtain basic computer skills, consider taking classes through a local adult education program, vocational school, community college, or from a local computer superstore (such as CompUSA).

For More Information
- One way to land a job as a receptionist quickly is to work with a temporary employment agency.
- Online job listings can be found at the general interest career-related web sites, such as Monster (www.monster.com) or Yahoo! Hot Jobs (http://hot jobs.yahoo.com).

Secretary (Administrative Assistant)

> ## AT A GLANCE
>
> SALARY POTENTIAL: Minimum wage to $50,000 (or more) per year.
>
> TRAINING/LICENSE/CERTIFICATION REQUIRED: None.
>
> OTHER REQUIREMENTS: A secretary must be organized, detail-oriented, able to follow directions, meet deadlines, multi-task, and perform a wide range of tasks within an office environment. Computer skills and proficiency using popular software applications, such as those found in Microsoft Office, are often essential.
>
> CAREER ADVANCEMENT OPPORTUNITIES: Secretaries can be promoted to executive assistants and hold other positions within an office or corporate environment.

A secretary is someone who assists a mid-level or executive staff member with a wide range of office-related tasks, such as answering the telephone, greeting visitors, scheduling, shipping packages, word processing, filing, opening and sorting mail, running errands, and organization.

Some secretarial positions are considered entry-level, whereas others require more skills than that of a receptionist. In many offices, secretaries are required to have computer and typing skills, plus be able to operate a wide range of office equipment (fax machine, copier, telephone system, etc.)

Computer skills can be self-taught or obtained by taking classes at a local computer center or adult education program. Secretarial jobs can be full time or part time. These jobs can be found at companies of all sizes and in virtually every industry. One way to land a job quickly as a secretary is to work with a temporary employment agency.

Depending on the employer, secretaries can be paid by the hour or be on salary. Most secretaries work traditional business hours (9:00 A.M. to 5:00 P.M., Monday through Friday), although this will vary by employer. Secretaries with specialized training can work for doctor's offices, law firms, or other specialized fields. Training for secretarial jobs in these specialized fields can be obtained from vocational and professional trade schools, as well as distance learning programs.

For More Information

- Administrative Jobs. Online job listings for secretaries and administrative assistants can be found at http://secretary.jobs.administrativejobsite.com.
- HelpWantedSite.com. Here you'll find online job listings for trained medical secretaries, http://medical.secretary.jobs.helpwantedsite.com/job search.asp.
- Legal Secretary Careers. Information and training opportunities for secretaries interested in working in the legal field are offered at this web site. Online job listings can also be found at www.legalsecretarycareers.com.
- Online job listings can be found at the general interest career-related web sites, such as Monster (www.monster.com) or Yahoo! Hot Jobs (http://hot jobs.yahoo.com).

Telephone Operator

> ### AT A GLANCE
>
> **SALARY POTENTIAL:** Minimum wage to $20 per hour.
>
> **TRAINING/LICENSE/CERTIFICATION REQUIRED:** None. On-the-job training is often provided by employers.
>
> **OTHER REQUIREMENTS:** A good speaking voice, patience, and an outgoing and friendly personality are helpful.
>
> **CAREER ADVANCEMENT OPPORTUNITIES:** With additional training, telephone operators can work as 9-1-1 operators, telephone receptionists, telemarketers, or for dispatchers in a variety of industries.

The job of an operator working for a telephone company has changed over the years, as most calls are now direct-dialed and don't require the assistance of an operator. Operators are, however, used to handle incoming directory assistance calls, collect calls and offer assistance to telephone users. In addition to telephone companies, large businesses, hotels, hospitals and other organizations that have a telephone switchboard still employ operators to answer calls and route them appropriately.

Because many companies have a need for operators around the clock, it's often necessary for people working in this field to have flexible schedules and be willing to occasionally work nights, weekends, and holidays.

The job requires highly repetitive tasks, plus speaking on the phone for many hours per day. Little or no physical movement is required. The job often involves working in a well-lit, climate-controlled office, or call center environment.

For More Information

- Federal Government Job Listings. This web site offers online job listings for operators within all branches and divisions of the federal government, http://federalgovernmentjobs.us/job-search/telephone-operator-0382.html.
- TelephoneOperatorJobs. This web site offers online job listings for operators and people interested in working within the telecommunications field, http://telephoneoperatorjobs.com.
- United States Telecom Association. This is a professional trade association for people in the telecommunications field, including operators. The organization's web site offers career-related information and other useful resources, www.usta.org.
- Contact the human resources department of your local phone company or any company that hires telephone operators.

Typist/Word Processor/Data Entry Keyer

AT A GLANCE

SALARY POTENTIAL: Minimum wage to $15 per hour.

TRAINING/LICENSE/CERTIFICATION REQUIRED: None, although applicants will typically be required to take a proficiency exam to prove they can accurately type or perform data entry. Microsoft offers a certification for its Microsoft Office suite of applications. Possession of this certification can make landing a job as a word processor easier.

OTHER REQUIREMENTS: Basic computer skills and proficiency using popular software applications is required for most jobs in this field. Employers look for people who are responsible, accurate, and efficient.

CAREER ADVANCEMENT OPPORTUNITIES: Limited. Higher paying jobs, such as a secretary, receptionist, or office assistant can be pursued with additional training.

Working as a typist, word processor, or data entry keyer is typically an entry-level position in an office environment. The job involves repetitive and mundane work, but requires limited skills. The job typically involves working in front of a computer for up to eight hours per day (or longer), either typing text or keying in data. On-the-job training is often provided, however, typing skills are a must. These jobs are available in many industries. One way to land work quickly is to work with a temporary employment agency.

For More Information

- Online job listings can be found at the general interest career-related web sites, such as Monster (www.monster.com) or Yahoo! Hot Jobs (http://hot jobs.yahoo.com).

Veterinary Assistant

AT A GLANCE

SALARY POTENTIAL: $15,000 to $20,000 per year.

TRAINING/LICENSE/CERTIFICATION REQUIRED: Certification or a degree as a veterinary assistant must be obtained through training. This can be obtained in one to two years, through traditional classroom training or distance learning programs. On-the-job training is also available, depending on the employer.

OTHER REQUIREMENTS: A veterinary assistant should be comfortable working with and handling animals in a veterinary office environment, under the supervision of a licensed veterinarian. Office skills, including proficiency using a computer, are required.

CAREER ADVANCEMENT OPPORTUNITIES: Limited.

A veterinary assistant job involves assisting a licensed veterinarian and handling a wide range of office management responsibilities. Part of this job involves interacting with pet owners and assisting the vet in handing many types of medical procedures. The job typically requires having a flexible work schedule. This is an entry-level position.

For More Information

- American Veterinary Medical Association. This is a professional trade association for licensed veterinarians and those working in the veterinary field, www.avma.org.
- Online job listings can be found at the general interest career-related web sites, such as Monster (www.monster.com) or Yahoo! Hot Jobs (http://hotjobs.yahoo.com).

CHAPTER

11

PHYSICAL
LABOR-INTENSIVE JOBS

The jobs in this chapter involve physical labor. Most involve working either in a factory or warehouse environment, or on location, as opposed to within a traditional office. As you'll discover, some of these jobs require specialized skills and training.

Apparel/Textile Worker

> **AT A GLANCE**
>
> **SALARY POTENTIAL:** Minimum wage to $12 per hour, plus overtime during peak production periods.
>
> **TRAINING/LICENSE/CERTIFICATION REQUIRED:** None.
>
> **OTHER REQUIREMENTS:** On-the-job training is typically provided.
>
> **CAREER ADVANCEMENT OPPORTUNITIES:** Limited.

Apparel workers are people who work in textile factories to manufacturer clothing. This job shouldn't be confused with that of a fashion designer, which is the person who actually designs the clothes and who has typically graduated with a degree from an accredited design school.

Within the apparel industry, there are a wide range of production worker jobs that involve cutting and sewing. These jobs often require working on an assembly line. Four out of 10 apparel workers are full-time sewing machine operators.

Because many of these labor-intensive jobs are being moved overseas, the U.S. Department of Labor projected that over 245,000 apparel worker jobs will be lost between 2002 and 2012. More than two-thirds of all apparel industry jobs can be found in Alabama, California, Georgia, New Jersey, New York, North Carolina, Pennsylvania, Tennessee, and Texas. Many jobs in this field are entry level and require highly repetitive work-related responsibilities.

For More Information

- Unite Here Union. A professional trade organization, (212) 265-7000, www.unitehere.org.

Cable TV/Satellite TV Installer/Communications Agent

> **AT A GLANCE**
>
> **SALARY POTENTIAL:** Hourly or salary-based compensation, depending on the employer.

> TRAINING/LICENSE/CERTIFICATION REQUIRED: On-the-job training is provided.
>
> OTHER REQUIREMENTS: CommTech 1 Certification (or equivalent).
>
> CAREER ADVANCEMENT OPPORTUNITIES: Limited.

Cable television companies (and their authorized agents), satellite television companies (and their authorized agents), and consumer electronics retailers are among the companies that hire cable television and/or satellite TV installers, which are also called communication agents.

Under limited supervision, the installer performs routine cable service reconnects; changes of service for residential and commercial video customers; disconnects all product lines; teaches customers how to use equipment; resolves billing and/or payment questions while on the premises; and upgrades company products and services. The job requires the use of basic hand tools and often requires working from high places. This can be a full-time or part-time job (but most employers look for people willing to work overtime, as needed).

For More Information

- Contact your location cable television company or consumer electronics retailer to learn about job openings.
- Online job listings can be found at the general interest career-related web sites, such as Monster (www.monster.com) or Yahoo! Hot Jobs (http://hotjobs.yahoo.com).

Carpenter

> AT A GLANCE
>
> SALARY POTENTIAL: $15 to $20 per hour or an annual salary of $32,000 to $47,000.
>
> TRAINING/LICENSE/CERTIFICATION REQUIRED: None.
>
> OTHER REQUIREMENTS: Having completed courses in carpentry, shop, mechanical drawing, and general mathematics in high school is helpful. A carpenter must work well with a wide range of tools and be physically fit.

> CAREER ADVANCEMENT OPPORTUNITIES: Carpenters can advance to higher pay-
> ing construction-related jobs, such as carpentry supervisor or general con-
> struction supervisor.

Carpenters with a wide range of construction skills find themselves gainfully employed rather easily, because they're able to work from blueprints to do everything from framing walls and partitions to installing doors and windows in homes and office buildings. Carpenters also work on a wide range of other structures, from buildings to boats, as well as in industrial plants.

Many of the skills acquired by carpenters are learned through on-the-job training or by participating in an apprenticeship program. The various unions, such as the United Brotherhood of Carpenters and Joiners of America and the Associated General Contractors have established training and apprenticeship programs.

Depending on the type of carpentry work you do, you may find jobs are more readily available during non-winter months. Some carpenters are self-employed and work as independent contractors. Others hold full-time jobs with construction companies or other types of employers. This type of work is extremely hands-on and labor intensive, although the type of work varies.

For More Information
- Associated General Contractors of America. This is a professional trade organization offering information and resources for people working in this field, www.agc.org.
- Home Builders Institute. This is a professional trade organization offering career-related information, training programs, and job listings, www.hbi.org.
- National Association of Home Builders. This is a professional trade organization offering information and resources for people working in this field, www.nahb.org.
- United Brotherhood of Carpenters and Joiners of America. This is a professional trade organization offering career-related information and training programs, www.carpenters.org.

Carpet Cleaner

> **AT A GLANCE**
>
> **SALARY POTENTIAL:** Minimum wage to $20 per hour.
>
> **TRAINING/LICENSE/CERTIFICATION REQUIRED:** On-the-job training is typically provided.
>
> **OTHER REQUIREMENTS:** The ability to lift and move furniture and use carpet cleaning equipment.
>
> **CAREER ADVANCEMENT OPPORTUNITIES:** Limited.

A carpet cleaner is someone who is hired to shampoo, vacuum, and clean carpeting using industrial strength chemicals and equipment. This often involves having to analyze and remove stains. Many people who work in this field are employed by locally owned and operated companies, including carpet cleaning franchises.

The work often involves moving furniture, inspecting and cleaning carpets, and putting everything back into its original location. The work can be repetitive and is considered an entry-level employment opportunity. The job involves traveling to the client's location, such as a home or office, and performing the cleaning work in a timely and responsible manner.

For someone looking to launch his or her own business with relatively low start-up capital (starting under $25,000), carpet cleaning could be a viable business opportunity. If you're simply interested in working for an established carpet cleaning business, contact the franchise or business operators in your area. Check the Yellow Pages under Carpet Cleaners for details.

For More Information
- Carpet Cleaning Equipment. This company sells carpet cleaning equipment to those working in this field, www.carpet-cleaning-equipment.net.
- CleanPro. Here you'll find details about one of many carpet cleaning franchise business opportunities available in the United States, www.cleanpro.com/carpetcleaningopportunity.html.
- Franchisegator. This is an online database of franchise opportunities, including carpet cleaning businesses, www.franchisegator.com.

- Sears Carpet Cleaning. The Sears department store offers a nationwide network of carpet cleaners. Employment opportunities are available, www.sears.ca/e/hc/carpcln.htm.
- Online job listings can be found at the general interest career-related web sites, such as Monster (www.monster.com) or Yahoo! Hot Jobs (http://hotjobs.yahoo.com).

Carpet, Floor, and Tile Installer

> **AT A GLANCE**
>
> **SALARY POTENTIAL:** Minimum wage to $30+ per hour.
>
> **TRAINING/LICENSE/CERTIFICATION REQUIRED:** None. On-the-job training and apprenticeship programs are available.
>
> **OTHER REQUIREMENTS:** Must be in good physical condition, have excellent manual dexterity, and be comfortable working with a range of tools. Careful measuring and cutting is also required. Good people skills are useful if you'll be interacting with clients.
>
> **CAREER ADVANCEMENT OPPORTUNITIES:** Advancement to supervisory positions or higher paid installation jobs is possible.

If you look down at your feet right now, chances are you'll see carpet, tile, hardwood, or other type of flooring. That flooring was installed by a professional. Carpet installers are hired by a wide range of companies, such as construction firms, flooring contractors, and retail flooring stores. Almost half of all carpet, tile, and hardwood floor installers are self-employed. Most floorers are trained on the job or through training programs provided by their employers. Apprenticeship programs are offered through several unions and professional trade organizations.

There are various specialties in this field which require specific skills. Installing carpet, tile, hardwood, and laminate floors each requires a different, but related skill set.

For More Information

- Certified Floor Covering Installers. An online career-related web site with job listings and a certification training program. A quarterly magazine, *The CFI Professional*, is also available, www.cfi-installers.org.

- Floor Covering Installation Contractors Association. This is a professional trade organization that offers training programs, career-related information, and information about training programs, www.fcica.com/index2.html.
- Floor Installation Association of North America. A professional trade organization offering a wide range of online resources, including training programs and job listings, www.fiana.org/html/Home.htm.
- National Association of Floor Covering Distributors. A professional trade association offering a self-study certification program, www.nafcd.org.

Closet Organizer

> ### AT A GLANCE
>
> SALARY POTENTIAL: Varies.
>
> TRAINING/LICENSE/CERTIFICATION REQUIRED: On-the-job training is provided.
>
> OTHER REQUIREMENTS: Top-notch organizational skills, creativity, and interpersonal skills, along with a keen attention to detail are important. You must also be comfortable working with tools.
>
> CAREER ADVANCEMENT OPPORTUNITIES: Limited.

A professional closet organizer's job is to assist someone in reorganizing his or her closet to make maximum use of the limited space available. This might including helping a client sort and organize wardrobe, as well as design, build, and install shelves, drawers, and other organizational fixtures within a closet. Some professional closet organizers are self-employed, whereas many work for companies or franchises that offer this type of specialized service. Having a flexible work schedule is important.

The best way to find jobs in this field is to contact the human resources department of a company that offers closet organization services in your area. These companies can be found online or in the Yellow Pages.

For More Information

- National Closet Group. This is a professional trade organization for closet organizers, (866) 624-5463, www.closets.com.

Construction Worker (Laborer)

AT A GLANCE

SALARY POTENTIAL: $15 to $22 per hour (or more) for entry-level laborers, more for skilled or semi-skilled craftworkers.

TRAINING/LICENSE/CERTIFICATION REQUIRED: Varies, based on the specific job. Some professions within the construction field require certifications and/or licenses, such as a plumber or electrician. Other, less skill-intensive jobs require no formal training, licenses, or certification.

OTHER REQUIREMENTS: Physical strength and stamina are important for success. Construction workers and laborers must be able to use a wide range of tools, plus lift and carry heavy objects.

CAREER ADVANCEMENT OPPORTUNITIES: Because the jobs available to construction workers are diverse, with additional training and apprenticeships, higher paying jobs can be sought if you become a skilled craftsworker, as opposed to a laborer.

The construction occupation is a broad field, with many specialties. Some require specialized training, whereas others require on-the-job training. Some of the specialties in the construction field include carpenters, construction equipment operators, brick masons, block masons, cement masons, concrete finishers, drywall installers, roofers, plasterers, pipe layers, sheet metal workers, electricians, plumbers, painters, and heating/air conditioning specialists.

Construction workers holding jobs that require little or no training or skill are considered laborers or helpers, whereas those with more advanced training are classified as semi-skilled or skilled laborers. Participating in training programs and apprenticeships will prepare you for higher paying jobs within the construction field.

Most people working in construction work more than 40 hours per week, which often includes evenings, weekends, and holidays (to deal with emergencies and to meet construction deadlines). A large percentage of construction workers are self-employed. In addition to building and remodeling homes and residential structures, construction workers help to build nonresidential buildings, highways, and work on a wide range of heavy and civil engineering construction jobs.

The job involves extensive physical labor and performing repetitive tasks in a wide range of construction environments, both indoors and outdoors.

For More Information

- Associated General Contractors of America, Inc. This is a professional trade organization, www.agc.org.
- iHireConstruction. An online resource featuring job listings and other career-related information, www.ihireconstruction.com.
- National Association of Home Builders. This is a professional trade association, www.nahb.org.
- U.S. Department of Labor's National Apprenticeship System. Learn about apprenticeship programs in the construction field, www.doleta.gov.

Electrician

AT A GLANCE

SALARY POTENTIAL: Varies, based on the type of work and the electrician's experience. This is considered a skilled labor job. Compensation can start at $20 per hour and go up considerably with experience.

TRAINING/LICENSE/CERTIFICATION REQUIRED: Most electricians participate in an apprenticeship program that lasts three to five years. This includes at least 144 hours of classroom instruction and 2,000 hours of on-the-job training each year of the apprenticeship. Some trade schools offer a three-year program to become an electrician. Most states require electricians to be licensed.

OTHER REQUIREMENTS: The job requires the ability to reach difficult areas, often by climbing ladders or by standing on scaffolding. A good understanding of math, mechanical drawing, electricity, science, and electronics is necessary.

CAREER ADVANCEMENT OPPORTUNITIES: There are a wide range of jobs for electricians in many different industries, such as construction. One career advancement opportunity is to become an electrical inspector.

Electricians work with electricity, providing light, power, air conditioning and refrigeration services to customers as they install, connect, test, and maintain electrical systems. An electrician must comply with the National Electronic Code, as well as all state and local codes, when installing any type of electrical wiring or system. Depending on the type of work an electrician does, the responsibilities and working conditions (along with the pay) will vary greatly. Aside from construction, electricians are hired in many other industries, which provides for a wide range of job opportunities. Most electricians join a union, which is the best resource for learning more about pursuing jobs in this field.

For More Information

- Independent Electrical Contractors. Information about independent apprenticeship programs and training options can be found at this web site, www.ieci.org.
- International Brotherhood of Electrical Workers. A trade union for electricians. The web site offers a wide range of information and resources, www.ibew.org.
- National Association of Home Builders. Information about independent apprenticeship programs and career information is offered here, www.nahb.org.
- National Electrical Contractors Association. This is a professional trade organization, www.necanet.org.
- National Joint Apprenticeship Training Committee. Information about training and apprenticeship programs can be found at www.njatc.org.

Fisherman

> **AT A GLANCE**
>
> **SALARY POTENTIAL:** Varies, typically $300 to $800 per week, often with no benefits. In many areas, the work is seasonal.
>
> **TRAINING/LICENSE/CERTIFICATION REQUIRED:** On-the-job training is typically provided. There are no minimum educational requirements. In many states or regions, a fishing license is required. This typically requires little more than paying a fee.

> OTHER REQUIREMENTS: Working as a fisherman requires long hours, sometimes in dangerous conditions, such as bad weather. If you'll be operating a large fishing vessel, you may be required to complete training offered by the U.S. Coast Guard.
>
> CAREER ADVANCEMENT OPPORTUNITIES: About half of all fishermen are self-employed and operate their own fishing vessels or work for captains of private fishing vessels. This job does not offer a stable work schedule and is often seasonal. A fisherman can become a fishing boat captain, skipper, first mate, or second mate, which are typically higher paying jobs.

The job of a fisherman is to catch or trap marine wildlife for food and other uses. In some cases, this is done from a small boat, however, some fishermen operate large fishing vessels that travel hundreds of miles to catch thousands of pounds of fish during each trip. The work involves long hours and requires completing highly repetitive tasks in a labor-intensive environment. This job can require being away from home for extended periods.

For More Information
- AgriSeek. Online job listings for fishermen and ship deckhands can be found at this web site, www.agriseek.com/work/e/Employment/Aquaculture/Fishing-Deckhand.
- CollegeGrad.com. Career-related information for fishermen is available at this web site, www.collegegrad.com/careers/farmi02.shtml.
- Maritime Technology Society. Information about schools that offer fishing and marine education programs, as well as career-related information is provided at this web site, www.mtsociety.com.

Fitness Instructor (also see Yoga Instructor)

> AT A GLANCE
>
> SALARY POTENTIAL: $21,000 to $55,000 per year. Private personal trainers tend to earn more than fitness instructors who teach classes.

> **TRAINING/LICENSE/CERTIFICATION REQUIRED:** Certification in your specific field must be obtained. Recertification is generally required every two years. This involves taking additional classes. Online certification programs are available.
>
> **OTHER REQUIREMENTS:** Fitness instructors must be strong, physically fit, energetic, outgoing, and full of enthusiasm to teach and motivate their students.
>
> **CAREER ADVANCEMENT OPPORTUNITIES:** Career advancement opportunities include becoming the fitness director at a health club or spa, or pursuing additional education to become a physical therapist.

As the fitness craze continues to spread across the United States, personal trainers, as well as aerobics, yoga, Pilates, and other types of fitness instructors continue to be in demand at places like health clubs, spas, weight loss centers, nursing facilities, schools, and hotels/resorts. There's also a growing need for private fitness instructors willing to work one-on-one with clients.

For More Information

- American Council on Exercise. An excellent resource for career-related information, salary information, online job listings, and certification options for personal trainers and fitness instructors, www.acefitness.org.
- Natural Healers. An online directory of schools offering certification training for fitness instructors and personal trainers, www.naturalhealers.com/feat-personaltraining.shtml.
- The National Personal Training Institute. Obtain the certification you need to become a personal trainer at one of this school's 16 nationwide locations. Most programs can be completed within six months, (800) 960-6294, www.nationalpersonaltraininginstitute.com.
- Work.com. Online job listings for fitness instructors, www.work.com/jobs_Fitness-Instructor.

Gunsmith

> **AT A GLANCE**
>
> **SALARY POTENTIAL:** Varies.

> TRAINING/LICENSE/CERTIFICATION REQUIRED: Earning a one-year certificate is required. In most states, a license is also required.
>
> OTHER REQUIREMENTS: In addition to adhering to strict safety and legal guidelines, a gunsmith must have a strong understanding of how guns work.
>
> CAREER ADVANCEMENT OPPORTUNITIES: Gun collectors, gun shops, and firearm manufacturers employ gunsmiths. With additional training, a gunsmith can become a Master Gunsmith.

A gunsmith is someone who earns a living cleaning, repairing, and customizing guns and rifles. It's a career path you can pursue after completing a home-study course or a relatively short and inexpensive post-secondary program. To succeed in this field, you must be comfortable working with firearms and ammunition. Many gun enthusiasts consider this type of work to be an art form.

For More Information

- National Rife Association. This is the official web site of the NRA. Here, you'll find information about firearms and can learn about career opportunities in the NRA and within the firearms industry. (The author of this book, nor its publisher, endorse the work of the NRA or its affiliated organizations.), www.NRA.org.
- PCDI. Information about a home study course to become a gunsmith is offered at this web site, www.career-courses.net.
- Thomson Education Direct. Information about a home study course to become a gunsmith is offered at this web site, www.educationdirect.com/gunsmith/CareerOutlook.html.

Handyman/Home Repairer

> AT A GLANCE
>
> SALARY POTENTIAL: Up to $80,000 per year.
>
> TRAINING/LICENSE/CERTIFICATION REQUIRED: Basic home repair and construction skills are necessary. It's also important to be fully insured and bonded. There is no minimum educational requirement.

> OTHER REQUIREMENTS: A proficiency using a wide range of tools is helpful. If you're self-employed, you'll need to own your own tools and equipment.
>
> CAREER ADVANCEMENT OPPORTUNITIES: A wide range of career advancement opportunities are available in the construction field, as well as working in a retail location, such as a hardware store. With additional training, a home repairer can learn appliance repair to increase his or her earning potential.

A handyman, as the name suggests, is someone who is strong, competent using tools, and on-call to assist a home owner with repairs, maintenance, installations, improvements, or light-duty carpentry around a home or property. These are jobs that would be considered too small for a carpenter or other construction professional. Handymen are often self-employed or employed by landlords to oversee apartments or condos.

The more expertise and experience a handyman has, the higher his or her income potential. Many skills used by a handyman are self-taught, learned on-the-job, or acquired through an apprentice program. Many people who typically work in the construction field do freelance handyman work to supplement their incomes.

Home repairers with an entrepreneurial spirit can become their own bosses by starting small businesses. Several franchise opportunities are available, such as Mr. Handyman (www.mrhandyman.com/MainCareers.aspx), which offers a turnkey opportunity for a handyman looking to establish his or her own business.

A self-employed handyman must self-market and advertise their business, plus strive to obtain referrals from existing customers. This is an excellent full-time or part-time opportunity.

For More Information

- Appliance Repair. Information about training as an appliance repair person is available at this web site, www.appliance-repair.org.
- Handyman Business. From this web site, you can gather information about how to start a handyman business, http://handymanstartup.com.
- iHireBuildingTrades. This is an online resource for career-related information and job listings, www.ihirebuildingtrades.com.
- Service Magic. Online job listings for freelance handymen are offered here, www.servicemagic.com.

Heating, Air-Conditioning, and Refrigeration Technician

AT A GLANCE

SALARY POTENTIAL: $10 to $30 (or more) per hour, depending on the work and employer.

TRAINING/LICENSE/CERTIFICATION REQUIRED: Completion of a post-secondary program from a technical/vocational school, certification, and state license is required. The training can take anywhere from six months to two years. Many people also participate in apprenticeship programs as part of their initial training.

OTHER REQUIREMENTS: Competence using a wide range of tools is necessary.

CAREER ADVANCEMENT OPPORTUNITIES: People with the skills to install, maintain, and repair heating, air-conditioning, and refrigeration systems are in demand by a wide range of companies.

A heating, air-conditioning, and refrigeration technician is someone qualified to install, maintain, diagnose, and repair these types of systems in homes or businesses. This is a labor-intensive field that involves working with a wide range of mechanical and electrical components, such as those found within major appliances. About 20 percent of the people working in this field belong to a union. The jobs in this field vary greatly, based on area of expertise and experience.

For More Information
- Air-Conditioning and Refrigeration Institute. This site offers information about training and education programs in this field, www.coolcareers.org.
- Air-Conditioning Contractors of America. This is a professional trade organization offering resources and career-related information, www.acca.org.
- Associated Builders and Contractors. This is a professional trade organization offering resources and career-related information, www.natex.org.
- North American Technical Excellence. Here you'll find information about nationally recognized certification and education programs, www.natex.org.

Housecleaner/Maid ✳

> **AT A GLANCE**
>
> SALARY POTENTIAL: Varies.
>
> TRAINING/LICENSE/CERTIFICATION REQUIRED: There is no minimum educational requirement. Some companies offer on-the-job training. This is an entry-level position.
>
> OTHER REQUIREMENTS: None.
>
> CAREER ADVANCEMENT OPPORTUNITIES: Limited.

A housekeeper or maid is someone who is paid, usually by the hour, to clean. Many housekeepers work for agencies or companies, such as Merry Maids. Some are self-employed. Responsibilities often include doing laundry, dusting, vacuuming, cleaning bathrooms and windows, and maintaining an organized home on behalf of the client. Maids can also be employed to clean office buildings. This is an entry-level, labor-intensive job. Self-employed workers tend to earn more money, however, they must also solicit their own business and become insured and bonded on their own.

For More Information
- International Executive Housekeepers Association. This is a professional trade organization for housekeepers, www.ieha.org.
- Merry Maids. This is one of the best known housekeeping franchises in America and an employer of housekeepers, www.merrymaids.com.
- Molly Maid. This is one of the best known housekeeping franchises in America and an employer of housekeepers, (800) 665-5962, www.molly maid.com/MainCareers.aspx.

House Painter (also see Wallpaper Hanger)

> **AT A GLANCE**
>
> SALARY POTENTIAL: $10 to $25 (or more) per hour.

> TRAINING/LICENSE/CERTIFICATION REQUIRED: None, however, the worker should be fully insured and bonded. On-the-job training is provided by many employers. This is typically an entry-level position with no minimum educational requirements.
>
> OTHER REQUIREMENTS: Painting equipment and supplies are needed.
>
> CAREER ADVANCEMENT OPPORTUNITIES: Limited.

Painters are hired to paint the interior or exterior of a home. Painters apply and remove paint, stain and/or varnish and must be able to select the appropriate materials to use for specific jobs while adhering to the customer's color preferences. The job often involves climbing ladders, being on your feet for extended periods and moving furniture and other household items.

Self-employed painters can work full time or part time and can typically set their own hours, while people working for a contractor (involved in new construction or renovations) typically work a standard 40-hour week.

For More Information

- HomeContractors.biz. This is an independent web site that offers referrals for people looking to hire housepainters or paperhangers, www.homecon tractors.biz.
- International Union of Painters and Allied Trades. This is a professional trade organization offering career-related information, www.iupat.org.
- Painting and Decorating Contractors of America. This is a professional trade organization offering career-related information, www.pdca.org.

Janitor (also see Housecleaner)

> AT A GLANCE
>
> SALARY POTENTIAL: $17,000 to $35,000 per year or minimum wage to $13 per hour.
>
> TRAINING/LICENSE/CERTIFICATION REQUIRED: None. On-the-job training is typically provided.

> OTHER REQUIREMENTS: This job involves being on your feet for long hours and utilizing a wide array of cleaning tools, including brooms, mops, vacuums, and various cleaning chemicals, soaps, and detergents.
>
> CAREER ADVANCEMENT OPPORTUNITIES: Limited. A janitor can pursue management or supervisory positions.

The difference between a janitor and a housekeeper is that a janitor typically works in a building, school, hospital, office, hotel, resort, factory, or other large commercial dwelling and is employed by a cleaning service. A housekeeper is often self-employed or works for a cleaning service and is responsible for cleaning homes, condos, or apartments.

In some cases, a janitor is hired to work after normal business hours. This is the case when working in most office buildings. In addition to cleaning floors and carpets, a janitor is often responsible for emptying trash, cleaning restrooms, and handling basic building maintenance tasks. This type of job has little career advancement potential, which limits your ability to earn raises, promotions, and ultimately earn a higher income.

For More Information

- International Executive Housekeepers Association. This is a professional trade organization for janitors, housekeepers, and others working in the cleaning profession, www.ieha.org.
- iSeek.com. This web site offers career-related information and online job listings, www.iseek.org/sv/13000.jsp?id=100349.
- To find janitor jobs in your area, use the Yellow Pages to find commercial cleaning services in your area and contact them directly. The more general career-related web sites, such as Monster (www.monster.com), will also list local jobs online.

Landscaper/Groundskeeper

> AT A GLANCE
>
> SALARY POTENTIAL: Minimum wage to $10 per hour for a groundskeeper, or $20,000 to $45,000 (or more) per year, depending on your level of training and experience as a landscaper.

> TRAINING/LICENSE/CERTIFICATION REQUIRED: None for a groundskeeper. To become a landscaper, completion of a certification program is required.
>
> OTHER REQUIREMENTS: This is a labor-intensive job that involves working outdoors using a wide range of tools.
>
> CAREER ADVANCEMENT OPPORTUNITIES: For a groundskeeper, the career path is limited without pursuing additional training and certification. For a landscaper, a wide range of career advancement opportunities are available.

Landing a job working at a gardening or landscaping company as an entry-level employee is a manual, labor-intensive job that offers on-the-job training and no minimum education requirements. This type of job is often referred to as a groundskeeper. A career as a landscaper, however, requires training and often certification.

As an entry-level employee working as a groundskeeper, responsibilities will include mowing, planting, watering, fertilizing, mulching, and pruning trees and shrubs. Certified landscapers will get involved with the layout and design of landscapes.

Groundskeepers and landscapers are often employed by private homeowners, homeowner's associations, golf courses, parks, schools, universities, corporate parks, playground operators, and state and local highway departments. Groundskeepers typically work for landscapers or other organizations, whereas a landscaper can be self-employed.

For More Information

- eLearners.com. Information about online-based training opportunities is offered at this web site, www.tradelearners.com/degrees/training-landscaping-3409.htm.
- LawnSite. Career-related information and online job listings are offered at www.lawnsite.com.
- Professional Lawn Care Association of America. This is a professional trade organization offering career-related information and training opportunities, www.plcaa.org.
- Tree Care Industry Association. This is a professional trade organization offering career-related information, www.TreeCareIndustry.org.

Locksmith

> **AT A GLANCE**
>
> **SALARY POTENTIAL:** $10 to $30 per hour, working part time or full time.
>
> **TRAINING/LICENSE/CERTIFICATION REQUIRED:** Certification is available through vocational schools and distance learning programs. On-the-job training is also provided by many employers. Many states require locksmiths to be licensed and bonded. A distance learning program can be completed in a few weeks for about $300.
>
> **OTHER REQUIREMENTS:** This job requires the use of tools along with having a flexible schedule, because many locksmiths are on call for emergencies.
>
> **CAREER ADVANCEMENT OPPORTUNITIES:** Hardware stores, construction companies, landlords, and locksmith stores are among the major employers of locksmiths. Some locksmiths, however, are self-employed. Some locksmiths also train to install and maintain security, alarm, and surveillance systems to increase their earning potential.

If you're looking for a key to unlock your future, yet don't have a lot of time or money to invest in your education or training, a career as a locksmith may be a viable option. A locksmith is someone who installs, repairs, maintains, and unlocks locks and safes, and also cuts keys and handles other related tasks for individuals and businesses.

When someone gets locked out of a home, car, or office, for example, it's the locksmith who often gets called to quickly repair a lock or create a duplicate key. Aside from training you'll receive as part of a certification program, good interpersonal skills are necessary.

Many locksmith companies that hire locksmiths do a complete background check on applicants for security reasons. Thus, this job isn't suitable for someone with a criminal record. This career, however, does offer the opportunity to launch a business with low start-up costs.

For More Information

- PCDI. Information about a self-paced, distance learning program for becoming a certified locksmith is offered at www.pcdicourses.com.

- Pick-A-Lock.com. Information about locksmith courses and supplies is offered at www.pick-a-lock.com.
- Thomson Education Direct. Career-related information, plus information about Thomson's distance learning program is offered here. The certification program is under $900, (800) 275-4410, www.educationdirect.com/lock smith/CareerOutlook.html.
- Online job listings can be found at the general interest career-related web sites, such as Monster (www.monster.com) or Yahoo! Hot Jobs (http://hot jobs.yahoo.com).

Mover

> **AT A GLANCE**
>
> **SALARY POTENTIAL:** Minimum wage to $25 per hour (or more).
>
> **TRAINING/LICENSE/CERTIFICATION REQUIRED:** None, however, if you're self-employed, bonding and insurance is highly recommended. Depending on the state you'll be working in, a license might be required.
>
> **OTHER REQUIREMENTS:** The ability to lift and carry heavy furniture, boxes, and objects. If you're self-employed, a moving truck or van is also necessary.
>
> **CAREER ADVANCEMENT OPPORTUNITIES:** Limited.

People move and businesses relocate. To make the moving process easier, it's common to hire a professional mover to assist with the packing and unpacking, loading and unloading of the truck, and driving the truck. Jobs working for professional moving companies require no previous experience or training. These are entry-level, labor-intensive jobs where the employer supplies the moving truck, moving supplies, insurance, and training. Employee benefits, including health insurance, are often offered.

Some experienced movers choose to become self-employed. The responsibilities involved with becoming a self-employed mover are greater, but the earning potential is significantly higher.

Moving companies often focus on the residential, commercial, or industrial market, or specialty markets, such as piano moving. In addition to having the physical stamina to move large and heavy items, good interpersonal skills are important. Customers expect the movers they hire to be prompt, professional, friendly, knowledgeable, reliable, and extremely careful when handling their fragile or valuable items.

For More Information

- Bekins Certified Professional Mover Training. Learn about a 25-hour training program for professional movers that offers certification as a Professional Mover upon completion, www.bekinsmoving.com/house/relo/train.htm.
- Certified Professional Mover Training Program. This web site offers information about a self-paced, interactive CD-ROM training program for professional movers, (703) 706-4985, www.promover.org/education/cpm.htm.
- Federal Motor Carrier Safety Administration (FMCSA). Information about licensing and other job requirements is offered at this web site, (202) 358-7000, www.fmcsa.dot.gov/factsfigs/licensing/OVERVIEW.htm.
- Professional Moving and Storage Association. This professional trade association's web site offers resources and career-related information, www.promover.org/membership/becomeamover.htm.
- Online job listings can be found at the general interest career-related web sites, such as Monster (www.monster.com) or Yahoo! Hot Jobs (http://hotjobs.yahoo.com).

Oil Change Technician

> **AT A GLANCE**
>
> **SALARY POTENTIAL:** Minimum wage to $15 per hour.
>
> **TRAINING/LICENSE/CERTIFICATION REQUIRED:** On-the-job training is typically provided by employers for this entry-level position.
>
> **OTHER REQUIREMENTS:** The ability to use a variety of tools, including computer diagnostic and reference tools.
>
> **CAREER ADVANCEMENT OPPORTUNITIES:** Limited. If employed by a company like Jiffy Lube, for example, promotion opportunities can lead to a higher paying management job.

An oil change technician is someone who performs standard oil changes on cars, SUVs, and trucks. In addition, the job requires handling a series of other common vehicle maintenance tasks, ranging from checking and replacing an air filter to changing windshield wiper blades or checking tire pressure. Oil change technicians are hired by gas stations, car dealerships, auto repair shops, and oil change shops, such as Jiffy Lube. The work involves highly repetitive tasks using basic tools. This is an entry-level position where on-the-job training is typically provided.

For More Information

- Automotive Oil Change Association. This is a professional trade association catering to oil change technicians. The web site offers career-related information, details about training opportunities, and potential employers, www.aoca.org.
- Jiffy Lube. Learn about career opportunities at Jiffy Lube, one of the country's largest chains of oil change companies, www.jiffylube.com/Company/cpy_CorpJobs.aspx.
- Online job listings can be found at the general interest career-related web sites, such as Monster (www.monster.com) or Yahoo! Hot Jobs (http://hotjobs.yahoo.com).

Personal Trainer (also see Aerobic Instructor and Yoga Instructor)

> ### AT A GLANCE
>
> SALARY POTENTIAL: $25 to $200 per hour.
>
> TRAINING/LICENSE/CERTIFICATION REQUIRED: Training and certification are required. Certification takes between two and three months.
>
> OTHER REQUIREMENTS: A personal trainer needs to be physically fit, health-oriented, outgoing, able to motivate others, reliable, detail oriented, and friendly.
>
> CAREER ADVANCEMENT OPPORTUNITIES: There is a wide range of career opportunities for personal trainers. With additional training, a personal trainer can become a nutritionist, massage therapist, or offer a wide range of other services to clients.

The demand for personal trainers continues to grow rapidly as everyone from professional athletes, working professionals, stay-at-home moms, students, and people from all walks of life are finding the need to incorporate physical fitness into their daily lifestyles to maintain their health. By taking on the role of educator, coach, and motivator, a personal trainer helps clients learn how to properly exercise, lose weight, and adopt a healthy lifestyle.

Some personal trainers are self-employed, whereas others work for health clubs, fitness centers, spas, hotels, resorts, cruise ships, universities, hospitals, or rehabilitation clinics.

For More Information

- LeisureJobs.com. Online job listings for personal trainers and careers in related fields can be found at www.leisurejobs.us.
- National Council on Strength and Fitness. A professional trade association offering information about certification programs and career-related advice for personal trainers is offered at this web site, (800) 772-6273, www.ncsf.org/school.
- Personal Training On The Net. This web site offers a variety of resources for personal trainers, as well as online job listings, www.ptonthenet.com/careers.aspx.
- Personal Training Schools. This web site offers a partial listings of schools that offer certification in personal training, www.naturalhealers.com/qa/personaltraining.shtml.
- The National Personal Training Institute. This is a chain of schools offering certification for personal fitness trainers, exercise consultants, and other fitness professionals, (800) 960–6294, www.nationalpersonaltraininginstitute.com.

Pest Controller/Exterminator

> **AT A GLANCE**
>
> **SALARY POTENTIAL:** $10 to $25 per hour.
>
> **TRAINING/LICENSE/CERTIFICATION REQUIRED:** Certification is required. This involves at least 10 hours of classroom training, plus 60 hours of on-the-job training. In some states, a license is also needed. Much of the needed education is provided through on-the-job training and apprenticeships.

> OTHER REQUIREMENTS: Pest controllers and exterminators must be willing and able to work in a wide range of spaces and not mind being directly exposed to infestations of bugs, rodents, and other creatures.
>
> CAREER ADVANCEMENT OPPORTUNITIES: Limited.

Mice, rats, roaches, termites, fleas, ticks, bees, ants, and a wide range of other creatures often find their way into homes, apartments, offices, and industrial buildings. When a can of over-the-counter bug spray or a few traps don't rid the area of the infestation, a pest controller or exterminator is called.

A pest controller must locate the problem, identify the cause, then kill, repel, or somehow control the problem using a wide range of traps, chemicals, and other tools of the trade. Like most jobs, there are several levels of pest controllers, including technicians, applicators, and supervisors.

The job requires good physical health, the ability to crawl into tight areas, climb ladders to reach high areas, and a willingness to work both indoors and out while wearing appropriate protective gear.

There are many locally owned and national pest control companies, such as Terminix, that hire and train pest controllers and exterminators.

For More Information

- National Pest Management Association. This is a professional trade association for people working in the pest control industry. The web site offers career-related information, online job listings, and a variety of resources, www.pestworld.org.
- Orkin. Learn about career opportunities available with Orkin, a national pest control and extermination company with over 400 offices throughout the United States, www.orkin.com/aboutorkin/careers.asp.
- Terminix. Learn about career opportunities available with Terminix, a national pest control and extermination company, with over 860 offices throughout the United States, http://jobsearch.terminix.newjobs.com.
- Online job listings can be found at the general interest career-related web sites, such as Monster (www.monster.com) or Yahoo! Hot Jobs (http://hot jobs.yahoo.com).

Physical Therapist Assistant

> ### AT A GLANCE
>
> SALARY POTENTIAL: $25,000 to $40,000 per year.
>
> TRAINING/LICENSE/CERTIFICATION REQUIRED: Physical therapists must pass a licensing exam from an accredited physical therapist educational program. Performing work as a Physical Therapist Assistant (PTA), however, does not require a license in most states. Training for this lesser-paying job is typically provided on the job, or can be completed in a two-year educational program (which results in an associate degree). Self-paced distance learning programs are available.
>
> OTHER REQUIREMENTS: This job involves working directly with patients in the medical field. Strong interpersonal skills and patience are important.
>
> CAREER ADVANCEMENT OPPORTUNITIES: With additional training, a physical therapist assistant can land a job as a licensed physical therapist, which greatly improves earning potential.

Working under the supervision of a licensed physical therapist, a PTA helps to provide services to patients to relieve pain, assist the patient in recovering from an injury, or helping a patient improve mobility if he or she is physically disabled or suffering from an illness. PTAs work with a wide range of patients with varying ailments or physical limitations. In addition to assisting a physical therapist perform treatments, it's the assistant's responsibility to maintain detailed patient records.

PTAs are employed by hospitals, clinics, rehabilitation centers, the private practices of licensed physical therapists, and nursing homes. Like many jobs in the medical field, working as a physical therapist assistant requires hard work, but can be extremely rewarding.

For More Information

- American Physical Therapy Association. This is a professional trade association for people working in the physical therapy field. Information about accredited training programs and online job listings are offered at this web site, (800) 999-2782, www.apta.org.

- Health Care Colleges Educational Directory. A listing of accredited educational and training programs for PTAs can be found here, www.health carecolleges.com.
- iHireTherapy.com. Online job listings for PTAs are offered at this web site, www.ihiretherapy.com.
- Rehab Options USA. Online job listings for PTAs are offered at http:// rehaboptions.com/phone.html.

Plumber

> ### AT A GLANCE
>
> **SALARY POTENTIAL:** $40,000 to $65,000 per year. Plumbers are among the highest paid workers in the construction field, however, salaries vary greatly based on the employer, type of work, geographic area, and the plumber's experience.
>
> **TRAINING/LICENSE/CERTIFICATION REQUIRED:** The licensing requirements for plumbers vary by state. Training is typically offered through apprenticeship programs, as well as postsecondary technical, vocational, and trade schools. United Association (UA) apprentices learn through both classroom and on-the-job training in what is considered by many to be the best construction industry apprentice program in the world. The five-year apprenticeship period is divided into one-year segments, each of which includes 1,700 to 2,000 hours of on-the-job training and a minimum of 216 hours of related classroom instruction.
>
> **OTHER REQUIREMENTS:** Plumbers must be comfortable working with a variety of tools in a wide range of environments. The job requires being in good physical condition.
>
> **CAREER ADVANCEMENT OPPORTUNITIES:** There is a wide range of career paths and advancement opportunities available to plumbers in related fields, such as working as a pipe layer, pipe fitter, and steamfitter.

Most people know plumbers as the professionals who come into their homes to install appliances and bathroom fixtures (such as sinks and toilets). However, plumbers also perform a wide range of other tasks and are integral to the construction of homes, offices, factories, and virtually any other type of building. In fact, plumbers are among the highest paid professionals in the construction field.

For More Information

- National Association of Plumbing-Heating-Cooling Contractors. This is a professional trade association for plumbers that offers a wide range of career-related information and resources, www.phccweb.org.
- Professional Career Development Institute. Information about one of many self-paced, distance learning programs for plumbers can be found here, www.pcdi.com/courses/pl/career.html.
- United Association of Journeymen and Apprentices in the Plumbing and Pipefitting Industry. A union for people working in the plumbing field. This web site offers information about apprenticeship training programs, (202) 628-5823, www.ua.org.
- Vocational Information Center / TCIDS. Details about training programs for plumbers, plus detailed career-related information is offered at this web site, www.tcids.utk.edu/cgi-bin/tcids/access/career_query.pl?number=498.

Postal Worker (also see FedEx/UPS/DHL Worker)

AT A GLANCE

SALARY POTENTIAL: $36,000 to $44,000 per year.

TRAINING/LICENSE/CERTIFICATION REQUIRED: Postal workers must be at least 18 years old and U.S. citizens. To qualify for a job in this field, a written examination is required. Contact your local post office for details. A wide range of traditional and distance learning training programs are available to help you prepare for the necessary exam.

OTHER REQUIREMENTS: Working within the U.S. Postal Service is not a traditional 9:00 A.M. to 5:00 P.M. job. Depending on your position, you may be required to work early mornings, nights, weekends, and even holidays.

CAREER ADVANCEMENT OPPORTUNITIES: There is a variety of different jobs and career paths within the U.S. Postal Service. Similar jobs are also available through shipping companies, such as FedEx, UPS, and DHL.

The U.S. Postal Service employs well over 850,000 people, including mail carriers, sorters, processors, and postal clerks. For a city mail carrier, the job involves carrying and moving heavy mail bags and trays, prolonged standing and walking, plus the willingness to work in all types of weather conditions. Depending on the type of postal job you're applying for, you must complete a written exam. For example, a city mail carrier must complete Exam 473. For details about these exams, call (866) 999-8777 or visit www.usps.com/employment.

For More Information

- DHL. The official DHL web site offers information about careers within the company, www.dhl-usa.com/HR/jobshome.asp?nav=Careers.
- FedEx. The official FedEx web site offers information about careers within the company, www.fedex.com/us/careers.
- Postal Jobs. Online job listings are offered here. This site also offers detailed information about the required written exams and information about study guides, www.postaljobs.com.
- United States Postal Service. The official web site of the United States Postal Service. Here you'll find a wide range of career-related information, www.usps.com/employment.
- UPS. The official UPS web site offers information about careers within the company, https://ups.managehr.com.

Prepress Technician

AT A GLANCE

SALARY POTENTIAL: Minimum wage to $25 per hour.

TRAINING/LICENSE/CERTIFICATION REQUIRED: On-the-job training is typically provided for entry-level positions.

OTHER REQUIREMENTS: None.

CAREER ADVANCEMENT OPPORTUNITIES: There is a wide range of jobs available in the printing industry, many requiring no formal education or training. Higher paying jobs are available in the printing and graphics design field, but require postsecondary training.

The job of a prepress technician will vary, based on the employer and equipment being used. In large printing houses, the prepress technician oversee and handles the prepress stage of the printing process, which includes creating the printing plates. Newer presses require the worker to be skilled using computers and related technology.

For More Information

- FedEx/Kinkos. Job listings and employment opportunities at FedEx/Kinkos print shops, www.fedex.com/us/officeprint/careers/index .html?link=5.
- iSeek. Detailed information about careers in the printing field are offered at www.iseek.org/sv/13000.jsp?id=100419.
- Printing Industries of America. This is a professional trade association for the printing industry. This web site offers useful career-related information, www.gain.net.
- Online job listings can be found at the general interest career-related web sites, such as Monster (www.monster.com) or Yahoo! Hot Jobs (http://hot jobs.yahoo.com).

Printing Machine Operator

AT A GLANCE

SALARY POTENTIAL: $10 to $20 per hour.

TRAINING/LICENSE/CERTIFICATION REQUIRED: On-the-job training is typically offered for entry-level positions. Training can also be obtained at a technical school or through an apprenticeship program.

OTHER REQUIREMENTS: None.

CAREER ADVANCEMENT OPPORTUNITIES: Limited.

Printing machine operators operate and maintain large presses at printing companies and newspapers, for example. The work can be tedious, as constant attention must be paid to the presses to keep them operating efficiently in order to meet deadlines and avoid waste. Newer printing presses require some computer knowledge. This job involves a high degree of manual labor.

For More Information

- Printing Industries of America. A professional trade association for the printing industry. This web site offers useful career-related information, www.gain.net.
- Online job listings can be found at the general interest career-related web sites, such as Monster (www.monster.com) or Yahoo! Hot Jobs (http://hot jobs.yahoo.com).

Roofer

AT A GLANCE

SALARY POTENTIAL: $10 to $25 per hour.

TRAINING/LICENSE/CERTIFICATION REQUIRED: Most roofers are trained through apprenticeship programs and on-the-job experience. An apprenticeship through a union, for example, can last up to three years.

OTHER REQUIREMENTS: Roofers should be proficient using a wide range of tools, physically fit, and not afraid to work outdoors at high elevations (on the roofs of homes and other buildings).

CAREER ADVANCEMENT OPPORTUNITIES: There are a wide range of jobs available in the construction field, however, many require additional training.

A roofer works in the construction industry and is responsible for installing, repairing, and replacing roofs on homes and a wide range of other buildings and structures. They're proficient using a variety of roofing materials and are capable of working on both flat and pitched (sloped) roofs. The work is physically taxing and requires being outdoors, sometimes in extremely hot temperatures. Extensive lifting, bending, climbing, and kneeling are required. The job involves some level of danger. Perhaps the biggest risk is actually slipping and falling off a roof.

Roofers work full time or part time for roofing contractors and are paid by the hour. Others are self-employed. This is one of many entry-level jobs in the construction industry.

For More Information

- ConstructionCareers.org. This web site offers information of interest to anyone interested in pursuing work in the construction field. Details about apprenticeship programs are provided, www.constructioncareers.org.
- National Roofing Contractors Association. This is a professional trade association for roofers. The web site offers career-related information and a variety of resources, www.nrca.net.
- United Union of Roofers. This is a union that supports roofers with a wide range of resources, including apprenticeship programs, www.union roofers.org.

Seamstress/Tailor

> **AT A GLANCE**
>
> **SALARY POTENTIAL:** Varies.
>
> **TRAINING/LICENSE/CERTIFICATION REQUIRED:** Most seamstresses and tailors learn from apprenticeship programs and on-the-job training. Some are self-taught.
>
> **OTHER REQUIREMENTS:** This job involves sewing by hand, using a traditional sewing machine, and perhaps an industrial quality sewing machine.
>
> **CAREER ADVANCEMENT OPPORTUNITIES:** Limited.

Working as a seamstress in a textile factory is typically an entry-level, minimum-wage job. Working as a seamstress or tailor for a retail tailor shop, dry cleaning establishment, dressmaker, bridal shop, or for a major department store's alterations department, for example, can result in significantly higher pay. The work is often tedious and requires a significant amount of sitting.

There are career opportunities for self-employed seamstresses to create one-of-a-kind dresses and wedding gowns, custom-tailored shirts, and suits, and a wide range of other garments for clients.

For More Information

- Custom Tailors and Designers Association. This is a professional trade organization for tailors and custom clothing makers. The organization offers a certification program for people working in the industry, (856) 423-1621, www.ctda.com.

- The Professional Association of Custom Clothiers. This is a professional trade organization for seamstresses, tailors and other people working in this trade, www.paccprofessionals.org.
- Online job listings can be found at the general interest career-related web sites, such as Monster (www.monster.com) or Yahoo! Hot Jobs (http://hot jobs.yahoo.com).

Shoe Repairer/Leather Worker (Cobbler)

> ### AT A GLANCE
>
> SALARY POTENTIAL: Minimum wage to $20 per hour.
>
> TRAINING/LICENSE/CERTIFICATION REQUIRED: Most people in this field receive training through an apprenticeship program.
>
> OTHER REQUIREMENTS: The dexterity to work with a wide range of hand tools.
>
> CAREER ADVANCEMENT OPPORTUNITIES: Limited.

Shoe repairers (cobblers) and leather workers are skilled at creating and repairing shoes and working with leather products, such as luggage and handbags. People in this field often work in factories or within small shops. Jobs in this field are somewhat limited due to declining demand. The job involves sitting for long periods and working with a wide range of handheld tools.

For More Information
- Shoe InfoNet. This web site is an online resource containing information of interest to shoe repairers. Details about training programs are provided, www.shoeinfonet.com.
- Shoe Service. This is a monthly, industry-oriented trade magazine for shoe repairers, http://shoeservice.msauk.biz.
- Society of Master Shoe Repairers. This is a professional trade association for shoe repairers and cobblers, http://somsr.msauk.biz/about.php.

Telephone Installer

> AT A GLANCE
>
> SALARY POTENTIAL: $15 to $40 per hour.
>
> TRAINING/LICENSE/CERTIFICATION REQUIRED: On-the-job training is provided by most employers, however, a high school diploma or GED is required.
>
> OTHER REQUIREMENTS: This job involves working with a wide range of tools in varied working conditions. Some knowledge of electricity and electronics is a plus. This can be obtained from a technical or vocational school, by completing a one-year certification program.
>
> CAREER ADVANCEMENT OPPORTUNITIES: With additional training, a telephone installer can also land work as a cable TV, alarm, or computer network installer, working with fiber optic cables, coaxial cables, telephone cables, or other technologies.

The job of a telephone installer, line installer, or repairer is to install and repair telephone lines. The job could require working for a telephone company or an independent company that specializes in offering this type of service. The job involves working on location, wherever new telephone lines or cabling are needed. This might mean digging underground, climbing utility poles or towers, working at construction sites, or within the walls or ceilings of existing homes or commercial buildings.

Depending on your employer, in addition to a 40-hour work week, you may be called to a site to deal with an emergency repair. Thus, a flexible schedule is necessary.

For More Information

- Communication Workers of America. This is a union comprised of professionals working in the telecommunications industry. Information and a variety of career-related resources can be found at the web site. Online job listings are also offered, www.cwa-union.org.
- International Brotherhood of Electrical Workers, Telecommunications Division. This is a union comprised of professionals working as electricians, telephone line installers, and in related fields. Information and a variety of career-related resources can be found at www.ibew.org.

- Online job listings can be found at the general interest career-related web sites, such as Monster (www.monster.com) or Yahoo! Hot Jobs (http://hot jobs.yahoo.com).

Toll Collector

> **AT A GLANCE**
>
> SALARY POTENTIAL: $30,000 to $50,000 per year.
>
> TRAINING/LICENSE/CERTIFICATION REQUIRED: None.
>
> OTHER REQUIREMENTS: The ability to quickly make change, provide receipts, and occasionally offer driving directions.
>
> CAREER ADVANCEMENT OPPORTUNITIES: Limited.

A toll collector is someone who sits in a tollbooth and collects tolls, makes change, provides receipts, and sometimes offers driving directors. The job involves extended periods of sitting or standing within a small, enclosed space, having five- to ten-second conversations with people hundreds of times per day, and having to deal with extreme hot or cold temperatures within your work environment, depending on the season. The work is extremely repetitive. The financial compensation is typically generous for a job that requires no formal education and minimal skills.

Obtaining a high-paying job working in a tollbooth can be extremely competitive. Finding a similar job working as a parking lot attendant, however, will be easier, although the pay will be anywhere from minimum wage to under $15 per hour.

For More Information
- The Toll Roads. This web site offers online job listings for tollbooth collectors and parking lot attendants, www.thetollroads.com/home/about_job .htm.
- Online job listings can be found at the general interest career-related web sites, such as Monster (www.monster.com) or Yahoo! Hot Jobs (http://hot jobs.yahoo.com).

Tool and Die Maker

> ### AT A GLANCE
>
> SALARY POTENTIAL: $15 to $30 per hour. (Approximately $45,000 per year.)
>
> TRAINING/LICENSE/CERTIFICATION REQUIRED: Participation in a postsecondary education training program at a technical or vocational school and/or an apprenticeship is typically required to land this type of job. The necessary training and/or apprenticeship can take upwards of five years.
>
> OTHER REQUIREMENTS: Proficiency using a computer, computer-controlled manufacturing equipment, along with computer-aided design (CAD) and computer-aided manufacturing (CAM) software is a job requirement.
>
> CAREER ADVANCEMENT OPPORTUNITIES: Tool and die makers can pursue higher paying supervisory positions or seek jobs in other areas of the manufacturing, engineering, or tool design fields.

Tool and die makers hold some of the most highly skilled jobs in the manufacturing industry. Thus, it typically requires up to five years of training (including participation in an apprenticeship program) to land the most lucrative jobs. The job involves working with a wide range of tools and equipment to manufacture many types of products, usually made from plastic or metal. Working as a tool and die maker involves highly complex, although often very repetitive, work. The work environment is typically within a factory or manufacturing facility.

Most entry-level positions in this field include working as a machine operator, welder, brazing worker, solderer, assembler, inspector, tester, or sorter.

For More Information
- CareersPrep. This site provides detailed information about career opportunities in the tool and die trade, as well as manufacturing-related jobs, www.careersprep.com/html/met_tool.html.
- National Tooling and Machining Association. In addition to learning about training and apprenticeship programs, this professional trade association is a great resource for learning about employers in this field, www.ntma.org.

- Precision Machine Products Association. This is a professional trade association offering a wide range of services and resources for people working in this field, www.pmpa.org.
- Precision Metalforming Association Educational Foundation. This organization offers information about accredited educational and training programs as well as apprenticeship opportunities, www.pmaef.org.

Transportation Security Administration (TSA) Officer

> AT A GLANCE
>
> SALARY POTENTIAL: $23,000 to $36,000 per year.
>
> TRAINING/LICENSE/CERTIFICATION REQUIRED: On-the-job training is provided, although job applicants must meet very strict employment requirements.
>
> OTHER REQUIREMENTS: TSA Officers must be able to follow directions and security procedures working within a busy airport environment.
>
> CAREER ADVANCEMENT OPPORTUNITIES: Limited.

TSA Officers are the people staffing the security checkpoints at all commercial airports. According to the TSA's web site, as a screener, job responsibilities include, "performing a variety of duties related to providing security and protection of air travelers, airports and aircraft. You will be responsible for identifying dangerous objects in baggage, cargo and/or on passengers; and preventing those objects from being transported onto aircraft. You are required to perform various tasks such as: wanding, pat down searches, operation of X-ray machines, lifting of baggage (weighing up to 70 pounds), and screening and ticket review using electronic and imaging equipment. As a Transportation Security Officer, you may perform passenger screening, baggage screening or both. You are expected to perform these duties in a courteous and professional manner."

TSA Officer jobs are available at all commercial airports nationwide. Applicants must be U.S. citizens, have a high school diploma (or GED), and meet a wide range of other requirements, all of which are detailed on the TSA's web site. The TSA is a branch of the U.S. federal government.

For More Information

- Transportation Security Administration Employment Office. This is the official web site of the TSA. Click on the Employment icon to learn about job opportunities at airports throughout the country, (800) 877-1895, www.tsa.gov.
- USAJobs.com. Online job listings for TSA Screeners and other jobs working for the U.S. federal government can be found on this web site, www.usa jobs.com.

UPS/FedEx/DHL Worker

AT A GLANCE

SALARY POTENTIAL: Minimum wage to $12 per hour or more, based on the job description and location.

TRAINING/LICENSE/CERTIFICATION REQUIRED: On-the-job training is provided for many of the entry-level positions within these shipping companies.

OTHER REQUIREMENTS: Depending on the job, the ability to lift and move packages (weighing up to 70 pounds) and/or customer service skills are required.

CAREER ADVANCEMENT OPPORTUNITIES: There is a wide range of job opportunities offered by these worldwide shipping companies.

Worldwide shipping companies hire a large number of entry-level employees to handle everything from customer service and telephone support to sorting and delivering packages. On-the-job training is required for many of these entry-level positions, plus with experience, promotions to higher paying jobs are available. Many of these shipping companies offer part-time opportunities to package handlers, drivers, warehouse staff, and customer service representatives.

For More Information

- DHL. Career opportunities available at DHL can be found at this web site. You can also contact the human resources department at your local DHL shipping office, www.dhl-usa.com/HR/jobshome.asp.

- FedEx. Career opportunities available at FedEx can be found at this web site. You can also contact the human resources department at your local FedEx shipping office, www.fedex.com/us/careers.
- UPS. Career opportunities available at UPS can be found at this web site. You can also contact the human resources department at your local UPS shipping office, http://ups.managehr.com.

Wallpaper Hanger (also see Painter)

> ### AT A GLANCE
>
> SALARY POTENTIAL: Minimum wage to $25 (or more) per hour.
>
> TRAINING/LICENSE/CERTIFICATION REQUIRED: None, although if you're running your own wallpaper hanging business, you'll want to be bonded and insured. Wallpaper hangers are typically trained on the job.
>
> OTHER REQUIREMENTS: Wallpaper hanging involves knowing how to prepare walls, measure and cut wallpaper and use the appropriate adhesives and tools to apply the wallpaper (or borders) to walls.
>
> CAREER ADVANCEMENT OPPORTUNITIES: Limited. Some wallpaper hangers also specialize in interior painting.

A wallpaper hanger is someone who prepares walls, measures and cuts wallpaper, and then applies wallpaper to walls using the appropriate adhesives. The job offers a flexible work schedule, but involves working in a variety of conditions, primarily homes, offices, and other types of buildings. A wallpaper hanger must be able to stand on his or her feet for extended periods, climb ladders and use a variety of tools.

Some wallpaper hangers also assist clients in choosing wallpaper, taking on the responsibilities of an interior designer. This requires the person to have excellent communication, sales, customer service skills, a flare for design and decorating, plus the skills needed to hang the wallpaper.

Many wallpaper hangers are self-employed and work as independent contractors. Others work for wallpaper retailers, home improvement retailers, interior painting companies, construction companies, or interior designers. This is an entry-level job that requires extensive manual labor. Many wallpaper hangers, however, have the luxury of setting their own work schedules, based around their clients' needs.

For More Information

- Online job listings can be found at the general interest career-related web sites, such as Monster (www.monster.com) or Yahoo! Hot Jobs (http://hot jobs.yahoo.com).

Warehouse Worker

> ### AT A GLANCE
>
> SALARY POTENTIAL: Minimum wage to $15 per hour.
>
> TRAINING/LICENSE/CERTIFICATION REQUIRED: None. On-the-job training is typically provided by the employer, as needed.
>
> OTHER REQUIREMENTS: Most warehouse jobs require lifting and moving of inventory, boxes, or other items. Thus, someone working in this type of job should be physically fit, free of back problems, and able to be on his or her feet for extended periods.
>
> CAREER ADVANCEMENT OPPORTUNITIES: Limited. This entry-level position could lead to supervisory or management-level jobs within a warehouse environment.

A warehouse worker is someone who works in a large warehouse environment and is responsible for moving around inventory, boxes, and any other items. This might involve physical lifting, the use of a dolly, or driving a forklift. Depending on the job, you may be responsible for accepting incoming shipments, preparing outgoing shipments, handling inventory management, or assisting with your company's order fulfillment operations. This is an entry-level job that sometimes requires basic computer skills, especially if the job involves inventory management responsibilities.

Depending on the employer, a warehouse worker job may involve a standard 9:00 A.M. to 5:00 P.M. work shift, early-morning, or late-night hours. A flexible schedule is sometimes required as is the ability to work overtime during peak business periods.

For More Information

- One quick way to land a job, at least temporarily, is to work with a temporary employment agency that specializes in filling warehouse positions.
- Online job listings can be found at the general interest career-related web sites, such as Monster (www.monster.com) or Yahoo! Hot Jobs (http://hot jobs.yahoo.com).

Welder

AT A GLANCE

SALARY POTENTIAL: $15 to $25 per hour.

TRAINING/LICENSE/CERTIFICATION REQUIRED: Most welders are trained on the job, a process that takes only a few weeks for most entry-level jobs in this field. Formal training can be obtained from vocational and technical schools, community colleges, and even private welding schools. For some welding jobs, a certification is required.

OTHER REQUIREMENTS: The ability to work with a variety of tools in varying conditions, including those found at traditional construction sites, shipbuilding sites, and factories is needed.

CAREER ADVANCEMENT OPPORTUNITIES: Limited.

Welding, soldering, and brazing workers are responsible for permanently joining metals parts together using extreme heat. People in this field work on all forms of metal. Thus, they're needed when ships, cars, houses, buildings, and a wide range of products are manufactured or built. Because welders work with extreme heat, the job involves dealing with a variety of potential hazards. The job also requires extensive manual labor and the handling of a variety of repetitive tasks. Most welders work full time, up to 70 hours per week. Many welders belong to a union, such as the International Association of Machinists and Aerospace Workers or the International Brotherhood of Boilermakers, Iron Ship Builders, Blacksmiths, Forgers, and Helpers.

For More Information

- American Welding Society. This is a professional trade association. This web site offers a variety of resources for welders, www.aws.org.

- GlobalSpec. Online job listings for welders can be found at this web site, http://welding-machines.globalspec.com.
- iHire Maintenance and Installation. This web site offers job listings for welders and those working in related fields, www.ihiremaintenanceand installation.com.
- Welding.com. Online job listings, career-related resources and information about training programs can be found at www.welding.com.

Woodworker

AT A GLANCE

SALARY POTENTIAL: Varies. Most woodworkers earn under $20 per hour.

TRAINING/LICENSE/CERTIFICATION REQUIRED: On-the-job training and apprentice-ships are available for entry-level positions, although formal training can be obtained through technical and vocational schools.

OTHER REQUIREMENTS: The ability to work with a wide range of tools used to build and create wood pieces. The more advanced tools are computer con-trolled, so for some jobs in this field, computer literacy is required.

CAREER ADVANCEMENT OPPORTUNITIES: Varies. There is a wide range of jobs in the carpentry, construction, and manufacturing fields that involve working with wood, including furniture building. The majority of woodworkers are employed by companies involved in manufacturing.

As the job title suggests, a woodworker is someone who earns his or her liveli-hood working with wood. This can involve working in construction or in more creative fields, like furniture building or cabinet making. Sawmills, furniture factories, kitchen cabinet manufacturers, hardwood flooring companies, musi-cal instrument manufacturers, construction companies, and others are among the employers who hire woodworkers. The primary job involves using tools to transform raw wood (lumber) into finished products. Working conditions vary dramatically based on the type of woodwork being done. The job, however, does require intense physical labor and the need to complete highly repetitive tasks.

For More Information

- Career Overview. This web site offers career-related information for anyone interested in entering this field, www.careeroverview.com/woodworker-careers.html.
- Vocational Information Center. This web site offers an online Carpentry Career Guide, which will be of interest to anyone looking to pursue a job as a woodworker, www.khake.com/page14.html.

CHAPTER

12

SALES-ORIENTED JOBS

For someone who enjoys the art of selling, any of the jobs in this section could be what you're looking for. The best sales jobs offer both a salary and some type of commission or bonus pay structure. Sales jobs require motivation, determination, and the ability to deal well with rejection. As you'll discover, some sales jobs require minimal training, but can be extremely lucrative.

Car Salesperson

> ### AT A GLANCE
>
> **SALARY POTENTIAL:** Varies, because this is typically a commission or salary plus commission-based job.
>
> **TRAINING/LICENSE/CERTIFICATION REQUIRED:** None. Some dealerships don't even require a high school diploma or GED.
>
> **OTHER REQUIREMENTS:** Top-notch sales and interpersonal skills, along with an understanding of cars (and their features) and auto financing is important.
>
> **CAREER ADVANCEMENT OPPORTUNITIES:** Ninety percent of car salespeople sell new cars, SUVs, passenger vans, and related vehicles for authorized dealerships. Salespeople can be promoted to sales managers or supervisors.

Car salespeople are hired by authorized new dealerships and used car lots. Because this is typically a commission-based sales job, your earning potential is directly related to your ability to make successful sales. The income potential is rather high for a job that requires no formal education or intense training.

This is typically a full-time job, although some dealerships offer part-time positions. Ideally, at least until you learn the job and start making steady sales, landing a car sales position that offers a salary or draw, plus commissions, will help ensure a steady income.

According to the National Automobile Dealers Association's web site, "Automobile salespeople are front-line professionals representing the dealership as well as the manufacturer of the products he or she sells. They must have an understanding of the products they sell, finance, insurance, state and federal laws, warranties and the automobile industry in general. Salespeople are organized self-starters who can stick to a tough daily routine and prospect for new customers by telephone, mail, and personal contacts. Most important, the sales staff should be excellent communicators who truly enjoy working with people."

For More Information
- Auto Jobs Today. This is an online resource for job listings and career-related information, www.autojobstoday.org.
- Auto Retailing Today. This is a professional trade organization offering training programs and other resources, www.autoretailing.org.

- National Automobile Dealers Association. This is a professional trade organization offering training programs and other resources, www.nada.org.

 CAREER SPOTLIGHT

eBay Trading Assistant

> AT A GLANCE
>
> SALARY POTENTIAL: Varies.
>
> TRAINING/LICENSE/CERTIFICATION REQUIRED: None, although eBay offers online-based and in-person training programs.
>
> OTHER REQUIREMENTS: Computer literacy, the ability to use the internet, a computer equipped with an internet connection, excellent writing skills, a good quality digital camera (for taking product photos), interpersonal skills, and sales skills are all needed.
>
> CAREER ADVANCEMENT OPPORTUNITIES: Limited.

Millions of people have discovered how to generate a part-time or even a full-time income buying and selling items, such as collectibles, on eBay. eBay is the world's largest online auction site. At any given minute, thousands of auctions are taking place.

While many people enjoy buying and selling items on eBay, even more people have items they'd like to sell, but they don't have the time, knowledge, or energy to actually use eBay and sell their own items. That's where an eBay Trading Assistant comes in.

According to eBay's web site, "Trading Assistants are experienced eBay sellers who will sell your items on eBay for a fee. Work with a Trading Assistant and enjoy these benefits: Save time and effort (the Trading Assistant handles every aspect of selling your item on eBay, from listing the item to shipping it to the buyer), take advantage of selling expertise (all Trading Assistants have experience selling on eBay and are in good standing in the eBay community. Many of them specialize in certain categories and know how to sell your type of item for maximum value), make money (when your item sells, the Trading Assistant passes the profit on to you, after taking out fees)."

An eBay Trading Assistant takes items from sellers and for a commission or pre-set fee, handles all of the work necessary to post the item up for auction on eBay, monitor the auction and then ship the item to the auction's highest bidder. A handful of different franchised businesses have opened up retail store fronts across America where people can simply drop off their items and have someone sell them on eBay on their behalf. To be a successful eBay Trading Assistant, you can work from home or get involved with one of these franchise opportunities.

Working as an eBay Trading Assistant requires a tremendous amount of creativity, since you'll need to write item descriptions and auction listings that capture people's attention. It may be necessary to perform research to determine what an item is actually worth, so you can set an opening bid price and a reserve price. You'll also need to develop skills as a photographer using a digital camera, so you can take and post photos of the products you're selling in conjunction with your listings.

While an independent eBay Trading Assistant can set his or her own work schedule, it's important to carefully monitor your auctions in order to quickly respond to questions from bidders. Thus, you'll probably find yourself spending several hours per day sitting in front of a computer that's connected to the internet. Another responsibility of the eBay Trading Assistant is collecting the money from winning bidders and then packing and shipping the items.

Here's My Story

Diana is a mother of two children. After successfully selling a wide range of items on eBay for herself, she began helping her friends sell their unwanted belongings using the eBay service. Before long, Diana established herself as an eBay Trading Assistant, working part time from her home to help people sell their stuff on eBay. For her services, Diana charges a flat fee plus a commission based on the selling price of the item.

"I started this business almost by accident. I had heard all about how people were selling their old, unwanted stuff on eBay and making a profit. In my basement and attic, I had a ton of stuff I no longer needed or wanted. It turned out that some of the stuff was actually valuable to other people. I began posting my own items on eBay and selling them. Within the first month, I made over $800. Not only was this profitable, it was fun too. With practice, I learned the intricacies of using eBay and started creating product listings that got noticed. I began telling my friends about my success and they asked for my help. Before long, I was managing over a dozen auction listings at a time," said Diana.

"When I discovered the eBay Trading Assistant program which is operated through eBay, I thought this would be a great opportunity for me to work part-time from home and generate some additional income. Initially, all of my business came from friends or referrals from friends. I eventually started promoting my business to generate more clients. I kept all of my expenses very low, however," added Diana.

If you want to be an eBay Trading Assistant, Diana believes you need to be an extremely well-spoken and friendly person. "You need to be able to generate business by getting potential clients to trust you. People need to give you their items in good faith, then you need to use your creativity to create listings and sell those items for the highest prices possible, taking full advantage of the various auction services eBay offers to sellers. I strongly recommend taking advantage of the online and in-person training classes that eBay offers through eBay University. Once you begin hosting many auctions simultaneously, there are various software packages and tools that will assist you in managing your eBay Trading Assistant business," said Diana.

According to Diana, "This is one of the very few jobs I could find that was fun, financially rewarding, that required little start-up capital, and offered a very flexible schedule. My biggest challenge was learning how to become more detail oriented, so as I handle many tasks simultaneously, nothing falls through the cracks."

For More Information

- eBay Trading Assistant Information. Learn more about eBay's Trading Assistant network, http://pages.ebay.com/tradingassistants/learnmore.html.
- eBay University Classes. Learn about the in-person training programs eBay hosts throughout the country. eBay offers three levels of training for sellers, including a training program called "eBay For Business." http://pages .ebay.com/university/classes.html.
- eBay University Online. Learn the basics of buying and selling items on eBay from this self-paced online training program offered by eBay, http://pages.ebay.com/university/index.html.
- iSoldIt. Learn about this independent franchise business opportunity that utilizes eBay Trading Assistant services. Required start-up capital is around $80,000 to establish and initially operate this type of retail store, www.i-sold it.com/your_store.asp.

Insurance Sales Agent

> **AT A GLANCE**
>
> **SALARY POTENTIAL:** $20,000 to $60,000 per year, depending on the employer, type of insurance being sold, and experience.
>
> **TRAINING/LICENSE/CERTIFICATION REQUIRED:** While many employers seek to hire college graduates for these positions, it's not a requirement. Insurance sales agents must obtain a state license, which typically requires the completion of a pre-licensing course.
>
> **OTHER REQUIREMENTS:** Being able to work well with clients, analyze their needs, and understand the insurance products you're selling are all important factors for success in this field. Having top-notch sales skills and telephone skills are also mandatory.
>
> **CAREER ADVANCEMENT OPPORTUNITIES:** Insurance sales jobs are available through independent insurance brokers and agents, as well as the insurance companies themselves. In addition to selling insurance, some people working in this field obtain the necessary training and licenses to sell financial products and services to supplement their incomes and further cultivate their client relationships.

The job of an insurance sales agent involves working directly with clients, analyzing their needs, matching those needs with appropriate insurance policies, and then selling those policies to clients. This is primarily a sales job that typically offers a small salary, plus commissions. Thus, your income potential is determined by your salesmanship abilities. The type of insurance you're selling will determine who your primary customers include. Soliciting new business is an important part of this job.

In the industry, insurance sales people are referred to as "producers." It's common for someone in this role to be able to sell several types of insurance, such as automobile insurance, homeowner's insurance, health insurance, long-term disability insurance, term life insurance, and/or whole life insurance. Much of the work is done from a traditional office or by making sales calls to potential and existing clients.

For More Information

- Independent Insurance Agents of America. This is a professional trade association offering career-related information and other resources relating to the insurance field, www.iiaa.org.
- Insurance Vocational Education Student Training. Information about training programs available for people interested in breaking into the insurance industry can be found at www.investprogram.org.
- InsuranceSalesJobs.com. Here you'll find online job listings and career information for insurance sales people, www.insurancesalesjobs.com.

Mall Cart Business Operator

AT A GLANCE

SALARY POTENTIAL: Varies.

TRAINING/LICENSE/CERTIFICATION REQUIRED: None, however, some basic business, managerial and bookkeeping knowledge is strongly recommended.

OTHER REQUIREMENTS: A successful mall cart business requires a good idea in regard to what you'll sell, dedicated employees, and the ability to catch the attention of mall shoppers as they walk by your cart.

CAREER ADVANCEMENT OPPORTUNITIES: Some mall cart operators franchise their original business ideas, expand into multiple mall locations, or build up their businesses until they are able to open within a traditional retail store environment.

If you're looking to start your own retail-oriented business but don't have the start-up capital to open a traditional retail store, consider launching some type of mall cart business. Most malls across the United States rent out cart space to small business owners. While space is limited, if your positioning within the mall is good, and you're offering the right type of product, the profit potential is excellent.

There are many franchise business opportunities and turnkey business solutions that utilize the mall cart business model. Many of these businesses are successful because they sell impulse purchase items that are highly profitable. Gifts, hand-crafted items, make-up, Tupperware, vitamins, sunglasses, T-shirts, balloons, perfume, watches, diet programs, language programs, gourmet dog treats, seasonal products, engraved gifts, embroidered baseball hats, and even pet hermit crabs are among the items that continue to do well as mall cart businesses.

Start-up costs vary based on fees paid to the mall, profit potential of items sold, and other costs of doing business. Plan on investing somewhere between $2,000 and $15,000 to launch this type of business. To learn more about mall cart business opportunities, visit the business office at your local mall or contact any of the franchisors that offer mall cart business opportunities. You'll find these opportunities advertised online or in business opportunity magazines, such as *Entrepreneur* (www.entrepreneur.com/bizopp/kiosk/0,6098,,00.html).

For More Information

- $125 per day. This web site sells an informative eBook that can be downloaded. It offers details about how to open and operate a mall cart business, www.125aday.com/ProductDetail.cfm?ID=66.
- Cart Marketing Tips. This is an informational resource for mall cart business operators, www.cartmarketingtips.com.
- Kiosk Expert. Information about how to launch a mall cart business is offered at www.kioskexpert.com.
- Simon Malls. Information about all of the 300+ malls in America owned and operated by Simon Property Group, Inc. can be found here, www.simon.com.

Manufacturing and Wholesale Sales Representative

AT A GLANCE

SALARY POTENTIAL: $30,000 to $100,000 (or more), based on what's being sold, your compensation package, the industry, and the employer. Salespeople can be paid in a variety of ways, including straight salary, salary plus commissions, commission only, or salary plus bonuses.

TRAINING/LICENSE/CERTIFICATION REQUIRED: The training and education needed will vary, based on the industry and what's being sold. Many sales jobs offer on-the-job training and require little more than a high school diploma or GED. Others require specialized training or a degree in a specific field.

OTHER REQUIREMENTS: Strong interpersonal, telephone, and written skills are critical for success in sales. You must also be detail-oriented, able to handle rejection well, have the patience to pursue difficult leads, and be able to maintain an upbeat and positive attitude about whatever you're selling. Staying motivated is one of the most difficult tasks a salesperson faces. An intimate knowledge of the product or service that's being sold is also critical.

CAREER ADVANCEMENT OPPORTUNITIES: Skilled salespeople are in demand in virtually every industry. Sales jobs in the wholesale and manufacturing field can be much more lucrative than traditional retail sales jobs. Once you have developed core sales skills and have sales experience, a wide range of career advancement opportunities will be available in many different industries.

Manufacturers and wholesalers in virtually every industry develop or import items that must be sold to distributors and ultimately retailers, typically in large quantities. This is the job of the wholesale or manufacturing salesperson, who must seek clients, cultivate existing business relationships, sell the company's products, and answer questions. Unlike selling in a retail environment, this type of sales often involves making in-person sales calls and doing extensive work on the telephone. Travel may be required.

For More Information

- A Career In Sales. This is an online resource offering career-related information and online job listings, www.acareerinsales.com.
- Manufacturer's Agents National Association. This is a professional trade organization for sales people, (714) 859-4040, www.manaonline.org.
- The Ladder. This is an informative web site offering career-related information and articles of interest to senior level salespeople. Online job listings are offered, http://sales.theladders.com.
- Online job listings, refer to any of the general interest career-related web sites, such as Monster (www.monster.com) or Yahoo! HotJobs (http://hotjobs.yahoo.com).

Online Business Operator (also see eBay Trading Assistant)

AT A GLANCE

SALARY POTENTIAL: Varies.

TRAINING/LICENSE/CERTIFICATION REQUIRED: None.

OTHER REQUIREMENTS: Computer literacy and creativity are important.

CAREER ADVANCEMENT OPPORTUNITIES: Many online businesses are scalable. They can start off small and grow, transforming a part-time job into a full-time business venture.

If you have a good idea, dedication, creativity, and a personal computer, launching your own online business has never been easier. In addition to selling products on eBay, there are a handful of complete, easy-to-use, and inexpensive turnkey solutions for creating and managing an e-commerce web site (online business). Two of these solutions are Yahoo! Small Business and eBay ProStores, both of which have a start-up cost of under $100, and provide all of the online tools you'll need to develop and launch your business. Using either of these turnkey solutions, all you'll need is a computer and an internet connection. No programming skills are required.

The first step to launching a successful online business is to find a unique product or service to sell. It's much easier to sell a hard-to-find, customized, or unique product or service than it is to offer something a customer can purchase at a local Wal-Mart or mall, for example. Find a product or service that caters to a specialized niche market, then focus on selling your product or service to that market via your web site. Many people have found success developing an online business around a hobby. If you surf the web, you'll discover that virtually anything can be sold online. The trick is to offer something that's new, unique, or somehow different than what's offered elsewhere.

As you develop your web site, make sure it looks professional. Visitors to your site must trust your company. Once you know what you'd like to sell online and begin developing your web site, you'll need to apply for a merchant account in order to accept credit card (Visa, MasterCard, Discover and American Express) payments. It's also important to become savvy at internet marketing to promote your business and generate traffic to your web site.

Many people from all walks of life launch online businesses as a part-time way of earning additional income. How successful your business becomes will depend on your idea, the quality of your web site, and how well you market your business. The start-up costs, however, are typically very low, which makes this an attractive opportunity for many people.

For More Information

- eBay ProStores. A powerful web site design and management tool that's inexpensive and allows people to develop and launch their online businesses relatively quickly, www.prostores.com.
- eBay.com. Selling items through eBay auctions is an ideal way to learn the basics of selling online, plus you can test out the viability of your business idea with virtually no initial investment. Millions of people earn a part-time income operating small businesses through eBay (also see "eBay Trading Assistant" within this book), www.ebay.com.
- Overstock.com. This is a resource for finding items to purchase at wholesale prices to potentially sell online, www.overstock.com.
- *The Unofficial Guide to Starting a Business Online* by Jason R. Rich (Wiley Publishing, 1999) offers an informative resource for anyone interested in launching an online business. The book is available at bookstores everywhere or at www.JasonRich.com.
- Yahoo! Small Business Solutions. This is a powerful web site design and management tool that's inexpensive and allows people to develop and launch their online business relatively quickly, http://smallbusiness.yahoo.com/merchant.

Product Demonstrator

AT A GLANCE

SALARY POTENTIAL: Minimum wage to $25 per hour (or more). Some jobs involve sales and also pay commissions.

TRAINING/LICENSE/CERTIFICATION REQUIRED: On-the-job training is provided.

OTHER REQUIREMENTS: Excellent verbal communication and interpersonal skills are critical for this type of work. It's also important for people working

> in this field to be well-maintained from a personal grooming standpoint. An outgoing personality and good sense of humor definitely help.
>
> CAREER ADVANCEMENT OPPORTUNITIES: Product demonstrators can also pursue work as models, public speakers, telemarketers, and/or salespeople.

The job of a product demonstrator involves being stationed at a trade show, convention, supermarket, retail store, department store, mall, or even on a street corner to showcase or demonstrate specific products to passersby.

This type of work might involve offering live demonstrations for groups of people or speaking one-on-one with potential customers. Product demonstrators are used to sell clothing, cosmetics, cleaning products, household goods, food products, and a vast array of other products using a live, interactive, and in-person infomercial type of presentation. The job might also involve actually selling the items after the demonstration.

Successful product demonstrators know everything about the product(s) they're showcasing and don't mind giving the same sales presentation dozens of times per day to potential customers.

For More Information

- Product demonstrators are often hired through modeling agencies. For a list of modeling agencies in your area, check the Yellow Pages or perform an online search. You can also contact the HR department of local department stores or retail shops.
- Online job listings, refer to any of the general interest career-related web sites, such as Monster (www.monster.com) or Yahoo! HotJobs (http://hot jobs.yahoo.com).

Real Estate Agent

> AT A GLANCE
>
> SALARY POTENTIAL: Varies, since this job typically involves a commission resulting from the sale or rental of properties.
>
> TRAINING/LICENSE/CERTIFICATION REQUIRED: Real estate agents need to obtain training, certifications, and licenses. Requirements vary by state.

> The necessary training can be obtained at vocational schools and through home study or online programs.
>
> OTHER REQUIREMENTS: Successful real estate agents are friendly, outgoing, have an upbeat personality, and are excellent salespeople. They also know a lot about the geographic regions where they're selling or renting properties.
>
> CAREER ADVANCEMENT OPPORTUNITIES: Real estate agents can work for agencies or be self-employed. Because compensation is based mainly on commissions, your success will be directly based on your skills.

A real estate agent is someone who sells or rents apartments, houses, condos, or commercial property to clients. Your job involves showing the properties to prospective buyers or renters, obtaining listings to show (from sellers), initiating negotiations between buyers and sellers, handling related paperwork, and helping to broker the sale or rental of real estate.

To prepare for the written exam needed to obtain a real estate agent's license, about a week's worth of training from an accredited school or training program is required. The training can be done in a traditional classroom setting, online, or via a distance learning program. Once you obtain your license, you'll initially need to work through a licensed broker.

This is one of the few jobs that requires minimal training but offers an extremely high earning potential, because you're paid a commission that's based on the sales you make. It can, however, take several months of hard work before making a first sale, so it's important to be able to support yourself while you're obtaining the initial on-the-job training and experience.

For More Information

- Century 21. Information about career opportunities at Century 21, one of the country's largest networks of real estate offices, with over 6,600 offices throughout the world, is offered at this web site, (888) 21-CAREER, www.century21.com/learn/careers.
- National Association of Realtors. This is a professional trade association for real estate agents, www.realtor.org.
- Real Estate Careers. This web site offers useful career-related information for prospective new real estate agents, www.restatecareer.com/relife.html.

- USA Real Estate License. Here, you'll find information about an affordable, self-paced CD-ROM training program for real estate agents, www.usareal estatelicense.com.
- Online job listings, refer to any of the general interest career-related web sites, such as Monster (www.monster.com) or Yahoo! HotJobs (http://hot jobs.yahoo.com).

Retail Assistant Manager

AT A GLANCE

SALARY POTENTIAL: Varies.

TRAINING/LICENSE/CERTIFICATION REQUIRED: On-the-job training is typically provided, although most retailers that hire assistant managers or managers look for applicants with extensive retail sales experience or promote from within. Some vocational schools, community colleges, and traditional colleges/universities offer degree programs in retail management.

OTHER REQUIREMENTS: In addition to having excellent retail sales skills, an assistant manager must be able to help manage employees, take direction from managers or other superiors, follow company guidelines, and help keep a retail business running smoothly. This often means filling in for workers who call in sick, assisting with inventory management, interacting with customers and solving their problems while working under the supervision of a store manager.

CAREER ADVANCEMENT OPPORTUNITIES: There is a wide range of career opportunities available in retail. As an assistant manager, advancement opportunities include getting a promotion to manager, district/regional manager, trainer, or securing a corporate job with the employer.

Working in a traditional retail environment, the job of the assistant manager is to assist the manager in the daily operation of a retail store. This includes handling a wide range of responsibilities and tasks above and beyond what's expected of retail sales associates. The assistant manager works under the supervision of the manager. On-the-job responsibilities vary greatly, depending on the employer.

Most assistant managers land their jobs as a result of promotions from traditional sales positions, after they've proven themselves to their employers, know the company's products/services, and have demonstrated management skills and the ability to take on additional responsibilities.

While working as a retail sales associate often involves having a pre-determined work schedule, an assistant manager must have a flexible work schedule and be able to fill in for the manager or other employees who don't show up for work. Depending on the employer, landing an assistant manager position can take anywhere from a few weeks to one year (or more) after being hired as a sales associate.

For More Information

- HCareers. Online job listings in the retail industry are offered at www.retailjobs.hcareers.com/seeker.
- Retail Industry Leaders Association. A professional trade association for workers in the retail industry, www.retail-leaders.org/new/index.aspx.
- Online job listings, refer to any of the general interest career-related web sites, such as Monster (www.monster.com) or Yahoo! HotJobs (http://hotjobs.yahoo.com).

Retail Sales Associate

AT A GLANCE

SALARY POTENTIAL: Minimum wage to $15 to hour (or more). Some retail sales positions offer commissions or bonuses based on sales performance.

TRAINING/LICENSE/CERTIFICATION REQUIRED: None. On-the-job training is typically provided.

OTHER REQUIREMENTS: Excellent personal communication and sales skills are important, although retail sales jobs are considered entry level. It's also important to have a thorough knowledge of what you're selling.

CAREER ADVANCEMENT OPPORTUNITIES: Retail sales associates can be promoted to assistant managers, managers, or to corporate positions.

At all retail stores, sales associates work on the front lines, interacting directly with customers. They're responsible for selling products or services, plus maintaining the cleanliness and organization within the retail environment. Sales associates work under the supervision of assistant managers and managers. In addition to actually selling and interacting with customers, responsibilities vary greatly from employer to employer.

Sales associates work either part time or full time. Most employers offer full-time workers benefits, in addition to an hourly wage. Some also offer sales commissions or bonuses, based on sales performance. Working in a retail environment can be tedious and often requires standing on your feet for hours at a time. Many retailers also require sales associates to wear uniforms or adhere to strict dress codes. Few employers, however, provide the clothing to meet that dress code, so it's an expense incurred by the employee.

Perhaps the biggest perk retail sales associates receive is a discount on the purchase of products or services bought from their employers. When seeking an entry-level position with a retailer, determine exactly how you'll be compensated and what expenses you'll incur. For example, some malls (where sales associates work) charge for daily parking, plus the sales associate is required to purchase and launder his or her own work clothes. The best retail sales jobs offer full-time employment (40 hours per week), plus pay overtime, commissions, and/or sales bonuses based on performance.

As a retail sales associate, be prepared to work evenings and weekends because most retail establishments are open for extended hours, seven days per week. Sales associates take direction from and answer directly to their assistant managers and/or managers.

For More Information

- HCareers. Online job listings in the retail industry are offered at www.retail jobs.hcareers.com/seeker.
- iHireRetail. Online job listings covering a wide range of job opportunities within the retail industry can be found at www.ihireretail.com.
- Retail Industry Leaders Association. A professional trade association for workers in the retail industry, www.retail-leaders.org/new/index.aspx.
- Online job listings, refer to any of the general interest career-related web sites, such as Monster (www.monster.com) or Yahoo! HotJobs (http://hot jobs.yahoo.com).

CAREER SPOTLIGHT

Retail Manager

AT A GLANCE

SALARY POTENTIAL: $25,000 to $75,000 per year. Unlike sales associates or even assistant managers, retail managers often receive an annual salary plus benefits, as opposed to an hourly wage.

TRAINING/LICENSE/CERTIFICATION REQUIRED: None. On-the-job training is typically provided, although some postsecondary schools offer a degree in retail management.

OTHER REQUIREMENTS: In addition to having excellent retail sales skills, a retail manager must be able to manage employees, oversee the basic finances/accounting related to the store, follow company guidelines, and help keep a retail business running smoothly. Store managers typically answer to district managers or owners.

CAREER ADVANCEMENT OPPORTUNITIES: Retail store managers can advance to other types of management positions in a wide range of industries, become district or regional managers, or take on corporate jobs within the retail industry.

Working as a retail store manager involves having extensive experience with retail sales, a proven ability to manage people and take on responsibilities, the ability to make decisions, and a willingness to follow directives passed down from superiors. At a retail location, such as a chain store at a mall, it's the manager who is in charge of hiring and firing employees, scheduling, overseeing inventory, maintaining the organization of the store, dealing with customer problems, handling basic accounting procedures on behalf of the store, and handling a wide range of other tasks.

A retail manager must be able to work well under stress, be proficient at multitasking and be prepared to work long hours, especially during peak sales periods. Store managers typically have extensive retail sales experience plus consider their work to be a career as opposed to a job. Many retailers promote from within, although once you have retail management experience, it's much easier to land similar jobs with other companies.

Here's My Story

Throughout high school, Peter held a variety of after-school jobs working in retail, primarily at his local mall. Upon graduating from high school, when it was clear that Peter would not be attending college full time, he decided to pursue a career in retail. Using the retail sales experience he already had, he selected a retail chain he was genuinely interested in working for and accepted a sales position, with the understanding that he'd be trained to take on assistant manager responsibilities once this type of job opened up at his location.

"The great thing about retail is that most of the major retail chains experience extremely high employee turn over rates. Thus, if you're able to prove yourself to be a hard working and dedicated employee, earning promotions quickly is relatively easy. Within three months after my high school graduation, I was promoted to assistant manager at the store I was working for. Two months after that, I was promoted to manager. For each new position, I received on-the-job training. Because I stuck with the same employer, I knew the company's products extremely well and was able to easily learn the extra skills needed to take on management-level responsibilities," explained Peter.

"When you're working as a retail sales associate, you answer to your assistant manager or manager. When you're the store manager, you answer to a district manager, but your job is to oversee all of the employees working at your location and to ensure the successful day-to-day operation of your store. This includes taking on a wide range of additional responsibilities, which vary greatly depending on where you work. In addition to hiring, firing, training, managing, and scheduling employees, I also oversee inventory, open or close the store, handle basic bookkeeping, put up and maintain store displays, make deposits at the bank, interact with mall management, and handle customer complaints and issues. Basically, I'm always on-call. If someone doesn't show up for work and I can't find someone to fill in, I need to take that employee's shift. Working as a retail store manager requires long hours and a lot of dedication to the company you work for. Sometimes your hard work is rewarded with a raise or bonus. Other times, you barely get a pat on the back," said Peter.

"If you're going to pursue a retail management career track, choose a company you really believe in. Find a company that values its employees and managers and that compensates them fairly. Know what you're getting into. Before taking on the role of manager, speak with other managers working within the chain and learn about their experiences," added Peter.

"One of the biggest misconceptions managers have is that they can remain friends with employees. This becomes very difficult when you are the boss. If you have friends working for you, they always try to take advantage, ask for extra time off, try to leave work early or don't always do what they're asked or obligated to do. You wind up having to cover for them. When you're a retail store manager, you're a decision maker and for that location, you're the boss. You need to have the respect, support, and dedication of your employees or your job is going to be very difficult," explained Peter. "Having good people skills, managerial skills, and organizational skills will be useful. As a manager, you'll often find yourself juggling many tasks at once and having both employees and your superiors counting on you."

For More Information

- HCareers. Online job listings in the retail industry are offered at www.retail jobs.hcareers.com/seeker.
- iHireRetail. Online job listings covering a wide range of job opportunities within the retail industry, www.ihireretail.com.
- Retail Industry Leaders Association. This is a professional trade association for workers in the retail industry, www.retail-leaders.org/new/index.aspx.
- The Retail Network. This is an executive search firm specializing in the retail industry. It helps match qualified and experienced managers and executive-level applicants with potential employers, www.retailnet work.com.
- Online job listings, refer to any of the general interest career-related web sites, such as Monster (www.monster.com) or Yahoo! HotJobs (http://hot jobs.yahoo.com).

Sales Trainer

AT A GLANCE

SALARY POTENTIAL: Varies.

TRAINING/LICENSE/CERTIFICATION REQUIRED: None.

> **OTHER REQUIREMENTS:** An outgoing personality, extensive sales experience, and the ability to teach others are important qualifications for this type of work.
>
> **CAREER ADVANCEMENT OPPORTUNITIES:** Sales trainers can pursue jobs in sales, management, marketing, public relations, and a wide range of other corporate jobs.

A professional sales trainer is someone who trains others on how to sell specific products or services. The sales trainer must have extensive sales experience, be proficient using and teaching a wide range of sales techniques, and be knowledgeable about the product/service he or she is training people to sell. Some sales trainers have previous teaching experience, while others have become expert sales people and have the natural ability and willingness to share their knowledge with others.

Sales trainers work for retail chains or large companies with a sales force. Some work directly for a specific employer, whereas others work as self-employed freelance consultants. This type of job primarily involves teaching, not actual sales. Extensive travel is often required.

For More Information
- National Association of Sales Professionals. Here you'll find information about training programs, certification, and resources for sales training professionals. Online job listings can also be found at www.nasp.com/Site Files/Certification/certifframe.html.
- Sales Training Association. This is a professional trade association for sales training specialists, http://freespace.virgin.net/sta.org.
- Online job listings, refer to any of the general interest career-related web sites, such as Monster (www.monster.com) or Yahoo! HotJobs (http://hot jobs.yahoo.com).

Telemarketer

> **AT A GLANCE**
>
> **SALARY POTENTIAL:** Minimum wage to $25 an hour (or more), based on salary, plus commissions and bonuses.

TRAINING/LICENSE/CERTIFICATION REQUIRED: None. On-the-job training is typically provided by the employer.

OTHER REQUIREMENTS: Basic computer literacy skills, a good telephone voice, and excellent verbal communication skills are useful for this type of work. Sales skills are also extremely useful in many telemarketing jobs.

CAREER ADVANCEMENT OPPORTUNITIES: Depending on the job, employers will sometimes pay experienced telemarketers a salary, plus commissions or bonuses. These opportunities can offer excellent earning potential.

A telemarketer (or telesales professional) is someone who uses the telephone as his or her primary business tool. Typically working from an office or call center (where dozens or hundreds of telemarketers work from cubicles simultaneously), a telemarketer typically makes outgoing sales calls on behalf of a company in order to sell products or services. The job involves calling dozens of people per hour, reciting a pre-written sales pitch and encouraging the person you're calling to purchase something or set up an appointment with an in-person sales agent.

Telemarketers can also accept incoming calls from people responding to radio, television, newspaper, or magazine ads, for example. In this case, it's the telemarketer's job to answer questions about the product or service being sold and then accept and process a order.

Telemarketing can require extremely repetitive work that involves receiving a lot of rejection. Thus, it's important to be able to keep yourself motivated as you make or receive call after call throughout your shift. Many telemarketers utilize computers to help them manage call logs and handle order processing tasks.

Companies in many different industries hire in-house telemarketers to handle outbound and inbound sales calls. There are also independent telemarketing companies, order-processing centers, and call centers that hire telemarketers to offer services to multiple clients simultaneously.

In most cases, telemarketing is a sales job, but one that requires no traveling to clients or even in-person interaction with clients or customers. Thus, expect to spend many hours per day speaking on the telephone to meet your job's responsibilities. Some telemarketers are able to work from "virtual call centers." Thanks to computer technology and the internet, this allows people to work from home or from other locations outside a traditional call center.

For More Information

- American Teleservices Association. A professional trade association for tele-marketers and telesales professionals. This web site offers useful career-related information for someone interested in this field, www.ata connect.org.
- CallCen.net. This web site offers online job listings for openings at call centers, www.callcen.net/jobs.htm.
- CallCenterJobs.com. Here you'll find online job listings for telemarketers, www.callcenterjobs.com.
- Tele-Plaza. This web site offers a listing of several professional trade associations of interest to telemarketers. From these links, you can find information about training programs, online job listings, and a wide range of other resources, www.teleplaza.com/trade.html.
- *Top Telemarketing Techniques* by Ellen Bendremer (The Career Press, 2003), www.careerpress.com. This 256-page book is an information-packed resource for all telesales professionals. It offers expert insight and proven strategies for utilizing the telephone as a powerful and effective sales tool. This book will give you the valuable information you need to develop, improve upon, and fully utilize your telephone sales skills, allowing you to close more sales over the telephone. This book is a "must read" for anyone interested in the telemarketing field.
- Online job listings, refer to any of the general interest career-related web sites, such as Monster (www.monster.com) or Yahoo! HotJobs (http://hot jobs.yahoo.com).

CHAPTER

SERVICE-ORIENTED JOBS

Service jobs involve helping or catering to the needs of others, such as customers or clients. Most of the jobs described in this chapter involve extensive interaction with other people throughout the work day.

Auto Body Repairer

AT A GLANCE

SALARY POTENTIAL: $15 to $22 per hour.

TRAINING/LICENSE/CERTIFICATION REQUIRED: On-the-job training is provided, however, most employers are looking for people who possess certification by the National Institute of Automotive Service Excellence (ASE).

OTHER REQUIREMENTS: Graduation from a accredited trade or vocational school is recommended, but not required.

CAREER ADVANCEMENT OPPORTUNITIES: A wide range of different skills and certifications can be obtained, which can greatly increase an auto body repairer's earning potential.

Not to be confused with an auto mechanic, an auto body repairer fixes the outer body of vehicles damaged in accidents. Straightening or removing dents, replacing windshields, replacing damaged parts, and making a vehicle look new after an accident are part of an auto body repairer's responsibilities. Employment opportunities are available from auto body shops, gas stations, and car dealerships. This is a $30 billion per year industry that continues to grow. It's easier to acquire a position and requires less training than becoming an automotive service technician/mechanic.

For More Information

- Automotive Service Association. A professional trade organization, www.asashop.org.
- National Automobile Dealers Association. A professional trade organization, wwww.nada.org.
- National Automotive Technician Education Foundation. This web site offers a directory of trade schools and accredited institutions that offer training in automotive body repair, www.natef.org.
- National Institute for Automotive Service Excellence (ASE). Information about training programs can be found at this web site, www.asecert.org.

Auto Detailer

> ### AT A GLANCE
>
> SALARY POTENTIAL: Minimum wage to $10 per hours (plus tips), or annual salary up to $35,000.
>
> TRAINING/LICENSE/CERTIFICATION REQUIRED: None.
>
> OTHER REQUIREMENTS: None.
>
> CAREER ADVANCEMENT OPPORTUNITIES: Limited.

Auto detailers are people who clean vehicles by hand, giving them that "like new" look. This often includes washing, vacuuming, waxing, shampooing the vehicle's interior and floor mats (and/or treating the leather interior), cleaning the wheel rims, and washing the windows.

Job opportunities are available from car dealerships, car wash facilities, and auto detailing shops. Some auto detailers choose to launch their own businesses and are self-employed.

For More Information

- Automotive Training Centers. This company offers hands-on training and certification for auto detailers, (888) 802-6481, www.autotraining centre.com/programs/automotive_detailing.asp.
- Thompson Education Direct. Learn about one of many distance learning programs that teaches auto detailing from this web site, http://educationdirect courses.com/html/career_diploma/Auto_Detailer.php.

Auto Mechanic/Automotive Service Technician

> ### AT A GLANCE
>
> SALARY POTENTIAL: Minimum wage to $30 per hour, or up to $50,000 per year, based on skills and experience.

> **TRAINING/LICENSE/CERTIFICATION REQUIRED:** Formal automotive technical training from a high school and/or postsecondary vocational school is required.
>
> **OTHER REQUIREMENTS:** None.
>
> **CAREER ADVANCEMENT OPPORTUNITIES:** Many levels of training and specialty training programs are available, offering greater earning potential and a wider range of career options. Specialty training includes transmissions, brake systems, exhaust systems, air conditioning systems, or working on specific makes/models of vehicles.

Over 820,000 automotive service technicians and mechanics currently work in the United States. Car dealerships, gas stations, auto body shops, and national chains (like Sears Tire & Auto, Pep Boys Auto, and Midas) are among the top employers.

The primary job of an automotive service technician or mechanic is to diagnose and repair a vehicle. This often involves using computers and other high-tech diagnostic tools to deal with the integrated electronic systems and computers that run most vehicles currently on the road. Hands-on work with a wide range of traditional tools in a garage or workshop environment is also a major part of this job.

For More Information

- Automotive Youth Education Systems (AYES). Information about training programs offered through high schools can be found at www.ayes.org.
- National Automobile Dealers Association. This is a professional trade organization, www.nada.org.
- National Automotive Technicians Education Foundation. This web site offers a directory of trade schools and accredited institutions that offer training in automotive body repair, www.natef.org.
- National Institute for Automotive Service Excellence (ASE). Information about certification training programs can be found at www.asecert.org.

Barber

> **AT A GLANCE**
>
> **SALARY POTENTIAL:** $15,000 to $36,000 (including tips).

> **TRAINING/LICENSE/CERTIFICATION REQUIRED:** In all states, barbers must be licensed. The requirements for the license, however, vary by state. The easiest way to obtain this license is to first attend a public or private vocational school offering barbering and cosmetology. This training will last between nine and 24 months. Additional work as an apprentice is also required.
>
> **OTHER REQUIREMENTS:** After obtaining a barbering license, additional training is required to stay up-to-date on the latest techniques and hairstyles.
>
> **CAREER ADVANCEMENT OPPORTUNITIES:** Income potential grows as a barber becomes more skilled and is able to offer a wider range of services beyond simply cutting and styling hair. Working in an upscale salon will also generate significantly higher revenues than holding a similar job at a lower-end barber shop or salon.

The work of a barber, hairdresser, and hairstylist is related, but somewhat different. Barbers primarily cut, trim, shampoo, and style hair. Some also fit hairpieces, offer shaves, scalp treatments and color, bleach, and highlight hair. Hairdressers, hairstylists, and cosmetologists offer a wide range of beauty services for both men and women.

Most barbers are hired by barber shops, salons, resorts, cruise ships, and nursing or residential care homes. Some barbers are self-employed and rent space at an existing salon or barber shop, while others are full-time or part-time employees. Another alternative, once you become a licensed barber, is to own your own barber shop or salon.

One key for generating the highest income from this type of job is to develop loyal clients who return regularly to have their hair cut or styled. This requires having top-notch skills as a barber/hairstylist, as well as extremely good interpersonal and conversational skills. Building long-term relationships with clients is important.

For More Information
- National Accrediting Commission of Cosmetology Arts & Sciences. This site offers a listing of accredited barbering and cosmetology schools and licensing requirements for each state, www.naccas.org.
- National Cosmetology Association. On this web site, you'll find information about careers in cosmetology, www.salonprofessionals.org.

- Stylist Online Job. This is a resource for finding job opportunities in cosmetology, www.stylistonlinejobs.com/jobseekers.php.

Bed and Breakfast Operator

AT A GLANCE

SALARY POTENTIAL: Varies.

TRAINING/LICENSE/CERTIFICATION REQUIRED: Varies by state.

OTHER REQUIREMENTS: You must have a large, clean home with extra bedrooms and be willing to host, clean up after, and cook for guests.

CAREER ADVANCEMENT OPPORTUNITIES: Working at a bed and breakfast (B&B) requires the same types of skills as working for a small hotel or motel. Owning and operating a B&B, however, allows you to earn an income, meet new people, and receive tax advantages relating to your home. Operating a successful B&B requires business, bookkeeping, marketing, and top-notch interpersonal skills. Experience working in the hospitality industry is highly recommended, but not required.

Opening your home to travelers looking for an alternative to staying at commercial hotels is a viable business, especially if you live in or near a popular tourist area. As a B&B operator or innkeeper, your job is to offer a clean and comfortable bedroom and bathroom for your guests, as well as a home-cooked breakfast. A wide range of other services can also be offered to improve a guest's stay and generate more revenue for you. Nightly fees charged by B&Bs vary greatly, based on location, time of year, amenities, and the quality of the room(s) you're offering.

For More Information

- B&B Associations. This web site offers a listing of regional B&B owner associations, www.businessplanworld.com/resource/book.cgi.
- Bed & Breakfast Inns Online. This web site is a wonderful, highly-informative resource for prospective innkeepers, www.bbonline.com/innkeeper/index.html.
- BedandBreakfast.com. This is an online directory of B&Bs throughout the world, www.bedandbreakfast.com.

- BusinessPlanWorld.com. Purchase a detailed business plan for operating a successful B&B. A business plan is a detailed starting point featuring plans for launching any type of business, www.businessplanworld.com/plan.htm.
- Inkeeping.com. An online resource for B&B innkeepers, including information on how to start a B&B, www.innsideinnkeeping.com.
- Land Lord Zone. This web site offers a wide range of information for innkeepers and B&B operators, www.landlordzone.co.uk/b&b.htm.

Butler

AT A GLANCE

SALARY POTENTIAL: $40,000 to $100,000+ (plus benefits).

TRAINING/LICENSE/CERTIFICATION REQUIRED: None.

OTHER REQUIREMENTS: You must be able to follow directions, multitask, be detail-oriented, manage other people while serving your employer, and take on a wide range of responsibilities.

CAREER ADVANCEMENT OPPORTUNITIES: Butlers can pursue different types of jobs, working for private households or within the hospitality industry (hotels, resorts, etc.) Each type of butler job offers different advancement opportunities.

Your name doesn't have to be Jeeves or Alfred to enjoy a career serving the rich and famous as a butler. There are over 50,000 butlers employed worldwide. Sometimes referred to as a "household manager," a butler's job involves working for a client and insuring that all aspects of his or her home or estate run smoothly. Some butlers work in private homes and aboard private yachts. Others are employed by luxury hotels, corporations, cruise ships, or resorts.

As the household manager, your responsibilities might include hiring and managing a staff of housekeepers, landscapers, chefs, and other household support staff members, while overseeing the day-to-day operations of the home or estate where you work. This includes answering the door and telephone, preparing for guests, catering to the needs of your employer, organizing meals and events, performing personal valet services, scheduling appointments and running errands.

Having a flexible work schedule is important. Some butlers are provided with room and board in addition to a salary plus benefits. Contrary to popular belief, there are female butlers.

For More Information

- Butler's Guild. This is a professional trade organization, www.butlers guild.com.
- FabJobs.com. Information about pursuing a career as a butler can be found here, www.fabjob.com/butler.asp.
- International Butler Academy. This is one of the world's foremost training academies for butlers. Job placement services are offered, www.butler school.com. For additional information about this career, visit this URL: www.butlerschool.com/links.htm.
- Magnums Butlers. Learn about online-based training program for butlers, www.magnumsbutlers.com/online_training.htm.

Buyer

> **AT A GLANCE**
>
> **SALARY POTENTIAL:** $35,000 to $60,000+ (plus benefits).
>
> **TRAINING/LICENSE/CERTIFICATION REQUIRED:** None.
>
> **OTHER REQUIREMENTS:** Many employers fill this position with college graduates, however, this is not always a pre-requisite.
>
> **CAREER ADVANCEMENT OPPORTUNITIES:** Entry-level positions in this field are called purchasing clerks, assistant buyers, or junior buyers. On-the-job training to learn the intricacies of your employer's business and experience successfully buying for that business are typically the prerequisites for a promotion to buyer or purchasing agent.

The job of a buyer (also called a purchasing agent) very greatly, depending on the type of company you work for. Manufacturing companies, wholesalers, retailers, farms, corporations, government offices, and many types of businesses have buyers on staff.

It's the buyer's job to negotiate the best possible deals when it comes to purchasing supplies, inventory, or anything the employer needs. This job often involves finding the best suppliers, negotiating the best prices, ensuring the necessary amount of inventory is always on-hand, and arranging for shipment of merchandise (which will be resold or used for manufacturing). Working with suppliers located overseas is often required, so understanding international business and shipping practices, plus being bilingual are beneficial.

Buyers typically work full time from traditional offices, however, traveling to see potential suppliers and attending trade shows is often part of the job's responsibilities.

For More Information

- The American Purchasing Society. This is a professional trade organization, features job listings and other career-related resources, www.american-purchasing.com.
- Institute for Supply Management. This is a professional trade organization, www.ism.ws.
- National Institute of Government Purchasing. This is a professional trade organization, www.nigp.org.
- BuyingJobs.com. Online job listings and career resources can be found at this web site, www.buyingjobs.com.

 CAREER SPOTLIGHT

Certified/Licensed Massage Therapist

> **AT A GLANCE**
>
> SALARY POTENTIAL: $25 to $100 per hour (or more), plus tips.
>
> TRAINING/LICENSE/CERTIFICATION REQUIRED: Certification and a state-issued license are required to become a massage therapist. Licensing regulations vary by state, however, completion of an accredited training program is typically required.
>
> OTHER REQUIREMENTS: In addition to being skilled at various massage techniques, a massage therapist must have a calming, cheerful, outgoing,

> patient, and understanding personality. Being a good listener and intuitive to other peoples' needs is also important.
>
> CAREER ADVANCEMENT OPPORTUNITIES: Massage therapists are hired by spas, resorts, cruise ships, physical therapy and rehabilitation centers, hotels, and health clubs. Many massage therapists choose to be self-employed because the income potential is greater. To generate higher revenues, massage therapists can offer more luxurious and exotic body treatments, in addition to standard massages.

A massage therapist is someone who is trained in the art of performing massage. Most accredited massage therapy schools offer training in a variety of different massage techniques, such as Swedish or deep tissue massage. Working in a spa or health club, a massage therapist will typically provide 30-, 60-, or 90-minute massages to clients in a private room. During this massage, the therapist must act professionally, keeping the client appropriately draped with a sheet or towel as the treatment is done.

Working at a spa, hotel, or resort requires the therapist to be an employee who is typically paid by the hour or an annual salary. While the spa might charge upwards of $100 or more per treatment, the therapist actually only receives a small part of that. The benefit to working for a spa, resort, or hotel is that all appointments are lined up on the therapists' behalf, and all supplies and treatment rooms are provided. The work schedule is dictated by the employer.

Massage therapists who choose to be self-employed must solicit their own clients, purchase their own equipment (such as a massage table, oils, towels, sheets, etc.), and either have a place in their homes or another locations to perform massages, or be willing to make outcalls and travel with their equipment to the client's homes or hotel rooms, for example. The biggest benefit to being self-employed is that a massage therapist can earn over $100 per hour, keep all revenues, and make his or her own hours. A self-employed massage therapist also has total control over whom he or she accepts as clients.

Whereas for the recipient of the massage, it's an extremely luxurious and relaxing experience, for the massage therapist, performing the massage is extremely physically and at times emotionally strenuous. Thus, being in good physical condition is important.

Here's My Story

Peter is a self-employed massage therapist living in Hollywood, California. He grew up on the east coast, but moved to California to enjoy the warm weather and the more laid-back lifestyle of the west coast. Peter invested six months of time to be trained as a certified and licensed massage therapist. He attended classes several nights per week while maintaining a day job in retail to pay his living expenses and tuition.

"I always knew I wanted to pursue a job where I could help people. I am a very caring and social person. Through massage, I have the ability to help people forget their troubles, relax, and be pampered. During many of my sessions, I engage in deep and meaningful conversations with my clients while the massage is taking place. People really open up to me, which is a rewarding experience onto itself. However, I always allow plenty of quiet time for the client to get lost in the relaxation they're experiencing," said Peter.

After graduating from massage school, Peter relocated to Hollywood and moved into a one-bedroom apartment with a living room and dining room area. He purchased a professional massage table and transformed the dining area into his treatment room. "Using lighting, soft classical or new age music, incense, and comfortable sheets, I've created a treatment room where my clients feel safe, warm and comfortable. This allows them to relax," said Peter.

"I decided to become a self-employed massage therapist because I wanted to have total control over my schedule and be selective in terms of my clientele. When doing research, I also heard stories about working for spas, health clubs, and hotels that didn't appeal to me in terms of the scheduling and how employees were treated. The significantly higher income from being self-employed also appealed to me. I charge $80 for a standard 60-minute massage, plus offer 90-minute massages for $100. This is usually accompanied by a $10 or $20 tip. In any given day, I won't schedule more than three or four appointments, because I want to be able to give each of my clients all of my attention and energy. Most of my clients work, so I tend to be busy in the late afternoon, nights, and on weekends. I don't accept appointments past 9:00 P.M., however," said Peter.

To find new clients, Peter runs classified ads in a variety of newspapers and locally published magazines. "I also post fliers at health clubs and on community bulletin boards, participate in online chat rooms, and rely heavily on word-of-mouth. I always offer special discounts to people who refer me to their friends. My goal is to generate as much repeat business as possible. I have a handful of clients who have a standing weekly appointment. It took some time to establish my client base, but after about six months, I began doing well," added Peter, who only accepts cash for his services.

"I have looked into accepting credit cards, but right now, I only accept cash. It's just easier. This has worked out fine for me. I really love my work and find it incredibly rewarding. I really enjoy meeting and getting to know new people. The best piece of advice I can offer to someone interested in entering this field is to make sure it's something you're comfortable doing. The job requires you to get extremely close with people in a totally non-sexual, but somewhat intimate way, both physically and emotionally. One thing I've made a point of doing is not pursuing friendships with my clients. Having that professional distance is important to me," said Peter.

For More Information

- American Massage Therapy Association. This is a professional trade association for certified and licensed massage therapists. The web site offers an abundance of resources and career-related information, www.amtamassage.org.
- Career Education Search. This web site offers an online directory of accredited massage therapy schools throughout the country, www.collegesurfing.com/ce/search/massage.
- hCareers.com. This web site offers online job listings in the hospitality field, which includes massage therapist positions at hotels and resorts, www.hospitalityjobs.hcareers.com/seeker.
- National Massage Therapy Institute. Information about training, licensing, and certification programs for massage therapists is offered. This is one of many accredited vocational schools throughout the country, www.studymassage.com.
- Salon Employment. This web site offers online job listings for massage therapists at salons and spas, www.massagetherapistemployment.com.
- TherapistJob.com. This web site offers online job listings for massage therapists and physical therapists, www.therapisthub.com/jobs/index.php.

Child Care Specialist

AT A GLANCE

SALARY POTENTIAL: Minimum wage to $20 per hour.

TRAINING/LICENSE/CERTIFICATION REQUIRED: Most states require child-care providers to obtain a license, which often means completing some type of

> training program. People in this job must pass a criminal background check and drug screening.
>
> OTHER REQUIREMENTS: Many employers look for applicants who have completed training in basic health and first aid. Creativity, patience, a nurturing personality, a willingness to teach, and administrative and organizational skills are important.
>
> CAREER ADVANCEMENT OPPORTUNITIES: There is a growing demand for child-care workers. Without additional training, career advancement opportunities are limited.

Child-care specialist is a broad title that encompasses many types of jobs relating to the care of infants, toddlers, and children under age five. Child-care services refer to working as a preschool teacher, teacher's assistant, a professional babysitter, or worker at a child-care facility.

This type of work can be extremely stressful because you're in charge of caring for and supervising multiple young children and ensuring their safety and well-being, while keeping them entertained. You must be constantly alert, able to deal with disruptive children, and understand that there's no such thing as a daily routine, since unexpected events happen constantly. Jobs are available from child-care centers, private households, nursery schools, preschools, and other organizations that offer child-care options to parents.

For More Information

- National Association for the Education of Young Children. This is a professional organization. The web site is an excellent source of information about careers in this field, www.naeyc.org.
- Center for the Childcare Workforce. This is a division of the American Federation of Teachers Education Foundation and is a professional organization that offers a wide range of resources for child-care workers, www .cce.org.
- National Child Care Information Center. This is a clearinghouse for information and resources pertaining to childcare, www.nccic.org.
- National Childcare Association. Information about training to become a Certified Childcare Professional is available from this web site, www.ncca net.org.

Concierge

> ### AT A GLANCE
>
> SALARY POTENTIAL: Varies. A salary or hourly wage, plus tips.
>
> TRAINING/LICENSE/CERTIFICATION REQUIRED: None, however, concierge training is available from colleges and vocational schools that offer programs in hospitality, tourism, and hotel management.
>
> OTHER REQUIREMENTS: The job requires top-notch customer service, multi-tasking and organizational skills, and the ability to access and act upon information quickly to answer questions and deal with requests from clients in a timely manner. Computer and telephone skills are also required.
>
> CAREER ADVANCEMENT OPPORTUNITIES: There are a growing number of opportunities in this field at a wide range of establishments that offer concierge services.

Upscale hotels, resorts, apartment buildings, shopping malls, airports, and even some large businesses offer their guests and clients a concierge service. A concierge is someone who is available to answer questions, provide recommendations, make reservations, acquire tickets for events or shows, handle errands, and perform a wide range of tasks on behalf of the client(s).

Going above and beyond when serving a client or hotel guest will often be rewarded with a tip. If you're working at an upscale hotel or resort, having extensive knowledge of local attractions, restaurants, public transportation, airports, and entertainment venues is critical. It is also necessary to provide referrals to local services, such as restaurants, local attractions, malls, internet access, massage therapists, beauty salons, churches, temples, hospitals (doctors, dentists, etc.), pharmacies, access to a fax and/or copy machine, overnight couriers, and other personal and business-related services. Providing driving directions and arranging for tours or transportation is also often part of a concierge's job, especially if you're working at a hotel or resort and catering to business travelers, vacationers, and tourists.

For More Information

- Concierge-In-A-Box. A comprehensive training guide for people interested in entering this field, (800) 863-5727, www.concierge-in-a-box.com.

- Triangle Concierge, Inc. This is a concierge training and consulting company offering career-related information, training programs, and other resources, www.traingleconcierge.com.

Consultant

AT A GLANCE

SALARY POTENTIAL: $25,000 to $100,000 (or more), based on your area of expertise and clientele.

TRAINING/LICENSE/CERTIFICATION REQUIRED: Varies, based on your area of expertise.

OTHER REQUIREMENTS: A consultant must be a problem solver who is detail-oriented, able to work well with people in a wide range of situations, and possesses knowledge and experience that's valuable to clients.

CAREER ADVANCEMENT OPPORTUNITIES: People who work as consultants typically have a specific area of expertise and are hired by the hour or by the job to help solve a particular problem a client is having. Some consultants are semi-retired experts in their fields, others work as consultants in between full-time jobs, and some specialists work as consultants in hopes of landing full-time employment with one of their clients.

Most consultants are self-employed and are considered freelancers. They're hired to work with individuals or companies to help solve specific programs, based on their areas of expertise. A computer consultant, for example, might be paid $50 to $200 per hour to assist a client in upgrading computers or maintaining a network. A marketing consultant might be hired by a company to help launch a new product. Consultants work in virtually every profession and industry and are hired by individuals and companies with varying needs.

As a consultant, it's important to keep up-to-date on the latest technology, information, or trends in your industry or area of expertise. If you're self-employed, part of your job will be soliciting new clients and managing your own consulting business, while your paychecks will come from the actual consultant jobs you work on. Your knowledge, experience, area of expertise, personality, and reputation will all play important roles when it comes to getting hired by clients.

Some consultants work for consulting firms, which are companies that help match consultants with clients (for a fee). This eliminates the need for a consultant to handle a lot of the administrative work associated with consulting, such as finding new clients and billing, for example.

For More Information

- eWork Markets. An online resource for helping consultants find new clients, www.eworkmarkets.com.
- SoloGig. An online source for job listings and opportunities for consultants and freelancers who work in a wide range of industries, including the IT field and general business, www.sologig.com/soloist/consulting_jobs.
- eLance. A fee-based online source of jobs for consultants who work in a wide range of fields relating to management, finance, sales, marketing, architecture, engineering, graphic design, art, legal, software and technology, training and development, web site development, writing, translation, or multimedia, www.eLance.com.

Correctional Officer

AT A GLANCE

SALARY POTENTIAL: Varies. $35,000 to $60,000 per year.

TRAINING/LICENSE/CERTIFICATION REQUIRED: Entry-level jobs require no training or certification. Career advancement opportunities are available to people who complete advanced training. Federal correctional officers, for example, must undergo at least 200 hours of formal training within their first year of employment, plus 120 hours of specialized training from the U.S. Federal Bureau of Prisons.

OTHER REQUIREMENTS: Job requirements vary by state. The American Correctional Association and the American Jail Association can provide specific employment guidelines.

CAREER ADVANCEMENT OPPORTUNITIES: With additional training and on-the-job experience, career advancement opportunities are available within the prison system.

A correctional officer or detention officer oversees people who have been arrested, convicted of a crime, or have been sentenced to serve time in jail or prison. The officer's job is to maintain order among inmates and prevent escapes. There are more than 3,300 jails, state prisons, and federal prisons in the United States that employ correctional officers. Most police and sheriff's departments across the country also hire correctional officers, as does the U.S. Immigration and Naturalization Service.

This type of job can be both stressful and hazardous. It requires a standard 40-hour work week (eight hours per day, five days per week), often with rotating shifts.

For More Information

- American Correctional Association. This is a professional trade organization with career-related information and job listings available, www.aca.org.
- American Jail Association. This is a professional trade organization with information about training and career-related information, as well as job listings, www.corrections.com/aja/index.shtml.
- Federal Bureau of Prisons. Career related information for correctional officers if offered at www.bop.gov.
- Office of Personnel Management. Job listings for correctional officers can be found at www.usajobs.opm.gov.

Court Clerk

AT A GLANCE

SALARY POTENTIAL: $10 to $20 per hour.

TRAINING/LICENSE/CERTIFICATION REQUIRED: High school diploma or GED. Community college or technical schools offer criminal justice degrees and courses in court operations and other areas that employers look for among applicants.

OTHER REQUIREMENTS: Court clerks must be detail-oriented, professional, and have excellent interpersonal skills. Basic office skills, including typing, filing, note taking, word processing, and telephone work are required.

> CAREER ADVANCEMENT OPPORTUNITIES: With additional training, career advancement options include promotions to court deputy or court administrator. Supervisory positions are also available to people with experience and the right skill sets.

The court clerk job involves preparing and scheduling a court's calendar of cases. It also involves communicating with plaintiffs, defendants, witnesses, and attorneys related to each case and maintaining a wide range of court-related documents, forms, files, and records. Outside of the courtroom, court clerks also file public records, such as mortgages and marriage licenses. The job involves handling repetitive and clerical tasks, and requires many office management and clerical duties, such as word processing, filing, and organizing.

For More Information

- Career Planer. Information about court clerk careers and job listings are offered on this web site, www.careerplanner.com/DOT-Job-Descriptions/COURT-CLERK.cfm.
- Criminal Justice Degree Programs. A listing of schools offering criminal justice degree programs can be found at www.education-online-search.com/legal_training/criminal_justice_degree/criminal_justice_degree.shtm.

Court Reporter

AT A GLANCE

SALARY POTENTIAL: $30,000 to $70,000 per year, based on the geographic location, level of certification possessed, the type of reporting job, and experience.

TRAINING/LICENSE/CERTIFICATION REQUIRED: Two to four years of post-secondary school training is typically required. Certification programs, requiring a one year or longer education commitment are available. In some states, a court reporter must also be a notary public.

OTHER REQUIREMENTS: Court reporters must be excellent listeners, skilled stenographers, detail oriented, deadline oriented, patient, and highly organized.

> CAREER ADVANCEMENT OPPORTUNITIES: Career advancement opportunities are available with the court system as well as the private sector.

The job of a court reporter is to document, word-for-word, everything that's said in a courtroom or during a deposition, and to create a complete and accurate transcript of court proceedings. Two different techniques—stenotyping and voice writing—are used to accomplish this objective. Court reporters work in court rooms, as well as for law offices and government agencies. The job involves sitting for extended periods and completing detailed and repetitive tasks.

For More Information

- National Court Reporters Association. This is a professional trade organization offering information about career opportunities and resources, www.ncraonline.org.
- National Verbatim Reporters Association. This is a professional trade organization offering information about career opportunities and resources, www.nvra.org.
- United States Court Reporters Association. This is a professional trade organization offering information about career opportunities and resources www.uscra.org.

Customer Service Specialist

> AT A GLANCE
>
> SALARY POTENTIAL: Minimum wage and up.
>
> TRAINING/LICENSE/CERTIFICATION REQUIRED: None.
>
> OTHER REQUIREMENTS: Excellent interpersonal, telephone, and problem-solving skills are necessary. Good listening skills, patience, and basic computer literacy are also important.
>
> CAREER ADVANCEMENT OPPORTUNITIES: Varies, depending on employer and industry. This is generally an entry-level position that can lead to career advancement opportunities within a company or industry.

All kinds of companies, in a wide range of industries, hire customer service representatives to communicate directly with their customers and clients. These people are responsible for taking orders, answering questions, dealing with problems, handling complaints, and ensuring that the customer's overall experience is as pleasant as possible. For the customer service representative, this might mean dealing with customers and clients in person, on the telephone, online, or via written correspondence.

Working conditions and hours vary greatly, based on the type of employer you're working for. You may find yourself working in a massive call center, for example, or sitting behind a desk in a retail store or showroom environment. In the United States, over two million people are employed as customer service representatives, creating plenty of jobs in this field.

Depending on who your employer is, in order to offer clients or customers the best support possible, it is necessary to become extremely familiar with the products and services you're supporting, plus develop a strong understanding of the average customer's wants and needs. As the job title suggests, this is definitely a service-oriented job where most of your time will be spent interacting with strangers. The job can be extremely repetitive and requires patience.

Because many companies offer extended hours for customer service availability, as a customer service representative, you may be required to work a 40-plus hour week, which might include evenings and weekends. Some call centers, for example, are open 24 hours per day, requiring customer services representatives to staff the phone lines constantly.

For More Information
- Contact companies in the industry you're interested in working.
- Online job listings, refer to any of the general interest career-related web sites, such as Monster (www.monster.com) or Yahoo! HotJobs (http://hot jobs.yahoo.com).

Day Spa Attendant

AT A GLANCE

SALARY POTENTIAL: Minimum wage and up. Some spas offer commissions to day spa attendants for selling treatments and related products. This dramatically increases earning potential.

TRAINING/LICENSE/CERTIFICATION REQUIRED: None.

OTHER REQUIREMENTS: Excellent people and organizational skills are an absolute must. This is a customer service-oriented business where clients expect to be pampered. You'll need a good understanding of the various treatments offered where you work, plus be able to recommend appropriate treatments and products to clients. Scheduling appointments is another key responsibility of a spa attendant.

CAREER ADVANCEMENT OPPORTUNITIES: With on-the-job experience and additional training, higher paying managerial and supervisory skills are available. You could also train to become a massage therapist or another type of certified professional capable of actually providing various spa treatments.

Day spas offer a wide range of body treatments, massages, manicures, pedicures, and other services designed to pamper clients. The job of a spa attendant is to greet clients, schedule appointments, sell skin, hair, and nail care products, assist with inventory management, and ensure the client's overall spa experience is enjoyable. The job often requires catering to a client's needs, recommending treatments, and coordinating therapists.

Day spas can be found in resorts, hotels, cruise ships, and as stand-alone business establishments. The easiest way to break into this business is to take an entry-level spa attendant position at a lower-end facility and work your way toward landing a job at an upscale or world-class spa, such as at a five-star resort where the pay is often higher and the work conditions are better. This job can involves working as a receptionist, salesperson, and/or incorporating other responsibilities related to the operation of the spa and the care of the clients.

For More Information
- BestSpaJobs.com. Online job listings and career-related information is provided at www.bestspajobs.com/jobs/jobbank.cfm.
- hCareers.com. Online job listings for spa-related jobs are offered, www.hospitalityjobs.hcareers.com/seeker.
- Salon & Spa Jobs. Career information and online job listings are offered at www.salonandspajobs.com.

Dog Groomer

AT A GLANCE

SALARY POTENTIAL: Varies.

TRAINING/LICENSE/CERTIFICATION REQUIRED: Specialized training and certification is required by most employers.

OTHER REQUIREMENTS: A love for animals and the ability to interact professionally with their owners is important. Creativity and personal style is also needed to incorporate the appropriate grooming procedures to various breeds of dogs and cats.

CAREER ADVANCEMENT OPPORTUNITIES: Dog groomers can be self-employed or work for an independent dog grooming business, veterinary office, or pet superstore (such as PetCo or PetSmart). There are also career opportunities as a groomer preparing dogs for dog shows.

The pet industry in the United States has become a $32 billion business, with 64.2 million households owning at least one pet. There are 68 million pet dogs in America, providing a large opportunity for professional groomers. Catering to these dogs are over 28,000 pet grooming businesses, plus countless self-employed groomers. This is a fast-growing industry with plenty of growth potential, especially for groomers with a flare for business and entrepreneurship.

Training to become a professional groomer can be done at a vocational school, through a distance learning program, or self-taught using DVDs and other self-paced training materials. Many dog grooming companies offer on-the-job training. It's possible to obtain entry-level work as a dog groomer, which can be more financially lucrative than working as a dog walker or pet sitter.

For More Information

- National Dog Groomers Association of America. This is a professional trade association comprised of dog groomers and related professionals. Information about certification programs, career information, and related resources is available at www.nationaldoggroomers.com.
- PetEdge. One of the country's largest pet supply wholesalers which offers a vast selection of grooming tools and products, (800) 738-3343, www.petedge.com.

- PetGroomer.com. This is an excellent resource for information about the dog grooming profession and the many training programs available, www.petgroomer.com.

CAREER SPOTLIGHT

Dog Trainer

> **AT A GLANCE**
>
> SALARY POTENTIAL: $20,000 to $35,000 per year or $20 to $100 per hour.
>
> TRAINING/LICENSE/CERTIFICATION REQUIRED: Certification from an accredited dog training school is required to work as a professional dog trainer. Tuition is typically under $5,000.
>
> OTHER REQUIREMENTS: In addition to being good working with untrained dogs, the job involves interacting with pet owners from all walks of life, plus being able to teach both the dog and its owner in a group or one-on-one situation.
>
> CAREER ADVANCEMENT OPPORTUNITIES: Limited.

When someone adopts a new dog and wants to teach it basic behaviors, they'll often hire a professional dog trainer for one-on-one instruction or participate in an organized training class held at a local pet superstore (like PetCo or PetSmart) or dog training school. Working as a dog trainer requires patience, a lot of physical exertion, excellent verbal communication skills, and the ability to teach others. The basic skills needed to teach dog training can be obtained by participating in an accredited course, which can take anywhere from several weeks to several months.

According to the Certification Council for Pet Dog Trainers, "A trainer who has received the Certified Pet Dog Trainer credential has met eligibility requirements and has successfully demonstrated his or her knowledge by passing the certification exam. To meet eligibility requirements, candidate trainers must have: at least 300 hours experience in dog training within the last five years; a high school diploma or equivalent; and one reference each from a veterinarian, a client, and a professional colleague. The certification testing covers knowledge of dog behavior and application of training techniques. The exam's five content areas include: Learning Theory, Instruction skills, Husbandry, Ethnology, and Equipment. Certified Pet Dog Trainers maintain their credential through continuing education such as workshops, conferences, and hands-on seminars for professional dog trainers. This continuing education requirement ensures that Certified Pet Dog Trainers are knowledgeable about the most current research, techniques, and thinking in the field."

Here's My Story

Erica is a certified dog trainer. Upon graduating from school, she held a full-time job working for one of the country's leading financial institutions and was extremely successful. When she settled down and got married, however, she decided to leave the fast-paced and hectic lifestyle of working in a corporate job. Instead, she decided to pursue her passion, which is working with animals. Thus, she decided to become a professional dog trainer.

After researching the best school to attend, she invested the time and money needed to become a certified dog trainer, then sought out a job working at a local dog training school located near her home.

"I have always loved animals and wanted to work with them. When I graduated from school, however, I needed to support myself and was forced to pursue a job that would pay enough money for me to do that. When I got married, as a couple, we had the financial stability for me to work on a part-time basis. So, instead of continuing in a job I didn't enjoy, I decided to try something entirely new," explained Erica.

"Working as a dog trainer for a small school, I am responsible for teaching about six to ten group classes per week. I am also available for private lessons through the school, which is something I do for an additional ten hours or so per week. Because I work for a small school, I am also responsible for helping with the school's day-to-day operations, so in addition to actually training dogs, I help run the small business," said Erica.

"If you're working as a dog trainer for the money, your best bet is to be self-employed and offer private, one-on-one training. You can build up clients through word-of-mouth and referrals from local pet shops, pet boarding houses, groomers and veterinarians. If you can afford to work for less money, becoming a dog trainer at a privately owned dog training school or at a pet superstore offers less responsibility," added Erica.

"The most rewarding part of this job is working with puppies over several weeks and watching them become eager to master new skills and overcome bad habits. As much as this job involves working with dogs, being able to interact well with the pet owners is just as important," she added.

For More Information

- Animal Behavior College. This is one of several companies that offer self-paced, distance learning programs for dog trainers, http://animalbehavior college.com/index.asp.
- Certification Council for Pet Dog Trainers. This is a professional trade association for dog trainers. The web site offers career-related information, plus details on the various ways to obtain the required certification to pursue this type of work, www.ccpdt.org.
- Dog-O-Mania. Online job listings for dog trainers, groomers, and others who work with pets can be found here, www.dogomania.com/ads/Jobs.shtml.
- PetCo. Learn about employment opportunities for certified dog trainers at the PetCo stores throughout the country, www.petco.com/Content/Content.aspx?PC=instructorswanted.
- PetSmart. Visit this web site and click on the "Careers" icon to learn about job opportunities for dog trainers at this chain of pet superstores, www.pet smart.com.
- Certified dog trainers are also employed by local dog training schools throughout the country. Check your local Yellow Pages for listings.

Dog Walker/Pet Sitter

> **AT A GLANCE**
>
> SALARY POTENTIAL: $15 to $50+ per hour.
>
> TRAINING/LICENSE/CERTIFICATION REQUIRED: None, however, it's wise to become bonded and insured if you'll be self-employed. This is an entry-level job.
>
> OTHER REQUIREMENTS: A love for dogs and a lot of stamina is important, as is the ability to interact professionally with the dog owners who hire you.

Being able to juggle a schedule with many daily appointments and keep track of the specific needs of each dog is also important.

CAREER ADVANCEMENT OPPORTUNITIES: With additional training, there are a wide range of jobs in the animal/pet care field, such as becoming a dog groomer, dog trainer, or veterinary assistant.

Out of the millions of dog owners in the United States, most work full time and are forced to leave their beloved dogs home alone. The job of a dog walker is to visit the pet owner's home, take the dog for a walk or run, feed the dog, and provide human interaction when the owner is away. Most professional dog walkers are self-employed, relying on word-of-mouth and local advertising to generate clients.

Dog walkers can charge for a variety of services, ranging from one-on-one playtime to feeding and even transportation to and from a grooming appointment. The fees charged by a dog walker vary by region, however, a fee of $15 to $20 for a 15- to 30-minute walk is average. Some dog owners opt to walk multiple dogs simultaneously, which can dramatically increase earning potential.

For a self-employed dog walker or pet sitter, it's advisable to become fully bonded and insured. Becoming familiar with basic pet first aid and training techniques, plus knowing the local veterinarians in case of an emergency, is also helpful.

Pet sitting, like babysitting, involves caring for pets for extended periods of time, up to several days, either in your own home or in the client's home. In addition to walking the dog, feeding, basic grooming, playing with and giving the appropriate medications to the dog may also be required.

For More Information

- Common Dog. This franchise business opportunity offers a complete, turnkey solution for starting your own homebased dog walking and dog sitting business, http://commondog.com/opp.php.
- Fetch Pet Care. This franchise business opportunity offers a complete, turnkey solution for starting your own, homebased dog walking and dog sitting business, (866) 338-2463, www.fetchpetcare.com.
- Home Business Forms. This web site offers a handful of written contracts and agreements used by self-employed dog walkers, pet sitters, and pet taxi services, www.businessformsstore.com.

- Pet Sitter's Network. An online resource for pet sitters and dog walkers, www.petsittersnetwork.com.

Doorman

> **AT A GLANCE**
>
> SALARY POTENTIAL: Minimum wage and up.
>
> TRAINING/LICENSE/CERTIFICATION REQUIRED: None.
>
> OTHER REQUIREMENTS: A friendly personality, attention to detail, and the ability to anticipate the needs of the people you work for.
>
> CAREER ADVANCEMENT OPPORTUNITIES: Career advancement opportunities are limited, but can include becoming a concierge.

Many upscale nightclubs, restaurants, hotels, and apartment buildings employ doormen. In addition to simply opening the door for people entering the building, a doorman might provide directions, hail taxicabs, sign for packages, or run basic errands. They might also be required to announce guests and/or check the identification of visitors and delivery people.

This is typically an entry-level position which could lead to a job as a concierge. In addition to the hourly wage, tips or holiday bonuses may comprise a significant percentage of your overall income, depending on where you work.

For More Information
- For doorman job at a hotel or resort, contact that establishment's human resources department. For a doorman job at an apartment building, for example, contact the property manager for the building you're interested in working at.
- Online job listings, refer to any of the general interest career-related web sites, such as Monster (www.monster.com) or Yahoo! HotJobs (http://hot jobs.yahoo.com).

Drycleaner

> ### AT A GLANCE
>
> SALARY POTENTIAL: Minimum wage to $12 per hour.
>
> TRAINING/LICENSE/CERTIFICATION REQUIRED: Training can be obtained at a vocational school, however, most people learn from on-the-job training. There are no minimum educational requirements for this type of work.
>
> OTHER REQUIREMENTS: The job involves a strong knowledge of fabrics and textiles, plus the ability to interact well with people. The job requires a significant amount of lifting, and standing and working in a hot and humid environment, often with chemicals.
>
> CAREER ADVANCEMENT OPPORTUNITIES: There is little career advancement opportunity in the drycleaning field, other than opening your own business or taking on managerial responsibilities.

There are several jobs within the drycleaning field, including people who do the drycleaning and laundering services, along with spotters (stain removers), pressers, and counter attendants. Many people who work in drycleaning are able to perform several or all of these job functions. Customers drop off their garments to be drycleaned, such as dresses, suits, tablecloths, curtains, blankets, and jackets. Drycleaners must be knowledgeable on how to care for these garments, without accidentally ruining them by exposing them to the wrong cleaning chemicals.

In addition to retail dry cleaning establishments where people drop off their clothing, many resorts, hotels, cruise ships, hospitals, and other institutions have dry cleaning facilities.

For More Information
- Institute of Industrial Launderers. This is a professional trade association catering to people working in the drycleaning field, (202) 296-6744.
- International Fabric Care Institute. This is a professional trade association catering to people working in the drycleaning field, (301) 622-1900.
- Online job listings, refer to any of the general interest career-related web sites, such as Monster (www.monster.com) or Yahoo! HotJobs (http://hotjobs.yahoo.com).

Emergency Medical Technician (EMT)/Paramedic

> ### AT A GLANCE
>
> SALARY POTENTIAL: The level of training and certification you have helps dictate your earning potential as an EMT or paramedic. Salaries vary dramatically by job and region. Expect to earn anywhere from $20,000 to $45,000 per year.
>
> TRAINING/LICENSE/CERTIFICATION REQUIRED: Formal training is required, but requirements vary by state. All states have a certification procedure that must be re-completed every two years.
>
> OTHER REQUIREMENTS: Compassion, the ability to work well under pressure, and the ability to deal with other people's stress, pain, injuries, and fear is critical.
>
> CAREER ADVANCEMENT OPPORTUNITIES: By obtaining higher levels of certification, EMTs can pursue higher paying and more demanding jobs. EMT-1 certification is required for entry-level work, while EMT-4 certification allows the EMT to carry out the most extensive pre-hospital care at the emergency scene or within an ambulance.

First, this job involves saving lives and helping others cope with medically-related emergencies. Job stress is common, but the rewards are plentiful. In some regions, EMTs work on a volunteer basis, while in many situations, this is a paid position working for and with a local police department, fire department, rescue squad, and/or ambulance service. Private ambulance services also hire EMTs.

The job of the EMT is to arrive at the scene of an emergency (often after being dispatched by a 9-1-1 operator) and quickly determining the nature and the extent of the patient's condition. Following strict rules, the EMT must then provide the appropriate medical treatments and help transport the patient to a medical facility, such as a hospital.

For More Information

- National Association of Emergency Medical Technicians. A professional trade organization offering career-related information and training opportunities, www.naemt.org.

- National Registry of Emergency Medical Technicians. A professional trade organization offering career-related information and training opportunities, www.nremt.org.
- Online job listings, refer to any of the general interest career-related web sites, such as Monster (www.monster.com) or Yahoo! HotJobs (http://hot jobs.yahoo.com).

Home Health Aide/Nursing Assistant

AT A GLANCE

SALARY POTENTIAL: Entry-level jobs typically start at minimum wage. Higher pay is offered to people with experience and training.

TRAINING/LICENSE/CERTIFICATION REQUIRED: A certification is required, which can be achieved in 6 to 12 months. Some companies will hire after the applicant completes as little as 75 hours of classroom and practical training.

OTHER REQUIREMENTS: People working in this field must be highly compassionate and have a flexible work schedule.

CAREER ADVANCEMENT OPPORTUNITIES: With additional training, there are a wide range of jobs in the medical field.

Home health aides and nursing assistants perform a wide range of tasks in the daily care of patients. This includes changing linens, feeding, grooming, dressing, and bathing of patients. Some home health aides choose to specialize in certain types of patients with special needs, such as the elderly, physically disabled, or mentally ill.

Employment is available in private homes (for individual patients), as well as within nursing homes and hospitals. This isn't necessarily a high-paying job, but it can be rewarding in many other ways. Most work done by home health aides is conducted under the supervision a registered nurse, doctor, or some type of licensed therapist.

For More Information
- Edu411. Information about schools offering certification programs and training can be found here. Most offer job placement assistance to graduates, www.edu411.org/Healthcare/healthcare_aide.php.

- National Association for Home Care. A professional trade association for home health care workers. Career-related information and additional resources are provided, www.nahc.org.
- Visiting Angels. This company is a placement service for home health care workers, www.visitingangels.com/employment_opp.htm.

Home Inspector

> **AT A GLANCE**
>
> **SALARY POTENTIAL:** Varies. A home inspector is typically paid a flat fee per job.
>
> **TRAINING/LICENSE/CERTIFICATION REQUIRED:** Training and certification is required. The required training can be done through a post-secondary school or by completing a home study program. A high school diploma or GED is required, in addition to the certification and a state-issued license.
>
> **OTHER REQUIREMENTS:** Home inspectors need to be detail-oriented, able to complete jobs in a timely manner, and able to work well with a wide range of clients.
>
> **CAREER ADVANCEMENT OPPORTUNITIES:** With additional training, home inspectors can train to become construction and building inspectors.

A home inspector is someone who inspects homes, townhouses, and condominiums, from basement to roof. This means examining a property's foundation, framing, interior finish, wiring, plumbing, heating, air conditioning, and electricity on behalf of home buyers, lenders, or contractors. Many home inspectors are self-employed and make their own hours.

For More Information

- Allied Home Inspection. Information about a home study training program can be found here, (800) 617-3513, www.homeinspectioncourse.com/Quick-Form.asp.
- American Society of Home Inspectors. This is a professional trade association offering career-related information, www.ashi.org.
- Center for Real Estate Education & Research. Information is provided at this web site about certification and training programs in the real estate field, www.recp.org.

- National Association of Home Inspectors. This is a professional trade association offering career-related information, www.nahi.org.
- Professional Career Development Institute (PCDI). Learn about one of many available home study training programs from this web site, www.pcdi courses.com.

Hotel Worker

> **AT A GLANCE**
>
> SALARY POTENTIAL: Minimum wage and up, depending on the position and employer.
>
> TRAINING/LICENSE/CERTIFICATION REQUIRED: None, for most entry-level hotel-related jobs. On-the-job training is typically provided.
>
> OTHER REQUIREMENTS: Hotels utilize a wide range of entry-level workers to handle many different jobs. Thus, the skills required will vary greatly based on the position.
>
> CAREER ADVANCEMENT OPPORTUNITIES: With additional training and experience, a wide range of career advancement opportunities are available within the hotel and hospitality industries. If you're interested in hotel management, consider pursuing a two-year degree from a community college or junior college.

Hotels and resorts hire people to fill a wide range of entry-level jobs, ranging from housekeeping to jobs in the food and beverage areas. When working in the hospitality industry, catering to the needs of guests and making them comfortable is typically the top priority. The majority of entry-level jobs within a hotel, resort, casino, boarding house, or bed and breakfast are service oriented and require a high degree of manual or physical labor.

For More Information
- hCareers.com. This web site offers online job listings for hotel, resort and hospitality jobs, www.hospitalityjobs.hcareers.com/seeker.
- International Council on Hotel, Restaurant and Institutional Education. Career-related information pertaining to the hospitality field is offered at www.chrie.org.

- International Executive Housekeepers Association. This is a professional trade association for people working in the hospitality field as housekeepers, www.ieha.org.

Income Tax Return Preparer

> ### AT A GLANCE
>
> SALARY POTENTIAL: $25,000 to $40,000.
>
> TRAINING/LICENSE/CERTIFICATION REQUIRED: Participating in vocational education program in accounting and computing will prepare you for a job in this field. It's also possible to acquire the necessary knowledge by participating in educational programs offered by large tax preparation firms (such as H&R Block).
>
> OTHER REQUIREMENTS: Top-notch organization and skills, attention to detail, basic math skills, and the ability to work well with people are all important for this type of job. Bookkeeping skills and proficiency using a computer are also helpful.
>
> CAREER ADVANCEMENT OPPORTUNITIES: Tax preparers can be self-employed or work for a large tax preparation firm, accounting firm, or a wide range of other employers. With additional training, career advancement opportunities include becoming a Certified Financial Planner, bookkeeper, accountant, or Certified Public Accountant.

The job of a tax preparer is to prepare income tax return forms for individuals and small businesses. This can be done manually or by using a personal computer equipped with an appropriate off-the-shelf tax software package. Responsibilities include: reviewing financial records (including prior tax return forms, income statements, and documentation of expenditures), interviewing clients to obtain additional information about taxable income, deductible expenses and allowances, computing taxes owed, and completing the appropriate tax forms.

A tax preparer is *not* a CPA or accountant, but is trained specifically to understand and complete income tax forms by following the necessary procedures and guidelines. For some tax preparers, this is seasonal work (January through mid-April), however, jobs are available on a year-round basis.

For More Information

- American Institute of Certified Public Accountants. This is a professional trade association for people who work in the accounting field, (212) 596-6200, www.aicpa.org.
- H&R Block. Information is offered at this web site about the company's tax training course, which is available in a traditional classroom environment or online. The online program requires a minimum of a 63-hour commitment to complete, www.hrblock.com/taxes/planning/tax_courses/index.html.
- Internal Revenue Service (IRS) Employment Program. This site provides information about careers as a tax preparer and offers an abundance of resources, www.irs.ustres.gov.
- National Society of Public Accountants. This web site is operated by a professional trade association for people who work in the accounting field, www.nsacct.org.

Language Translator/Interpreter

AT A GLANCE

SALARY POTENTIAL: $40,000 to $100,000 (or more) per year.

TRAINING/LICENSE/CERTIFICATION REQUIRED: Being fluent in two or more languages is a must. Certification is available in some cases through the American Translators Association and/or the U.S. Department of State, however, this is not a requirement for many jobs. To become a sign language interpreter, certification is required through the National Association of the Deaf or the Registry of Interpreters for the Deaf.

OTHER REQUIREMENTS: Listening, organizational, and conversational skills are necessary. Translators and interpreters also need to be outgoing, detail-oriented, patient, and able to communicate well in writing and verbally.

CAREER ADVANCEMENT OPPORTUNITIES: There are many career advancement opportunities for experienced translators interested in working in the corporate sector, U.S. government, the United Nations, courts, the U.S. military, publishing industry, or in the educational field.

For someone who is fluent in two or more languages, there is a wide range of career opportunities available as a translator or interpreter. For someone able to communicate using sign language, interpreter jobs for the deaf are also available. Translator and interpreter jobs enable cross-cultural communication, which is extremely important in today's global economy. In addition to being able to simply translate words, the job of an interpreter or translator is to communicate ideas and sometimes complex concepts, often taking into account specific cultural differences or similarities.

Technically, being an interpreter and translator are different, but related professions, although many people have the skills necessary for both jobs. Interpreters translate one language into another when it's being spoken (often in real time). Translators, however, convert written materials from one language into another.

There is no nationally recognized certification or educational path to follow to pursue this type of career. Various employers have different qualifications, although a high school diploma or GED is almost always required. Several associations offer certification programs which will make it easier to land certain types of jobs in this field.

Within the United States, the most commonly needed translators and interpreters are between English and Portuguese, French, Italian, German, Spanish, Chinese, Japanese, and Korean. There's also a demand for sign language translators for the deaf community.

Salaries for these jobs vary greatly, depending on the industry you're working in, your experience level, and the type of translation or interpreting you'll be doing. In many cases, this type of career involves travel.

For More Information

- American Literary Translators Association. This is a professional trade organization for translators working in the publishing field, www.literary translators.org.
- American Translators Association. This is a professional trade organization offering career-related information, www.atanet.org.
- Translators and Interpreters Guild. This is a professional trade organization offering career-related information, www.ttig.org.
- U.S. Department of State, Office of Language Services. Information about government-related jobs as a translator or interpreter can be found at www .state.gov.
- United Nations. This web site offers a wide range of information about this international organization, www.un.org. For job listings available within

the UN, point your web browser to: https://jobs.un.org/Galaxy/Release3/vacancy/vacancy.aspx.

- Online job listings for translators and interpreters can be found at www.translatorsbase.com, www.multilingual.com, eLance.com, www.translationdirectory.com and http://groups.yahoo.com/group/ translation-jobs.

Marketing Specialist

> ### AT A GLANCE
>
> SALARY POTENTIAL: $30,000 to $50,000 (or more) depending on the industry and employer.
>
> TRAINING/LICENSE/CERTIFICATION REQUIRED: No formal certification or license is required. A two- or four-year degree in marketing is often sought by employers, but not always required. This type of degree can be obtained through a distance learning program or from a traditional college or university.
>
> OTHER REQUIREMENTS: Marketing specialists must have superior communication and interpersonal skills, be creative, detail-oriented, and able to work in a team-oriented environment.
>
> CAREER ADVANCEMENT OPPORTUNITIES: A wide range of career opportunities is available with companies in all industries, as well as within specialized marketing and/or public relations firms and advertising agencies. Some experienced marketing specialists work as self-employed consultants.

When a company has a product or service to sell or needs to boost awareness about its existence, this responsibility often falls to the marketing, advertising, promotions, and public relations departments (which at some companies are the same). When a company doesn't have the in-house resources to fulfill the demands of these jobs, they often hire a marketing, advertising, and/or public relations firm, which is staffed by experienced professionals in the marketing, advertising and public relations fields.

Marketing people work closely with a company's top-level executives, as well as its research and development and sales team (as appropriate) to develop, implement, and manage the company's overall marketing campaigns. The job involves a strong understanding of the company, its products and/or services, the industry and the competition, and an ability to effectively reach the company's target audience with a powerful marketing message.

Marketing, advertising, promotions, and public relations jobs are similar in scope and are inter related, yet each has its own skills and primary objectives. For example, the advertising department might handle the company's paid advertising, whereas the public relations department works with the media to generate positive publicity for the company in the press. Meanwhile, the marketing department might work with retailers to develop innovative ways to communicate directly or indirectly with the company's target customers.

For More Information

- American Association of Advertising Agencies. This is a professional trade association for people involved in the advertising industry, www.aaaa.org.
- Careers In Marketing. This is an online resource offering information, recommended books, and links for people interested in the marketing field, www.careers-in-marketing.com.
- KnowThis. This is an online resource for anyone interested in the marketing field, www.knowthis.com/careers/careersmkt.htm.
- Public Relations Society of America. This is a professional trade association for people involved in the public relations field, www.prsa.org.

Proofreader

AT A GLANCE

SALARY POTENTIAL: Varies.

TRAINING/LICENSE/CERTIFICATION REQUIRED: None, although training as a journalist is helpful.

OTHER REQUIREMENTS: A strong knowledge of written language, grammar, punctuation, and an extensive vocabulary are needed.

CAREER ADVANCEMENT OPPORTUNITIES: Proofreading work can lead to becoming an editor, writer, or other jobs in the publishing field.

A proofreader is someone who takes a document, such as a book, manuscript, or article and edits it to correct spelling errors, grammar, and punctuation mistakes. Once a manuscript is typeset, the proofreader will review the pages for typos and other mistakes. The job involves extensive reading and sometimes requires working under a tight deadline. Book publishers, newspapers, magazines, and a wide range of other companies involved in publishing (including website development) utilize proofreaders.

The work of a proofreader can often be done from home and does not always require working from a traditional office. The work schedule is typically flexible and can be done on a part-time or full-time basis, depending on the employer. Some proofreaders work on a consulting basis and are self-employed.

With experience and perhaps additional training, career advancement opportunities include becoming some type of editor, such as a copyeditor or line editor.

For More Information

- eLance. Online job listings for freelance proofreaders are offered at this web site, www.elance.com.
- Grammatika. Online job listings for freelance proofreaders are offered at this web site, http://grammatika.com/freelance.htm.
- LearnProofreading.com. Information about a two-day course on how to become a professional proofreader is offered here, (212) 369-8945, www.learnproofreading.com.
- ProofreadingJobs.org. Online job listings and other resources for proofreaders are offered at this web site, www.proofreadingjobs.org.
- Online job listings, refer to any of the general interest career-related web sites, such as Monster (www.monster.com) or Yahoo! HotJobs (http://hotjobs.yahoo.com).

Property Manager

> ### AT A GLANCE
>
> SALARY POTENTIAL: $15,000 to $60,000 per year. One benefit is that landlords or property owners sometimes offers free or greatly reduced rent to their property managers.

> TRAINING/LICENSE/CERTIFICATION REQUIRED: None. On-the-job training is often provided.
>
> OTHER REQUIREMENTS: The ability to perform basic home/apartment/condo maintenance and repairs is necessary.
>
> CAREER ADVANCEMENT OPPORTUNITIES: Limited.

A property manager works on behalf of a property owner/landlord to maintain a house, apartment building, or condo complex. The work involves performing basic repairs and maintenance, dealing with tenants, collecting rent, and coordinating services (such as landscapers and major repairs). The property manager often lives on the property he or she manages and is available to tenants on an ongoing basis, especially to handle emergencies. It's also often the property manager's job to show empty apartments to prospective tenants (and/or work with real estate brokers).

Property managers also work as liaisons between the property owners and their tenants, handling disputes between neighboring tenants and ensuring the well-being of the property as a whole. In addition to being handy with tools, good interpersonal skills are beneficial for this type of work.

For More Information
- ApartmentCareers.com. Online job listings for property managers can be found at www.apartmentcareers.com.
- Institute of Real Estate Management. This is a professional trade association for property managers. This agency offers accreditation to professionals working in the industry, (312) 329-6000, www.irem.org.
- JobSearchSite.com. Online job listings for property managers can be found at http://property.management.jobs.jobsearchsite.com.
- National Association or Realtors. This web site offers the "Field Guide to Property Management," an informative resource for people interested in this field, www.realtor.org/libweb.nsf/pages/fg412.

CAREER SPOTLIGHT

Public Relations Specialist (Account Executive)

> AT A GLANCE
>
> SALARY POTENTIAL: $20,000 to $150,000 per year.
>
> TRAINING/LICENSE/CERTIFICATION REQUIRED: None.
>
> OTHER REQUIREMENTS: A public relations specialist must have superior written and verbal communication skills, plus be detail and deadline oriented. This job requires extensive creativity and the ability to network and build strong working relationships, especially with members of the media.
>
> CAREER ADVANCEMENT OPPORTUNITIES: Public relations specialists can work for public relations firms, as independent consultants or inhouse, within the public relations/marketing department of a company. Public relations specialists work in all industries.

A publicist, public relations (PR) specialist, or public relations account executive is someone who specializes in creating, launching, and managing public relations campaigns on behalf of client(s) or employer(s). This involves promoting the company's message, generating positive publicity within the media, and perhaps hosting special events. PR people work closely with advertising and marketing people to help promote companies, products, services, business leaders, authors, celebrities, and professional athletes.

PR work typically involves writing and distributing press releases, coordinating publicity events, creating press kits, interacting with reporters, scheduling interviews for client(s), and developing innovative ways to promote their clients or employers to the general public and the media.

While there is no formal training or license requirements to work in the PR field, many PR specialists have some education in marketing, advertising, writing, or journalism. Much of the knowledge needed is learned through on-the-job training.

The best way to land a public relations job is to first participate in an organized internship program through your school. Many of the larger PR firms hire inexperienced, entry-level publicists and provide training. Most PR firms special-ize in working with clients in a specific industry. Medium- and large-sized com-panies in virtually all industries often have PR departments inhouse.

PR work is typically done from a traditional office, however, in some jobs, travel is required. Some freelance PR specialists who are self-employed work from their homes. The earning potential this type of work offers varies greatly. A senior account executive at a PR firm who has extensive experience and a large network of media contacts can earn several hundred dollars per hour, while an entry-level publicist might earn minimum wage or up to $15 per hour, depend-ing on the employer and the type of PR work. Even within the PR field, there are many specialties, such as press release writing, interview coordination, and event planning.

Though it's certainly possible to pursue work in the PR field without a college degree, many college graduates with a degree in marketing, advertising, journal-ism, writing, or business communication find it easier to land higher paying jobs in the public relations field upon graduation. This field offers a wide range of opportunities.

Here's My Story

Julie is a publicist working for a well-known PR firm in Chicago. The firm handles a wide range of clients, from celebrities and television production companies to household cleaning products and fast food restaurants. While still a junior in high school, Julie landed an unpaid internship program at a PR firm. This transformed into a summer job and ultimately a full-time position upon graduation.

During her internship, she learned all about the PR field and gathered valu-able real-world experience. Upon graduation, she was offered a full-time job from the firm she interned with. Participating in an internship program while still in high school is rare, but many PR firms hire entry-level employees who are high school or recent college graduates.

"Public relations work is a broad term that means different things to different companies. Some companies hire a PR firm to generate publicity in the media for a new product they're launching. Others hire a PR firm to boost general awareness about their company. The job in definitely all about being creative and finding innovative ways to promote a company, product, service, or individual to the gen-eral public, often utilizing the media," said Julie.

"This job definitely involves knowing how to communicate and get attention. Having good writing skills is essential, especially if you'll be writing press releases or other types of press materials on behalf of your clients. My best piece of advice is to choose an industry that really interests and excites you, then choose to work in PR for a company within that industry or for a PR firm with clients in that industry. Being excited about what you're promoting is really important for keeping yourself motivated and for being as creative as possible," said Julie. "Depending on the projects you're working on, working above and beyond a traditional 40-hour week is common."

For More Information

- CollegeGrad.com. This web site offers a detailed article about career opportunities in public relations and describes some of the best ways to break into this field, with or without a college education, www.collegegrad.com/entrylevel/entrylevelpublicrelationsjob.shtml.
- Entry Level Jobs. This web site offers online job listings for entry-level positions in a variety of fields, including public relations, www.entryleveljobs.com.
- Public Relations Society of America. This is a professional trade association for people working in the public relations field. The web site offers career-related information, job listings, and a variety of other useful resources, www.prsa.org.
- Variety. The official web site for *Daily Variety* magazine offers online job listings for public relations jobs in the entertainment industry, www.variety.com/index.asp?layout=variety_careers.
- Online job listings, refer to any of the general interest career-related web sites, such as Monster (www.monster.com) or Yahoo! HotJobs (http://hotjobs.yahoo.com).

Resort Worker (Hospitality Worker)

> **AT A GLANCE**
>
> **SALARY POTENTIAL:** Varies.
>
> **TRAINING/LICENSE/CERTIFICATION REQUIRED:** None, for most entry-level jobs within a resort.

> OTHER REQUIREMENTS: This will depend on the type of resort job you pursue. Most require an outgoing and friendly personality, plus a willingness to cater to guests' needs.
>
> CAREER ADVANCEMENT OPPORTUNITIES: From entry-level positions within a resort, a wide range of higher level jobs can be earned, such as becoming a supervisor, assistant manager, or manager.

Hotels, resorts, cruise ships, golf clubs, tennis clubs, theme parks, and country clubs hire a wide range of skilled and unskilled people to help cater to guests. These are referred to as hospitality jobs. Working at a resort can be a fun experience, however, it's important to understand that as a resort employee, you're expected to work, not be on vacation like the paying guests.

Resort jobs are available at tourist destinations throughout America and around the world. Some are seasonal, while others hire for year-round employment. In addition to general hospitality jobs, with additional training, it's possible to land higher paying and specialized jobs at resort properties. Lifeguards, tennis instructors, spa workers, scuba diving instructors, and a wide range of other skilled employees are always in demand.

While resort jobs typically don't offer high pay, many provide food and/or accommodations, plus offer a fun work environment and the ability to utilize the facilities when you're not on the job.

For More Information

- CoolWorks. Job listings for positions at ski resorts around the world are offered at www.coolworks.com/ski-resort-jobs.
- Disneyland. Discover hospitality jobs available working at Disneyland in Anaheim, California, http://disney.go.com/disneycareers/disneyland.
- HCareers. Online job listings for positions at resorts around the world can be found at www.hospitalityjobs.hcareers.com/seeker.
- IHireAccommodationandFood.com. Online job listings for positions at resorts around the world can be found here, www.ihireaccommodation andfood.com.
- ResortJobs.com. Online job listings for positions at resorts around the world can be found at www.resortjobs.com.
- TropicJobs.com. Hospitality jobs working for resorts in the Caribbean are listed at www.tropicjobs.com.

Security Guard

AT A GLANCE

SALARY POTENTIAL: $15,000 to $35,000 per year.

TRAINING/LICENSE/CERTIFICATION REQUIRED: Depending on the job, martial arts and/or firearms training may be required. Some security jobs are entry level, however. Some employers look for applicants with military training and/or former law enforcement experience. Many states require private security guards to have a license. To obtain a license, one must undergo a background check, pass a written exam, be a U.S. citizen, and be at least 18 years of age.

OTHER REQUIREMENTS: Knowledge of basic first aid is useful. Completion of a course in lethal weapons training (which takes at least 40 hours) is also beneficial and will help an applicant land a security guard job.

CAREER ADVANCEMENT OPPORTUNITIES: There is a wide range of jobs as a private security officer working for businesses, nightclubs, shopping malls, stores, banks, schools, and private security firms. With specialized training, private security officers can work as prison guards, airport security screeners, armored car drivers, or body guards.

A private security guard job typically involves guarding something or someone against unwanted intruders or danger. Unlike jobs as a prison guard, for example, the work of a private security officer typically involves sitting for extended periods of time, working alone for long hours, checking IDs, and monitoring video surveillance systems. Some private security officers carry weapons. Others, however, are armed with nothing more than a flashlight and a two-way radio or cell phone.

Many entry-level private security guard jobs offer on-the-job training and require no formal training or licenses. Higher-level security work typically involves carrying a firearm and completing advanced training. For these jobs, employers typically seek people with previous security experience, former military training, or previous law enforcement experience. It's important to understand that working as a private security guard is different from pursuing a career as a police or law enforcement officer.

Work as a private security guard can be done on a full-time or part-time basis. The job often involves working nights, weekends, or early mornings, plus having a flexible work schedule.

For More Information

- iHireSecurity. Online job listings for private security guard positions can be found at www.ihiresecurity.com.
- iSeek. Information about careers as private security guard is available at this web site, www.iseek.org/sv/13000.jsp?id=100190.
- Vocational Information Center. Information about careers as private security guards is available at www.khake.com/page28.html.
- Online job listings, refer to any of the general interest career-related web sites, such as Monster (www.monster.com) or Yahoo! HotJobs (http://hot jobs.yahoo.com).

Swimming Pool Cleaner

> **AT A GLANCE**
>
> **SALARY POTENTIAL:** Minimum wage to $15 per hour.
>
> **TRAINING/LICENSE/CERTIFICATION REQUIRED:** None. On-the-job training is typically provided.
>
> **OTHER REQUIREMENTS:** None.
>
> **CAREER ADVANCEMENT OPPORTUNITIES:** Limited.

A swimming pool cleaner is hired by private pool owners, health clubs, resorts, hotels, and schools to clean and maintain swimming pools, whirlpools, and hot tubs. This involves testing the water and equipment, insuring that the water and filtering system is clean, mixing and utilizing chemicals, and maintaining the pool so it's safe for people to swim in.

Most swimming pool cleaners work for pool cleaning companies, whereas some are self-employed. This is considered an entry-level position that involves a significant amount of physical labor. In many areas, this is seasonal work.

For More Information

- Online job listings, refer to any of the general interest career-related web sites, such as Monster (www.monster.com) or Yahoo! HotJobs (http://hot jobs.yahoo.com).

Teaching Assistant/Teacher's Aide

AT A GLANCE

SALARY POTENTIAL: $15,000 to $23,000 per year.

TRAINING/LICENSE/CERTIFICATION REQUIRED: Teacher's aide certification can be obtained from a post-secondary school or by completing a distance learning program. Certification and licensing requirements vary by state. Degree programs are also offered at many two-year colleges.

OTHER REQUIREMENTS: Teacher's aides must enjoy working with students under the supervision of a teacher and be able to handle a wide range of tasks.

CAREER ADVANCEMENT OPPORTUNITIES: With additional training, a teacher's aide can pursue his or her teaching license to become a full-time teacher or child-care worker.

Teacher's aides are hired by public and private elementary and secondary schools to assist teachers in the classroom. Job responsibilities include grading homework, helping develop lesson plans, supervising students, taking attendance, and record keeping, as opposed to actually teaching the students. This is an entry-level, full-time or part-time position. Like teachers, teacher's aides have their summers off.

For More Information

- American Federation of Teachers, Paraprofessional and School Related Personnel Division. This union represents teachers and teacher's aides. The web site offers a wide range of resources for people working in education, www.aft.org/psrp.
- National Resource Center for Paraprofessionals. This is a professional trade association for teacher's aides, www.nrcpara.org.

- Online job listings, refer to any of the general interest career-related web sites, such as Monster (www.monster.com) or Yahoo! HotJobs (http://hotjobs.yahoo.com).

Tour Guide

> **AT A GLANCE**
>
> **SALARY POTENTIAL:** Varies.
>
> **TRAINING/LICENSE/CERTIFICATION REQUIRED:** None, although education and training in tourism and/or hospitality is helpful.
>
> **OTHER REQUIREMENTS:** Tour guides should be outgoing, friendly, knowledgeable about the areas they are touring, patient, and well spoken. Public speaking skills are crucial. It's also necessary to be able to manage groups, stay on a schedule, and be detail oriented.
>
> **CAREER ADVANCEMENT OPPORTUNITIES:** There are career opportunities for tour guides at museums, tourist attractions, tour companies, and with the department of tourism of almost any city, state, or region.

A tour guide is someone who provides a detailed tour offering information, insight, and historical background about a location, tourist attraction, museum exhibit, or geographic area. The job involves escorting people, providing detailed commentary, staying on schedule, and being able to answer questions. Working conditions, pay, and job requirements vary greatly based on the employer and type of work.

For More Information

- CruiseJobFinder. This web site offers online job listings for tour guides, http://cruisejobfinder.com/fm/tourguides.
- Professional Guides Association of America. This is a professional trade association comprised of tour guides and others working in the tourism industry, (703) 892-5757.
- Tourism Offices Worldwide Directory. This is an online listing of tourism offices and related companies throughout the world, www.towd.com.
- In addition to tourism offices, contact public relations companies that specialize in tourism.

Travel Agent

AT A GLANCE

SALARY POTENTIAL: $20,000 to $50,000 per year. This job typically offers a salary, plus commissions, so earning potential is based on your success meeting the job requirements and booking travel for clients.

TRAINING/LICENSE/CERTIFICATION REQUIRED: Training is available from postsecondary vocational schools and accredited distance learning programs. Many travel agencies offer on-the-job training. In some states, a license or certification is required.

OTHER REQUIREMENTS: Travel agents must be outgoing, friendly, good communicators, detail-oriented, and knowledgeable about a wide range of travel destinations. Proficiency using computers and the internet is necessary.

CAREER ADVANCEMENT OPPORTUNITIES: There are employment opportunities helping vacationers plan their travel, however, some travel agents focus exclusively on corporate travel, booking cruise vacations, planning honeymoons, or putting together vacation packages to specific destinations.

A travel agent assists vacationers and business travelers in booking airline tickets, hotels, rental cars, tours, cruise vacations, and other types of getaways. The job involves assessing clients' wants and needs, finding travel options that fit within their budgets, and booking that travel on behalf of the client. A travel agent offers recommendations and must be knowledgeable about a wide range of destinations. For international travelers, travel agents also assist with acquiring passports, visas, certifications of vaccinations, and other paperwork.

Most travel agents work in a traditional office environment. Because much of this work is done using the internet, it's possible for some travel agents to work from home and to set their own hours. The job involves working directly with clients, either in-person or over the telephone, then working with the various travel service providers (airlines, hotels, cruise ship companies, tour operators, etc.) to make the necessary travel arrangements.

This is a customer service-oriented job that requires catering to clients' needs, promptly addressing their concerns, and often handling last-minute travel-related emergencies. Most travel agents are employed by travel agencies. One of the biggest perks of working as a travel agent is the ability to travel throughout the world, either for free or at greatly reduced rates.

For More Information

- The American Society of Travel Agents. This is a professional trade association offering information about careers in the travel and tourism industries, plus details about certification programs for travel agents, www.asta net.com. The web site offers a downloadable, 25-page eBook about how to launch your career as a travel agent.
- The Travel Institute. Learn about a variety of training and certification programs for travel agents, www.icta.com. The web site also offers extensive career-related information and resources of interest to someone first entering this field.
- Travel Jobs. This web site offers online job listings for travel agents, www.traveljobs.com.
- Online job listings, refer to any of the general interest career-related web sites, such as Monster (www.monster.com) or Yahoo! HotJobs (http://hot jobs.yahoo.com).

Tutor/Education Consultant

AT A GLANCE

SALARY POTENTIAL: Minimum wage to $25 or more per hour.

TRAINING/LICENSE/CERTIFICATION REQUIRED: Depending on where you're employed, a teaching license or qualifications to work with learning disabled or challenged students may be required.

OTHER REQUIREMENTS: Like any teacher, a tutor must be patient, outgoing, well-organized, detail-oriented, enjoy working with children and teens, plus have a strong knowledge in one or more subjects.

CAREER ADVANCEMENT OPPORTUNITIES: In addition to working as an independent private tutor for elementary, middle school, high school, and/or college students, a qualified tutor can pursue work at a private learning and tutoring center.

A tutor is someone hired to help a student learn a specific subject. A tutor might be required because the student has fallen behind or is facing additional challenges, such as being learning disabled. A tutor will typically work one-on-one with a student after school, at night, or on weekends.

Especially at the high school and college levels, tutors are needed for virtually every subject, requiring the tutor to have a strong understanding of specific subjects, such as English, various aspects of math, history, science, or foreign languages. In addition to being well educated on his or her specialty subject, a tutor must also possess teaching skills to properly instruct their students.

Many people with teaching licenses pursue tutoring work to supplement their teaching incomes or until they find teaching jobs. Graduate students and even high school and college students with high grades often work part time as tutors. Unless you're working for a tutoring service, it is your responsibility to market your services and line up students as clients to generate work on a consistent basis.

For More Information

- International Tutor Association. This is a professional trade association for tutors that offers a variety of resources to people working in this field, www.itatutor.org. The organization offers a nationally recognized certification program for tutors.
- Kumon Learning Centers. This is a national chain of independent tutoring centers, www.kumon.com/about/career.asp.
- Sylvan Learning Centers. This is a national chain of independent tutoring centers, www.educate.com.
- TutorNation. Online job listings for tutors can be found at (866) TUTOR-90, www.tutornation.com.
- TutorsTeach. Online job listings for tutors can be found at www.tutors teach.com.
- Online job listings, refer to any of the general interest career-related web sites, such as Monster (www.monster.com) or Yahoo! HotJobs (http://hot jobs.yahoo.com).
- The best way to generate clients when working as a tutor is to run classified ads in newspapers and post ads on bulletin boards at or near schools. You can also generate leads from teachers and guidance counselors at schools.

TRANSPORTATION JOBS

The jobs in this section involve travel or assisting others with their travel, either by car, bus, train, boat, or airplane. As you're about to discover, jobs in the transportation field vary greatly.

Airline Flight Attendant

> ### AT A GLANCE
>
> SALARY POTENTIAL: $15 to $60 per hour, or an annual salary of between $48,000 and $93,000, depending on the airline.
>
> TRAINING/LICENSE/CERTIFICATION REQUIRED: At least three to eight weeks of training will be provided by the airline once you're hired. A high school diploma or GED is required. Some (but not all) airlines also require at least a two-year college degree.
>
> OTHER REQUIREMENTS: Each commercial airline has its own minimum age, height, weight, vision, and appearance guidelines for this position. Union membership is also typically required.
>
> CAREER ADVANCEMENT OPPORTUNITIES: Flight attendants earn more and receive additional perks based on experience and seniority. Perks include free travel, scheduling flexibility, choice of routes, and paid over-time.

The primary job of a flight attendant is to ensure the safety of passengers aboard commercial aircrafts. Secondary responsibilities involve catering to a passenger needs, by helping people find their seats, assisting with the stowage of baggage, reviewing safety procedures before take-offs, and serving meals and drinks. Thus, having superior people skills is critical.

A flight attendant working for a major airline can expect to fly 65 to 85 hours per month, plus spend an additional 50+ hours per month helping to prep aircraft, writing reports, and participating in other administrative (ground-based) duties. Having a flexible schedule and a willingness to be away from home for extended periods is required.

With recent cutbacks and airline mergers, competition for these jobs has become fierce. To learn about the hiring practices of a specific airline, visit its web site and click on the Careers, Employment Opportunities, or Jobs icon.

For More Information

- AirlineJob.net. Online job listings can be found here, www.airlinejob.net/flight-attendant-jobs.htm.

- Association of Flight Attendants (Union). This is a professional trade organization. You'll find career-related information and resources on the organization's web site, (202) 434-1300, www.afanet.org.
- Flight Attendant Careers. Career-related information can be found on this web site, www.flightattendantcareer.com.
- Flight Attendant Recruitment Agency. Online job listings are offered at (800) 676-5034, www.inflightcareers.com.

Airline Reservations Specialist/Ticket Agent/ Customer Service Agent

> ### AT A GLANCE
>
> SALARY POTENTIAL: Minimum wage to $15 per hour, or $30,000 to $40,000 per year.
>
> TRAINING/LICENSE/CERTIFICATION REQUIRED: None.
>
> OTHER REQUIREMENTS: Excellent customer service, telephone, and verbal communication skills are necessary. Basic computer literacy is also required. Training is typically provided by the employer. Being bilingual is a plus.
>
> CAREER ADVANCEMENT OPPORTUNITIES: In addition to airlines, reservations specialists are hired by hotels, resorts, travel-related web sites, cruise ship companies, bus lines, and railroad companies.

At any major airline, thousands of people handle the customer service needs of passengers. This includes booking and confirming reservations, ticketing, and checking in passengers and their baggage at the airport.

These jobs are offered on a full-time (40 hour per week) or part-time basis. It's often necessary, however, to have a flexible schedule and work nontraditional hours and/or on weekends. Because of internet travel-related web sites, electronic ticket options, and automated check-in procedures at airports, competition for these positions is increasing as fewer jobs are available.

For More Information
- Air Transport Association of America. This is a professional trade organization. Here, you'll find resources for people working in this industry, www.airlines.org / www.air-transport.org.

- Bureau of Labor Statistics. Detailed career-related information can be found at this web site, www.bls.gov/oco/ocos135.htm.
- Visit the web site of the airline or hotel chain, etc. you're interested in working for and click on the Employment, Careers, or Jobs icon.

Baggage Porter/Bellhop

AT A GLANCE

SALARY POTENTIAL: Minimum wage to $50,000 per year (including tips).

TRAINING/LICENSE/CERTIFICATION REQUIRED: None.

OTHER REQUIREMENTS: Must be able to lift heavy luggage and enjoy working with people.

CAREER ADVANCEMENT OPPORTUNITIES: Limited.

The job of a baggage porter or bellhop is to assist people with their luggage at places like hotels, resorts, cruise ships, and airports, plus direct guests or passengers to their rooms or cabins, and/or assist them in hailing taxis. While the base pay for these jobs is relatively low, someone with a good personality who is also highly efficient can dramatically supplement his or her income from tips.

Bellhop jobs at high-priced, luxury hotels and resorts, especially in tourist areas, tend to generate the most tips from satisfied guests. At high-traffic resorts, like those in Las Vegas, bellhops have extremely high income potential. It's often necessary, however, for a team of bellhops to pool tips in certain jobs.

Another job to consider is that of a valet parking attendant in terms of income potential. To be a valet parking attendant a valid driver's license is required and it's necessary to be able to drive manual and automatic transmission vehicles.

For More Information
- iHireHospitalityServices. A career web site and job listing service for the hospitality industry, www.ihirehospitalityservices.com.
- Contact the human resources department of the hotel or resort where you're interested in working to learn about job openings.

Bus Driver

> ### AT A GLANCE
>
> SALARY POTENTIAL: $10 to $20 per hour.
>
> TRAINING/LICENSE/CERTIFICATION REQUIRED: A commercial driver's license is required. Contact your local Registry of Motor Vehicles to discover your state's requirements for obtaining this type of license. Several weeks of on-the-job training is typically provided by employers.
>
> OTHER REQUIREMENTS: You must be able to stay alert while on the job, always focusing on your passengers, as well as other traffic on the road and pedestrians. Bus drivers must be able to deal with stress and have a flexible work schedule. Drivers must be at least 21 years old, in good physical health, and have at least 20/40 vision.
>
> CAREER ADVANCEMENT OPPORTUNITIES: Varies, based on the type of bus you drive. There are a variety of different types of opportunities for bus drivers.

Bus drivers can work for local transit systems, motor coach companies, tourism companies, or school bus companies. This can be a full- or part-time job. About one-third of all bus drivers work part time. Training and job-related responsibilities will vary greatly, based on the type of bus you drive and your employer. After obtaining a commercial driver's license, expect to receive between two and eight weeks of training by your employer.

Some bus drivers belong to the Amalgamated Transit Union, the Transport Workers Union of America, the United Transportation Union, or the International Brotherhood of Teamsters. Full-time drivers typically receive benefits, such as health insurance, sick leave, and paid vacations. The job involves a lot of sitting and possibly the repetition of following the same routes multiple times per day, everyday.

For More Information
- 800drivers. Online job listings for bus drivers can be found at (800) DRI-VERS, www.1800drivers.com.
- Amalgamated Transit Union. This union represents bus drivers and offers a wide range of resources and information, www.atu.org.

- International Brotherhood of Teamsters. This union represents bus drivers and offers a wide range of resources and information, www.teamster.org.
- National Association for Pupil Transport. This is a professional trade association, www.napt.org. The web site offers information about careers as a school bus driver is offered.
- Transport Workers Union of America. This union represents bus drivers and offers a wide range of resources and information, www.twu.org.
- United Transportation Union. This union represents bus drivers and offers a wide range of resources and information, www.utu.org.

Chauffer/Limousine Driver (also see Taxi Driver)

> **AT A GLANCE**
>
> **SALARY POTENTIAL:** Minimum wage to $20 per hour (including tips).
>
> **TRAINING/LICENSE/CERTIFICATION REQUIRED:** The hack license and the requirements for obtaining it vary by state. Contact your local Registry of Motor Vehicles. In addition to a standard driver's license, obtaining the necessary hack license will typically require passing a written exam, a driving exam, and participating in a specialized training program.
>
> **OTHER REQUIREMENTS:** Having a good driving record and a flexible work schedule is required because weekend, early morning, daytime, and/or night work is often required.
>
> **CAREER ADVANCEMENT OPPORTUNITIES:** Driving a private limousine pays better than working as a taxi driver, however, career advancement opportunities are somewhat limited. Self-employed drivers can earn more, but they must purchase or lease, as well as maintain their own vehicle(s), while drivers working for an employer will be provided with a vehicle.

As opposed to taxi drivers, chauffeurs and limousine drivers operate limousines, town cars, vans, and other types of vehicles and are hired by wealthy individuals, companies, and government agencies. Unlike driving a taxi, all services are pre-arranged with the client, such as a trip to or from an airport or to a special event.

Chauffeurs and limousine drivers are expected to be prompt, courteous, and professional. They're expected to open the vehicle's door for a client, assist with luggage, hold an umbrella (if it's raining) as they enter or exit the vehicle, and provide extras within their vehicles, such as beverages, newspapers, or magazines.

In addition to providing top-notch customer service, a chauffer or limousine driver must also know local geography, understand all traffic and driving laws, and always practice safe driving techniques. The job requires extensive driving, patience when dealing with traffic or difficult passengers, and a flexible work schedule.

For More Information

- National Limousine Association. This web site provides information about working as a limousine driver or chauffer, www.limo.org.
- Limousine & Chauffeured Transportation Magazine. An industry-oriented magazine and online-based resource for chauffeurs and limo drivers, www.lctmag.com.

Cruise Ship Worker

AT A GLANCE

SALARY POTENTIAL: Minimum wage and up, depending on your job aboard the ship.

TRAINING/LICENSE/CERTIFICATION REQUIRED: Entry-level jobs require no previous experience, however, certain jobs require licensing, certification, or training.

OTHER REQUIREMENTS: Working on a cruise ship requires you to be on the job almost all the time, however, all of your room and board (including meals) are included. Depending on the type of job you're doing, the skills you need will vary dramatically.

CAREER ADVANCEMENT OPPORTUNITIES: Entry-level positions can help prepare you for more skilled positions aboard a cruise ship.

A cruise ship is like a luxurious city on the sea that operates constantly. It takes a crew of over 1,000 to keep a large cruise ship operational for its 3,000 or more passengers. Though working on a cruise ship definitely has its perks, such as free travel and the ability to spend a lot of time visiting exotic locations, anyone who has held this type of job will tell you it's anything but a paid vacation. Most cruise ships hire people for six months at a time. The best way to find out what jobs are available is to contact the popular cruise ship companies directly.

This is a great job for someone who enjoys traveling and doesn't mind being away from friends and family for months at a time. It's ideal for recent high school graduates or people taking time off from college, for example.

In addition to entry-level jobs, cruise ships have an ongoing demand for people with a wide range of specialized skills. These jobs tend to pay competitive wages. Crews are divided into several main categories, including shipboard hotel operations, entertainment jobs, and technical/nautical jobs.

For More Information

- Cruise Job Finder. An online resource for job listings with all of the major cruise lines, www.cruisejobfinder.com.
- Cruise Ship Jobs. An online resource for job listings available with all of the major cruise lines, www.cruiseshipjobs.tk.
- Hospitality Jobs. Online job listings in the hospitality field that are available aboard cruise ships, as well as at resorts and hotels, can be found here, www.hospitalityjobs.hcareers.com/seeker.
- Royal Caribbean Cruise Lines. Employment information relating to Royal Caribbean Cruise Lines. Be sure to visit the web sites of all of the popular cruise line companies to learn about job openings, www.royalcaribbean .com/ourCompany/career.do.

Taxi Driver

> ### AT A GLANCE
>
> SALARY POTENTIAL: $15,000 to $35,000 per year or $5 to $15 per hour (plus tips).
>
> TRAINING/LICENSE/CERTIFICATION REQUIRED: In most states, taxi drivers must obtain a hack license, and all states require a valid driver's license.
>
> OTHER REQUIREMENTS: The ability to drive a taxicab, patience, and knowledge of the geographic area where you'll be driving is needed.

> CAREER ADVANCEMENT OPPORTUNITIES: Experienced taxi drivers can pursue higher paying jobs as limo drivers or chauffers.

A taxi driver can work part time or full time. The job involves a lot of driving, navigating through traffic, and interacting with passengers. Most taxi drivers must maintain a flexible work schedule and could be required to work nights, weekends, and/or holidays. This is considered an entry-level job.

Depending on the employer, some taxi drivers own or lease their vehicles and work as independent contractors for taxi companies. Others are full-time or part-time employees working for a taxi company.

For More Information

- For licensing information, contact the Taxi & Limousine Commission or the Department of Transportation in your area. Contact information can be found in the telephone book.
- Online job listings can be found at the general interest career-related web sites, such as Monster (www.monster.com) or Yahoo! Hot Jobs (http://hotjobs.yahoo.com).

Truck Driver

> AT A GLANCE
>
> SALARY POTENTIAL: Minimum wage to $25 per hour.
>
> TRAINING/LICENSE/CERTIFICATION REQUIRED: Depending on the size and weight of the trucks you'll be driving, a special driver's license is required. Each state has its own licensing guidelines, plus there are federal regulations that must be adhered to. In a short time, a truck driving school will provide the skills needed for this job.
>
> OTHER REQUIREMENTS: Because this job involves an extensive amount of driving, you'll be sitting for hours at a time. Patience is also required, especially when dealing with high traffic situations. Navigational and map-reading skills are also useful, particularly if you'll be working as a long haul or local

> delivery driver. In some situations, a truck driver is required to load and unload his or her vehicle, requiring some physical stamina and strength.
>
> CAREER ADVANCEMENT OPPORTUNITIES: A wide range of companies employ truck drivers for anything from local deliveries to cross-country hauls.

Truck drivers are responsible for insuring the safe and timely transport of a wide range of goods using the country's roads and highways. Because the work involves extensive driving, one of the job's biggest challenges is dealing with traffic and controlling road rage. When behind the wheel, the driver must remain alert at all times, and adhere to all local, state, and federal driving laws.

During a seven-day period, a long-distance driver can not work for more than 60 hours, plus for every 11 hours of driving, the driver must rest for at least 10 hours. While adhering to these and other regulations, the driver must make on-time deliveries and contend with a wide range of weather and road conditions.

Drivers required to travel long distances are away from home for extended periods and typically work alone in their vehicles. To avoid traffic, the job often requires drivers to work through the night, on weekends, and on holidays. Potential drawbacks to the job include loneliness, boredom, and fatigue.

There are over three million truck drivers employed in the United States and the demand for qualified drivers continues to grow. For the right type of person, driving a truck can provide a stable and well-paying career opportunity. Some drivers work for trucking companies, while others own their own vehicle(s) and are self-employed, working as independent contractors for a variety of clients.

For More Information

- American Trucking Association. This is a professional trade association offering resources, information about training, and career-related information, www.trucking.org.
- Best Driver Jobs. Online job listings for truck drivers can be found at www.bestdriverjobs.com.
- C1 Truck Driver Training. Learn about a training program for truck drivers that combines classroom instruction with behind-the-wheel experience driving 18-wheel trucks. This is a two- to four-week program. The school has five campuses throughout the country. This is one of many truck driver training programs available throughout the country, www.c1training.com.
- Looking For Drivers. Online job listings for truck drivers can be found at www.lookingfordrivers.com.

- Professional Truck Driving Institute. This is one of many accredited schools that teaches the skills needed to become a truck driver. This training will prepare you to pass your state's written exam and driving test that's typically required to obtain a license, www.ptdi.org.

 CAREER SPOTLIGHT

Valet Parking Attendant

> ### AT A GLANCE
>
> SALARY POTENTIAL: Minimum wage to $200 per shift (or more). Tips account for the majority of compensation within this profession. The average valet parking attendant earns under $20,000 per year.
>
> TRAINING/LICENSE/CERTIFICATION REQUIRED: A valid driver's license and the ability to drive both automatic and manual transmission vehicles is essential. Most employers perform background checks and do mandatory drug tests on their valet parking attendants.
>
> OTHER REQUIREMENTS: Having an outgoing and friendly personality and working quickly will help generate high tips.
>
> CAREER ADVANCEMENT OPPORTUNITIES: Limited.

Hotels, resorts, upscale restaurants, some airports, conference, and convention centers, parking garages, and other places of business often offer valet parking as a convenience for their guests or customers. A valet parking attendant stands near the entrance of an establishment, greets guests, and parks their cars for them. When the guest is ready to leave, the valet parking attendant fetches the car in a timely manner.

Most valet parking attendants are paid a low hourly salary. The true earning potential is through tips. Depending on where you work, an average tip can be anywhere from $1 to $10. For a valet parking attendant working at a resort hotel in Beverly Hills or a resort in Las Vegas, earning several hundred dollars per shift in tips is common.

The trick to making the most money as a valet parking attendant is working for an upscale place of business, such as a four-star resort, and insuring that the employer doesn't require its valet parking attendants to either pool their tips or share a percentage of their tips with the house.

For the most part, working as a valet parking attendant involves minimal stress, but requires performing a high degree of repetitive tasks. The job typically involves working outdoors (in all weather conditions) and always paying careful attention to the vehicles, insuring you don't get them dirty or damage them in any way. This is definitely considered an entry-level position and one that's often highly competitive to land because of the high income potential.

Here's My Story

Jared is a former valet parking attendant. He moved to Los Angeles to pursue acting, but quickly found that despite his charm and good looks, landing a starring role in a television series, commercial, or movie was a lot harder than he thought. Because he needed to have a flexible schedule in order to attend auditions, acting classes, and open casting calls, he figured working as a valet parking attendant would provide the income he needed, yet also give him plenty of flexibility in terms of scheduling. His goal was to work evenings, nights, and weekends.

"I started off applying for valet parking jobs only at the most exclusive and prestigious resorts, hotels, restaurants and nightclubs in Hollywood. It took several weeks, but I finally landed a valet parking job at a top-ranked and world famous hotel, right in the heart of Beverly Hills," recalled Jared.

"The job paid just minimum wage, however, the tips were amazing. The problem was, as I discovered after I accepted the job, all valet parking attendants needed to pool their tips at the end of the night, plus a small percentage went to the hotel. Thus, while I would hustle throughout my shift to park and retrieve several hundred cars, and I'd earn between $1 and $20 per car in tips, at the end of the night, I'd wind up giving up a large portion of my earnings. Few of the other valet parking attendants were as dedicated as I was. I worked hard and was extremely friendly to the guests for the sole purpose of receiving tips. There were several times I received a $100 tip, which was amazing," said Jared.

"I would never have accepted a basic valet parking job for an establishment that didn't have a truly upscale clientele, because the potential for tips would be much lower. Ultimately, I got fed up having to share my tips and started not reporting some of them. Within a week or so of doing this, I was caught by my boss. After about four months on the job, I decided to seek a valet parking attendant job at another hotel, that didn't require us to pool tips or pay a percentage to the hotel. My income immediately went up," said Jared.

Working as a valet parking attendant was a job Jared held for over eight months in total. He ultimately moved away from Los Angeles and returned to his hometown when he realized that he wasn't cut out to become a professional actor. "I wouldn't recommend becoming a valet parking attendant as a long-term career. It is, however, an easy way to make some cash when you're in between jobs or want a job that doesn't require a whole lot of hard work."

For More Information

- iHire Hospitality. This web site offers online job listings for valet parking attendants and other positions in the hospitality industry, www.ihirehospitalityservices.com.
- Online job listings can be found at the general interest career-related web sites, such as Monster (www.monster.com) or Yahoo! Hot Jobs (http://hotjobs.yahoo.com).
- Contact the human resources department of any business, hotel, resort, or restaurant that offers valet parking to its customers or guests.

CHAPTER

15

UNUSUAL JOB OPPORTUNITIES

For people who don't enjoy the traditional work schedule or want to pursue something a bit unusual as a career, this section is for you! Discover some of the more unusual job and career paths available. Using a bit of creativity, you could find yourself doing something you love and earning a salary, without having to conform to the demands of corporate America.

Antique Broker/Collector

> AT A GLANCE
>
> SALARY POTENTIAL: Varies.
>
> TRAINING/LICENSE/CERTIFICATION REQUIRED: None.
>
> OTHER REQUIREMENTS: A strong working knowledge of history, art, collectibles, and antiques.
>
> CAREER ADVANCEMENT OPPORTUNITIES: Opportunities are available at antique stores, galleries, flea markets, and online (using eBay, for example).

Buying and selling artwork and antiques requires a strong knowledge of what you're selling. It's also necessary to build a strong and credible reputation among your clients. Jobs are available at antique stores, however, it's also possible to be your own boss, working at flea markets or even using eBay, to buy and sell collectibles, antiques, and art.

For More Information

- Antique & Collectibles National Association. This is a professional trade organization for people involved with buying and selling antiques, www.antiqueandcollectible.com.
- Antique.Org. This web site is an online resource relating to this career, www.antique.org.
- Contact the Antique Dealer's Association in your state.

Bridal Consultant/Wedding Planner

> AT A GLANCE
>
> SALARY POTENTIAL: $25,000 and up.

> TRAINING/LICENSE/CERTIFICATION REQUIRED: None.
>
> OTHER REQUIREMENTS: Wedding planners and bridal consultants must be extremely detail and deadline oriented, social, organized, and hard working. This is not a typical 9 to 5 job. Long hours working evenings and weekends is a must.
>
> CAREER ADVANCEMENT OPPORTUNITIES: Limited.

As a wedding planner and/or bridal consultant, your job is to ensure that your client's wedding is properly planned and happens without a flaw. This includes everything from coordinating the photographer, florist, musicians, and caterers, to sending out invitations and insuring that the wedding dress is properly tailored. This is a fun and rewarding career opportunity that offers freedom, flexibility, and financial independence. It's a job that's dominated by women.

Every year, more than 2.5 million weddings take place in America. With engaged couples being so busy with work and other obligations, hiring a wedding planner or bridal consultant has become as common as hiring a florist, disc jockey, band, or caterer. Many wedding planners and bridal consultants are self-employed and rely heavily on word-of-mouth and referrals to generate business. Others work for wedding chapels, resorts, casinos (such as those in Las Vegas), cruise ships, restaurants, function rooms, and other places where weddings are held.

For More Information

- Lulu. This is an online bookstore for wedding planners, www.lulu.com/lovegevity.
- Thomson Education Direct. Learn about training for bridal consultants at (800) 889-9593, www.educationdirect.com/bridalconsultant.
- Wedding Planner Career Information. This web site offers information about career opportunities and details about how to break into this industry, www.fabjob.com/weddingplanner.asp.
- Wedding Planner Institute. This school offers a two-year degree program for Professional Wedding Planners, as well as a Wedding Planning Certification program (which takes less time to complete), (877) 597-8166, www.weddingplanninginstitute.com.

CAREER SPOTLIGHT

Casino Dealer

AT A GLANCE

SALARY POTENTIAL: $30,000 and up per year. Casino dealers typically receive a salary, benefits, plus tips.

TRAINING/LICENSE/CERTIFICATION REQUIRED: Completion of a recognized training program in one or more of the popular casino table games is required. These courses offer approximately 100 hours of training and can be completed in two to four weeks. Additional training will be provided by the employer. In many states where gambling is permitted, a license is required for this type of work.

OTHER REQUIREMENTS: Basic mathematical skills, an outgoing personality, the ability to be on your feet for extended periods, and knowledge of house rules are required. You must also be at least 21 years of age to enroll in a casino dealer training program.

CAREER ADVANCEMENT OPPORTUNITIES: Limited. Casino dealers can earn promotions to pit boss or seek out more lucrative jobs within a casinos.

Las Vegas, Atlantic City, Lake Tahoe, Reno, Indian reservations, riverboat casinos, and cruise ships are some of the places where casino dealers are employed. With as little as a few weeks of training from a recognized casino dealer school, you to can pursue work in a casino as a dealer for poker, blackjack, craps, roulette, or any number of other popular table games. Calculating and paying winning bets and collecting losing bets quickly is perhaps the most challenging aspect of this job, because it requires some mathematical ability and concentration while working in a crowded and noisy environment.

Here's My Story

Eric is a blackjack dealer who currently works at a popular Atlantic City casino. He's a high school graduate who grew up in Connecticut. Prior to moving to Atlantic City, Eric completed a several week training program which provided him with the education needed to pursue work as a dealer at a casino. "If you use any internet search engine, you'll find dozens of casino dealer schools located throughout the country. The trick is to find one that offers excellent job placement services in areas where you want to work. Since I knew I wanted to work in Atlantic City, I made a point to seek out a dealer school that demonstrated success placing its graduates at casinos in Atlantic City," explained Eric, who borrowed the money for his tuition from friends and family.

"Upon graduating, I began my job search efforts and applied for jobs at multiple casinos. Initially, the process was the same as for any other job. The interview process, however, included me demonstrating my skills as a dealer," recalled Eric. "I think the casinos are looking for competent people in terms of their skills, but personality and appearance are also carefully evaluated."

Eric explained, "The biggest challenge of working in a casino is being watched all the time by the gamblers at your table, passers by, supervisors, and video surveillance cameras. Everything you do while on the job is watched carefully. That takes some getting used to. Also, as a dealer, you need to know the rules of the game better than anyone else at your table and you need to be able to perform lots of mathematical calculations in your head very quickly without getting distracted. There's absolutely no room for error. No matter what's happening in the casino around you, it's vital for the dealer to stay totally focused. At the same time, you need to make every person at your table feel comfortable, like they're a high roller. This is what generates the best tips."

As for the biggest misconception people have about working in a casino, Eric stated, "When you visit Atlantic City or Las Vegas and you step into a casino, you're there to have fun. If you're working, however, it's totally different. This is a job. As a dealer, you're not there to have fun. People don't necessarily understand that. The best advice I can offer to someone who wants to be a casino dealer is to meet and speak with people who are doing exactly what you want to do, where you want to do it. This will offer you a more realistic perspective of what the job is all about. Working as a dealer in an Atlantic City casino is very different from working in Las Vegas or on an Indian reservation casino, so make sure you understand the culture and environment where you'll be working, before accepting the job. The atmosphere and work environment also varies within the different casinos in Atlantic City."

Working as a casino dealer may seem like a fun, rewarding, and glamorous job. "While the job does have its perks and benefits, its important for people to really do their research to understand exactly what they're getting into, especially if they'll be moving across the country, to a place like Las Vegas, to pursue their career goals," concluded Eric, who suggested that if your state offers legalized gambling, you might want to land a job as a dealer locally before relocating to insure working in a casino is really what you want to do.

For More Information

- American Gaming Association. A professional trade association comprised of casino workers, www.americangaming.org. This web site offers an abundance of resources and career-related information.
- California Dealer School. An accredited casino dealer school located in California that provides the training needed to land a job as a dealer in a casino, www.californiadealerschool.com.
- Casino Dealer College. This network of casino dealer schools offers training for under $1,000, www.casinodealercollege.com. It requires under two weeks to complete.
- For employment information at any of the major casinos in America, visit the "employment" or "careers" section of that casino's web site.

eBook Publisher

AT A GLANCE

SALARY POTENTIAL: Varies.

TRAINING/LICENSE/CERTIFICATION REQUIRED: The ability to write and sell electronic eBooks via the internet. This requires some writing skills, plus the ability to develop, manage, and promote a web site.

OTHER REQUIREMENTS: eBook publishers are typically self-employed. They write or acquire text-based information that can be sold online in the form of eBooks.

CAREER ADVANCEMENT OPPORTUNITIES: Limited.

An eBook is a text-based document that is often the length of a book. However, instead of using traditional printing and distribution methods to publish the book, it's created into an electronic file, called an eBook, which can be distributed online.

When someone purchases an eBook, it can be paid for and downloaded directly from a web site or e-mailed to the recipient by the publisher.

eBooks are a way to distribute how-to information, novels, or any other type of written material in an electronic format. Many eBook publishers develop specialized content that's of interest to a niche market, then promote and sell their eBooks online via a web site. The demand for eBook products is limited, but growing. Sales potential relies mainly on the need for the information being provided and the ability of publishers to successfully market their eBooks to potential readers.

An eBook can be created using a word processor and specialized software, such as Adobe Acrobat (www.adobe.com), which is available from computer retail stores. To generate sales for an eBook, the publisher (who is often the author as well), must promote his or her product(s) and make them available online for purchase.

Writing, publishing, and distributing eBooks is a great part-time business opportunity because of the extremely low start-up costs involved. Even if you don't consider yourself a writer or author, you can still license eBook content and focus on the marketing and distribution of that content to generate profits.

For an example of how a professional dog trainer created an eBook-based dog training program and how she markets and sells it online, visit www.mydogbehaves.com.

For More Information

- Digital Publishing 4 Profit. This web site offers the tools needed by eBook publishers to create, market, and distribute their products online, www.digitalpublishing4profits.com.
- eBook Publishing Tools. From this web site, you'll learn about a wide range of software products, online tools, and resources of interest to eBook writers and publishers, www.ebook-publishing-tools.com.
- Knowledge Download. This web site offers the tools needed by eBook publishers to create, market, and distribute their products online, www.knowledge-download.com.
- Publishing eBooks Made Simple. This web site offers information about how to create and market your own eBooks, www.00ebooks.com.

Feng Shui Practitioner

> **AT A GLANCE**
>
> **SALARY POTENTIAL:** Varies.
>
> **TRAINING/LICENSE/CERTIFICATION REQUIRED:** In-person, video, audio, and multi-media training programs are available, along with a wide assortment of books. There are no minimal education requirements in terms of traditional education, but there are various levels of certification a practitioner can obtain in terms of their Feng Shui training.
>
> **OTHER REQUIREMENTS:** A belief and understanding in the principles of Feng Shui is important.
>
> **CAREER ADVANCEMENT OPPORTUNITIES:** Limited.

Feng Shui, pronounced "fung shway," is an ancient Chinese practice designed to help people live in harmony with their environments. Feng Shui assists many in obtaining prosperity, health, and improving their relationships. A Feng Shui Practitioner is a trainer, consultant, and counselor for others. In addition to understanding and believing in Feng Shui fundamentals and principles, a practitioner must have strong interpersonal and communication skills.

Most Feng Shui practitioners are self-employed and charge clients for their services. It's important to understand that this isn't a religion, but a belief system that goes back thousands of years.

For More Information

- About.com. This is a web site offering a good introduction to what Feng Shui is all about, http://fengshui.about.com/od/basics/a/fsbasics1.htm.
- China Studies. Learn about one of many training programs for practitioners, (800) 551-2482, www.chinastudies.com.
- The Feng Shui Training Center. One of the many training programs offered throughout the country that offers Feng Shui practitioner certification, (877) 470-7769, www.thefengshuitrainingcenter.com.
- Western School of Feng Shui. A Feng Shui training program. Tuition for this one week program is $2,750. This web site also offers information about pursuing a career as a practitioner, (800) 300-6785, www.wsfs.com/training.htm.

Gift Basket Business Operator

> AT A GLANCE
>
> SALARY POTENTIAL: Varies.
>
> TRAINING/LICENSE/CERTIFICATION REQUIRED: None.
>
> OTHER REQUIREMENTS: Creativity is necessary to create visually appealing gift baskets that recipients will appreciate.
>
> CAREER ADVANCEMENT OPPORTUNITIES: This is typically a homebased business for someone interested in being self-employed. Positions are also available at florists.

Creating attractive, often themed gift baskets can be a viable business for someone interested in being self-employed and working from home, or who wants to work at a florist or corporate gift company. A gift basket is comprised of candy, flowers, fine cheeses, plush toys, and other small items packaged nicely within a basket suitable to be presented as a gift.

This business requires minimal training and a small initial financial investment. Once your business is operational, you'll need to discover innovative ways to advertise, market, and promote it in order to generate business. *Entrepreneur* magazine reports the average profit before taxes for gift basket businesses is $65,700.

For More Information

- eGiftBaskets.com. This is a turnkey business opportunity for launching your own gift basket business, www.egiftbaskets.com. Training, materials, inventory, and resources are included.
- Gift Basket Business World. An online resource for people interested in launching their own gift basket businesses, www.giftbasketbusinessworld .com. Training is provided.
- GiftBasketBusiness.com. Information about starting a gift basket business, as well as listings of suppliers is offered at www.giftbasket business.com.
- The Gourmet Gift Company. Information about starting a successful gift basket business is available from this web site, www.gourmetgiftcom pany.com/opportunity.htm.

Hypnotherapist

> ## AT A GLANCE
>
> SALARY POTENTIAL: Varies. $25 to $150 per hour.
>
> TRAINING/LICENSE/CERTIFICATION REQUIRED: There are a variety of courses (which can be completed in several days) to become a certified hypnotherapist.
>
> OTHER REQUIREMENTS: You must be a good communicator, intuitive, and compassionate, plus have a belief in what hypnotherapy can offer.
>
> CAREER ADVANCEMENT OPPORTUNITIES: Limited.

Imagine yourself in a beautiful meadow. Picture the meadow in your mind's eye, with the wind blowing, the birds chirping, and the water from a stream flowing smoothly. You feel yourself getting relaxed. As I count from ten to one, you will become increasingly more relaxed . . . .

The work of a certified hypnotherapist involves hypnotizing someone for therapeutic purposes. Once someone is in a relaxed state and his or her mind is open to suggestion, you, as the therapist, can guide him or her toward overcoming a bad habit or dealing with a traumatic experience from the past, for example. The work involves working one-on-one with clients and providing them with a comfortable and safe environment as you hypnotize them.

Most certified hypnotherapists are self-employed and charge by the session. Unlike other forms of therapy, this one requires the client to truly believe in the benefits of hypnosis and to be a willing participant.

For More Information

- Hypnodyne Foundation. This organization offers a wide range of training programs, including a home study course, to become a certified hypnotherapist, (727) 536-2960, www.hypnodyne.com.
- Hypnosis Information. This web site offers information about hypnosis and hypnotherapy, www.hypnosis-information.com.
- Hypnotherapy Training Institute. Obtain information about training programs to become a Certified Hypnotherapist from this web site, www.hypnotherapy.com.

Inventor

> **AT A GLANCE**
>
> SALARY POTENTIAL: Varies.
>
> TRAINING/LICENSE/CERTIFICATION REQUIRED: None.
>
> OTHER REQUIREMENTS: Creativity, the ability to work with tools to transform ideas into viable products.
>
> CAREER ADVANCEMENT OPPORTUNITIES: Companies in a wide range of industries hire inventors to work within their research and development or new product development departments.

Inventing and brainstorming is often referred to as "research and design" work within the corporate arena. An inventor is someone who is creative and able to conceive new product ideas, develop prototypes for those ideas, and take the steps necessary to bring those new products to market. An inventor might also create new and innovative uses for existing products or modify a product to improve it.

Depending on what you're inventing, various skills and/or levels of expertise may be required. If you come up with an idea, consider obtaining the appropriate trademarks, copyrights, and/or patents prior to sharing your idea with others. Also, beware of the many scams out there that solicit original ideas with promises of large profits.

For More Information
- United States Copyright Office. Information about how to file a copyright is provided at www.copyright.gov.
- United States Patent and Trademark Office. Information about how to file a patent and/or trademark is provided at this web site, www.uspto.gov/web/offices/tac/tmfaq.htm.

Mystery Shopper

> **AT A GLANCE**
>
> SALARY POTENTIAL: Minimum wage to $25 per hour.
>
> TRAINING/LICENSE/CERTIFICATION REQUIRED: None.
>
> OTHER REQUIREMENTS: A passion for shopping and dining out.
>
> CAREER ADVANCEMENT OPPORTUNITIES: Limited.

When retail stores or restaurant owners want to evaluate the experience their customers receive, they often turn to market research companies and utilize mystery shoppers. Mystery shoppers call on retail businesses and restaurants, posing as ordinary customers, then provide detailed evaluations of their experiences. After visiting the store or restaurant, the mystery shopper will prepare a detailed written report for the client.

This job is typically part-time and requires a flexible work schedule. When applying for this type of job, beware of scams. Seek legitimate opportunities with market research companies.

For More Information

- About.com. Career-related advice for breaking into the mystery shopping field can be found here, http://jobsearch.about.com/od/mysteryshopper/a/mysteryshopper.htm.
- Mystery Shoppers Providers Association. A professional trade organization for mystery shoppers. This site offers information about job opportunities with legitimate employers, as well as other career-related information, (972) 406-1104, www.mysteryshop.org.
- National Shopping Service. One of the largest mystery shopper employers in the United States. Career information and job listings are offered online, (800) 800-2704, www.nationalshoppingservice.com.

Personal Shopper/Stylist

> ### AT A GLANCE
>
> SALARY POTENTIAL: $25 to $200 per hour. Some personal shoppers work for upscale stores and are compensated through sales commissions.
>
> TRAINING/LICENSE/CERTIFICATION REQUIRED: None.
>
> OTHER REQUIREMENTS: A personal shopper must have good taste, be reliable, detail-oriented, able to multitask, and have excellent communication skills. Excellent customer service and retail sales skills are important.
>
> CAREER ADVANCEMENT OPPORTUNITIES: Limited.

A personal shopper is someone who assists a client in handling a wide range of errands and shopping-related tasks. Some personal shoppers are self-employed and hired on an hourly basis by clients. Others work for upscale stores and are responsible for giving important clients highly personalized attention. Many personal shoppers are hired to shop for clothing on behalf of their client(s). Thus, a good understanding of current fashion trends and each client's personal taste and needs is required. Many celebrities and top-level business people use personal shoppers, also referred to as stylists, to purchase and select outfits on their behalf.

For More Information

- FabJobs.com. Information about a self-paced distance learning program for becoming a personal shopper is offered at this web site, www.fabjob.com/personalshopper.asp.
- Great Shopping Jobs. This web site offers online job listings and career advice for personal shoppers, www.greatshoppingjobs.com/ShoppingJobs/personal-shopper-jobs.php.
- I Hire Retail. Online job listings for personal shopper jobs at major retailers can be found at www.ihireretail.com.

Professional Gambler

> **AT A GLANCE**
>
> SALARY POTENTIAL: Varies dramatically.
>
> TRAINING/LICENSE/CERTIFICATION REQUIRED: No formal training is required.
>
> OTHER REQUIREMENTS: The ability to focus, perform complex mathematical equations in your head, and read nonverbal communication signals from others are skills utilized by professional gamblers. A tremendous amount of discipline and some luck are also required.
>
> CAREER ADVANCEMENT OPPORTUNITIES: Limited.

A professional gambler is someone whose office is a casino. These people spend countless hours playing their favorite casino table games, such as poker, blackjack, or craps, in an effort to earn a full-time living. Being a professional gambler offers no job security, significant financial risk, and no traditional benefits (such as a retirement plan or health insurance). Working as a professional gambler is very different than spending a weekend vacationing in Las Vegas or Atlantic City.

Outside of traditional casinos, professional gamblers can utilize online-based casinos or earn money by successful betting on sports, horse races, or dog races. This is definitely not a career path most people should pursue. There can be a fine line between earning a living as a professional gambler and being addicted to gambling in a negative way (which could lead to high levels of debt, or worse).

For More Information
- ProfessionalGambler.com. Information for professional gamblers can be found at www.professionalgambler.com/gambleholic.html.
- Card Player. This is an informative online resource for professional and amateur poker players, www.cardplayer.com.

Psychic/Astrologer/Tarot Card Reader

> **AT A GLANCE**
>
> SALARY POTENTIAL: Varies.

> TRAINING/LICENSE/CERTIFICATION REQUIRED: None.
>
> OTHER REQUIREMENTS: If you're a believer, a psychic, astrologer, and/or tarot card reader needs to have supernatural psychic abilities and be intuitive.
>
> CAREER ADVANCEMENT OPPORTUNITIES: Limited.

People from all walks of life, from world leaders to homemakers, are intrigued by what some psychics, astrologers, and tarot card readers have to say about their futures. After all, some people believe their destiny is predetermined and someone who knows the future can offer a preview of what's to come. Psychics, astrologers, and tarot card readers are typically self-employed, have their own storefronts or "offices" and work one-on-one with clients. Some offer their services online, via telephone, or in-person at new-age bookstores and are paid by the minute or by the session. Others work at fairs, carnivals, or at popular tourist attractions.

Though most believe that to be psychic you need to be born with this skill, it is possible to learn how to perform tarot card readings and work with astrology. Training is available through books, video courses, and classes taught through many new-age bookstores and adult education programs. Those who are successful in this field are intuitive and extremely good communicators. Aside from simply offering someone a glimpse into the future, psychics, astrologers, and tarot card readers often perform basic counseling, helping clients overcome fears, problems or obstacles in their lives.

Compensation in this field varies dramatically. A tarot card reader can charge anywhere from $10 for a five-minute reading to several hundred dollars for an in-depth reading.

For More Information

- Ankida. Discover how to perform tarot card readings through this online resource and instructional tool, www.ankida.com/ankida/positions/tools/tarot/tarot.htm.
- Free Tarot Training MSN Group. This is an online community of tarot card readers that offers free online training and resources, http://groups.msn.com/FreeTarotTraining.
- Tarot.com. This web site offers a variety of resources and tools for people interested in tarot cards, psychics, and related fields, www.tarot.com/tarot/index.php.
- There are a wide range of books that teach astrology and tarot card reading. Visit your local bookstore or any new-age bookstore.

Singles Event Coordinator

AT A GLANCE

SALARY POTENTIAL: Varies. This type of job typically involves being paid a salary, plus commissions.

TRAINING/LICENSE/CERTIFICATION REQUIRED: None, although experience with event planning is helpful.

OTHER REQUIREMENTS: Singles event coordinators must be friendly, outgoing, well-organized, understanding, skilled at promoting and marketing, plus be detail oriented.

CAREER ADVANCEMENT OPPORTUNITIES: Singles event coordinators can pursue jobs coordinating other types of events, such as weddings or corporate parties.

With many people looking for love, but being too busy to utilize traditional methods of meeting new people, a large number of dating services, matchmaking companies, and companies that host singles events have popped up across the United States. Singles event coordinators seek groups of single people looking for love and then coordinate some type of fun event to facilitate an easy way for people to meet and interact. Speed dating events, for example, have become extremely popular.

For More Information
- 8-Minute Dating. Career opportunities and information about 8-Minute Dating, a well-known speed dating service, can be found at this web site, www.8minutedating.com/host.shtml.
- Great Expectations. Discover job opportunities working for this nationwide dating service, www.ge-dating.com/Careers.aspx.
- Rainbow Dating. Learn about job opportunities working for a leading dating service catering to the gay and lesbian community, www.rainbowex pressdating.com/jobs.html.
- Speed Dating. Career opportunities and information about Speed Dating, a well-known speed dating service, can be found at this web site, www.off linespeeddating.com.

Yoga Instructor

AT A GLANCE

SALARY POTENTIAL: Varies. Working at a health club, for example, pays significantly less than working as a private yoga instructor, which can generate revenues of $25 to $150 (or more) per hour.

TRAINING/LICENSE/CERTIFICATION REQUIRED: Certification and training is required, depending on the type of yoga you plan to teach.

OTHER REQUIREMENTS: A yoga instructor teaches people how to relax, breath, and become well-balanced through exercise and meditation. Thus, the instructor needs to be skilled at yoga and teaching, plus have excellent verbal communication skills, and an outgoing personality.

CAREER ADVANCEMENT OPPORTUNITIES: Yoga instructors are employed by health clubs, yoga studios, upscale hotels, resorts, and cruise ships. Some instructors are self-employed and offer one-on-one instructor or small group classes.

According to Wikipedia (http://en.wikipedia.org/wiki/Yoga), "Yoga is a family of spiritual practices that originated in what in the present-day is known as India, where it is seen primarily as a means to enlightenment. Traditionally, Karma Yoga, Bhakti Yoga, Jnana Yoga, and Raja Yoga are considered the four main yogas. In the West, yoga has become associated with the asanas (postures) of Hatha Yoga, which are popular as fitness exercises. Yoga as a means to enlightenment is central to Hinduism, Buddhism, and Jainism . . . . Yoga entails mastery over the body, mind, and emotional self, and transcendence of desire."

A yoga instructor is someone who has mastered one or more types of yoga, plus has undergone the necessary certification training to become a yoga instructor. The job involves teaching yoga to students, often in a yoga studio or in a health club environment. Like aerobics, yoga has become an extremely popular way for people to relax, mediate, and stay physically fit. Thus, there's a large and ever-growing demand for yoga instructors. A related job involves becoming a certified Pilates instructor.

For More Information

- National Exercise and Sports Trainers Association (NESTA). This professional trade association offers a home study course for becoming a certified sport yoga instructor, www.nestacertified.com/sportyoga.html.
- Natural Healers. This web site offers a comprehensive list of schools that train and certify yoga instructors, www.naturalhealers.com/find.shtml.
- Spa & Beauty Schools. This web site offers a listing of schools and training programs for yoga instructors, www.spabeautyschools.com.
- Yahoo! Yoga Career Training. This web site lists a wide range of yoga training programs and information about how to become a certified yoga instructor, http://dir.yahoo.com/business_and_economy/business_to_business/health_care/fitness/career_training/Yoga.
- Yoga Teacher Training. Here you'll find information about one of many online training and certification programs for yoga instructors, www.yoga-teacher-training.org.
- Yoga.com. This web site is a clearing house of information and resources for all topics relating to yoga, www.yoga.com.
- Online job listings can be found at the general interest career-related web sites, such as Monster (www.monster.com) or Yahoo! Hot Jobs (http://hotjobs.yahoo.com). Also, contact the human resources department at your local health clubs and yoga studios.

INDEX

500,000 people earn a living on eBay. What do they know that you don't?

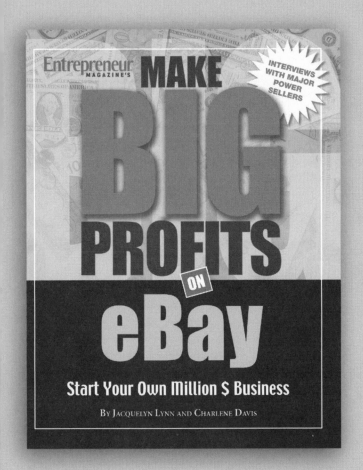

The secrets are in this book.

When *Entrepreneur* applies over 25 years of business experience to the eBay world, you get:

· The scoop on how to take advantage of all eBay's features

· Tips from PowerSellers who have made it big

· The lowdown on current eBay trends, products and markets

· Hidden ways to make money without selling a thing

· Essential information on customer service, marketing and business operation

Pick up your copy today!

EP
Entreprene
Press

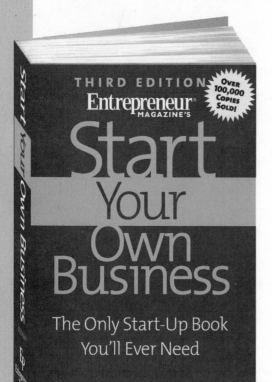